Cambridge IGCSE™

Extended Mathematics

EXAM PREPARATION AND PRACTICE

Nick Asker, Nick Hamshaw & Tom Wolstenholme

with Digital access

Shaftesbury Road, Cambridge CB2 8EA, United Kingdom

One Liberty Plaza, 20th Floor, New York, NY 10006, USA

477 Williamstown Road, Port Melbourne, VIC 3207, Australia

314–321, 3rd Floor, Plot 3, Splendor Forum, Jasola District Centre, New Delhi – 110025, India

Cambridge University Press & Assessment is a department of the University of Cambridge.

We share the University's mission to contribute to society through the pursuit of education, learning and research at the highest international levels of excellence.

www.cambridge.org

Information on this title: www.cambridge.org/9781009829519

First published 2026

Exam Preparation and Practice to support Third edition 2023

20 19 18 17 16 15 14 13 12 11 10 9 8 7 6 5 4 3 2 1

Printed in Malaysia by Vivar Printing

A catalogue record for this publication is available from the British Library

ISBN 978-1-009-82951-9 Exam Preparation and Practice with Digital Access (2 Years)

ISBN 978-1-009-82952-6 Digital Exam Preparation and Practice (2 Years)

ISBN 978-1-009-82954-0 Exam Preparation and Practice - eBook

Additional resources for this publication at www.cambridge.org/9781009829519

Cover image LPETTET/Getty Images

Contents

Extra digital questions, in the form of **Multiple-choice questions** and **Flip cards**, for all chapters can be found online at Cambridge GO. For more information on how to access and use your digital resource, please see inside the front cover.

How to use this series

This suite of resources supports learners and teachers following the Cambridge IGCSE™ and IGCSE (9–1) Mathematics syllabuses (0580/0980). Up-to-date metacognition techniques have been incorporated throughout the resources to meet the changes in the syllabuses content and develop a complete understanding of mathematics for learners. All of the components in the series are designed to work together.

The coursebook contains 24 chapters that together offer complete coverage of the syllabus. We have worked with NRICH to provide a variety of project activities, designed to engage learners and strengthen their problem solving skills. Each chapter contains opportunities for formative assessment, differentiation and peer and self-assessment offering learners the support needed to make progress. Cambridge Online Mathematics is available through the digital/print bundle option or on its own without the print coursebook. Learners can review content digitally, explore worked examples and test their knowledge with quiz questions and answers. Teachers benefit from the ability to set tests and tasks with the added auto-marking functionality and a reporting dashboard to help track learner progress quickly and easily.

The digital teacher's resource provides extensive guidance on how to teach the course, including suggestions for differentiation, formative assessment and language support, teaching ideas and PowerPoints. The Teaching Skills Focus shows teachers how to incorporate a variety of key pedagogical techniques into teaching, including differentiation, assessment for learning, and metacognition. Answers for all components are accessible to teachers for free on the Cambridge GO platform.

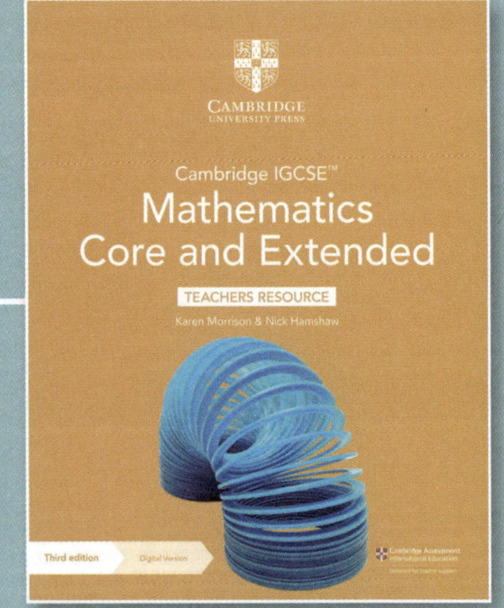

A Practice Book is available for learners who want to have extra questions to work through. This resource, which can be used in class or assigned as homework, provides a wide variety of extra maths activities and questions to help learners consolidate their learning and prepare for assessment. Tips are also regularly featured to give learners extra advice and guidance on the different areas of maths they encounter. Access to the digital versions of the practice books is included, and answers can be found either here or in the back of the books.

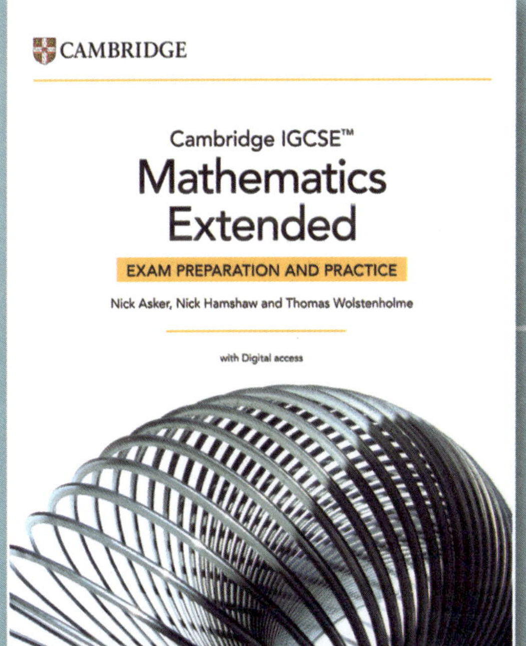

The Exam Preparation and Practice resource provides dedicated support for learners in preparing for their final assessments. Hundreds of questions in the book and the accompanying digital resource will help learners to check that they understand, and can recall, syllabus concepts. To help learners to show what they know in an exam context, a checklist of exam skills with corresponding questions and past paper question practice is also included. Self-assessment and reflection features support learners to identify any areas that need further practice. This resource should be used alongside the coursebook, throughout the course of study, so learners can most effectively increase their confidence and readiness for their exams.

How to use this book

This book will help you to check that you **know** the content of the syllabus and practise how to **show** this understanding in an exam. It will also help you be cognitively prepared and in the **flow**, ready for your exam. Research has shown that it is important that you do all three of these things, so we have designed the Know, Show, Flow approach to help you prepare effectively for exams.

Know You will need to consolidate and then recall a lot of syllabus content.

Show You should demonstrate your knowledge in the context of a Cambridge exam.

Flow You should be cognitively engaged and ready to learn. This means reducing test anxiety.

Exam skills checklist

Category	Exam skill
Understanding the question	Recognise different question types
	Understand command words
	Mark scheme awareness
Providing an appropriate response	Understand connections between concepts
	Keep to time
	Know what a good answer looks like
Developing supportive behaviours	Reflect on progress
	Manage test anxiety

This **Exam skills checklist** helps you to develop the awareness, behaviours and habits that will support you when revising and preparing for your exams. For more exam skills advice, including understanding command words and managing your time effectively, please go to the **Exam skills chapter**.

Know

The full syllabus content of your IGCSE Extended Mathematics course is covered in your Cambridge coursebook. This book will provide you with different types of question to support you as you prepare for your exams.

KNOWLEDGE FOCUS

Knowledge focus boxes summarise the topics that you will answer questions on in each chapter of this book. You can refer back to your Cambridge coursebook to remind yourself of the full detail of the syllabus content.

You will find **Knowledge recall questions** to make sure you understand a topic, and **Recall and connect questions** to help you recall past learning and connect different concepts. It is recommended that you answer the Knowledge recall questions just after you have covered the relevant topic in class, and then return to them at a later point to check you have properly understood the content.

Knowledge recall question

Testing yourself is a good way to check that your understanding is secure. These questions will help you to recall the core knowledge you have acquired during your course, and highlight any areas where you may need more practice. They are indicated with a blue bar with a gap, at the side of the page. We recommend that you answer the Knowledge recall questions right after you have covered the relevant topic in class, and then return to them at a later point to check you have properly understood the content.

« RECALL AND CONNECT 1 «

To consolidate your learning, you need to test your memory frequently. These questions will test that you remember what you learned in previous chapters, in addition to what you are practising in the current chapter.

UNDERSTAND THIS TERM

These list the important vocabulary that you should understand for each chapter. Definitions are provided in the glossary of your Cambridge coursebook.

This icon shows you where you should complete an exercise without using your calculator.

Show

Exam questions test specific knowledge, skills and understanding. You need to be prepared so that you have the best opportunity to show what you know in the time you have during the exam. In addition to practising recall of the syllabus content, it is important to build your exam skills throughout the year.

EXAM SKILLS FOCUS

This feature outlines the exam skills you will practise in each chapter, alongside the Knowledge focus. They are drawn from the core set of eight exam skills, listed in the exam skills checklist. You will practise specific exam skills, such as understanding command words, within each chapter. More general exam skills, such as managing text anxiety, are covered in the Exam skills chapter.

Exam skills question

These questions will help you to develop your exam skills and demonstrate your understanding. To help you become familiar with exam-style questioning, these questions follow the style and use the language of real exam questions, and have allocated marks. They are indicated with a solid red bar at the side of the page.

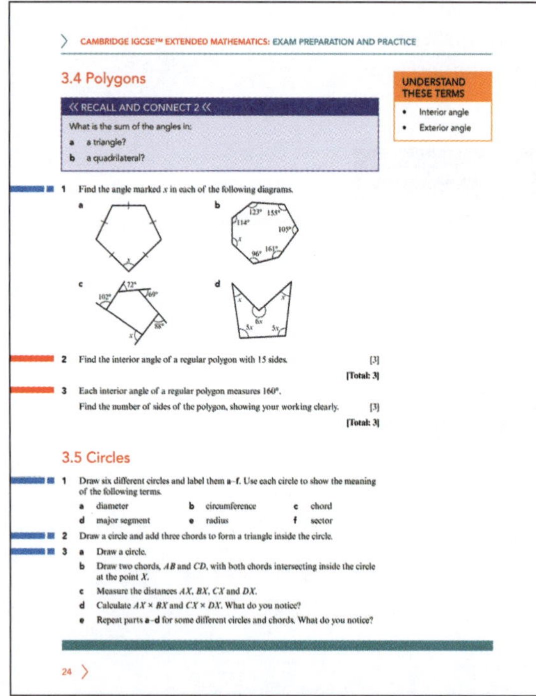

CAMBRIDGE IGCSE™ EXTENDED MATHEMATICS: EXAM PREPARATION AND PRACTICE

3.4 Polygons

UNDERSTAND THESE TERMS
- Interior angle
- Exterior angle

« RECALL AND CONNECT 2 «

What is the sum of the angles in:

a a triangle?

b a quadrilateral?

1 Find the angle marked x in each of the following diagrams.

2 Find the interior angle of a regular polygon with 15 sides. [3]

[Total: 3]

3 Each interior angle of a regular polygon measures 160°.

Find the number of sides of the polygon, showing your working clearly. [3]

[Total: 3]

3.5 Circles

1 Draw six different circles and label them **a**–**f**. Use each circle to show the meaning of the following terms.

a diameter **b** circumference **c** chord

d major segment **e** radius **f** sector

2 Draw a circle and add three chords to form a triangle inside the circle.

3 **a** Draw a circle.

b Draw two chords, AB and CD, with both chords intersecting inside the circle at the point X.

c Measure the distances AX, BX, CX and DX.

d Calculate $AX \times BX$ and $CX \times DX$. What do you notice?

e Repeat parts **a**–**d** for some different circles and chords. What do you notice?

24

Looking at sample answers to past paper questions helps you to understand what to aim for.

The **Exam practice** sections in this resource contain example student responses and examiner-style commentary showing how the answer could be improved (both written by the authors).

Flow

Preparing for exams can be stressful. One of the approaches recommended by educational psychologists to help with this stress is to improve behaviours around exam preparation. This involves testing yourself in manageable chunks, accompanied by self-evaluation. You should avoid cramming, and build in more preparation time. This book is structured to help you do this.

Increasing your ability to recognise the signs of exam-related stress and working through some techniques for how to cope with it will help to make your exam preparation manageable.

REFLECTION

This feature asks you to think about the approach that you take to your exam preparation, and how you might improve this in the future. Reflecting on how you plan, monitor and evaluate your revision and preparation will help you to do your best in your exams.

SELF-ASSESSMENT CHECKLIST

These checklists return to the Learning intentions from your coursebook, as well as the Exam skills focus boxes from each chapter. The statements that relate to Exam skills are indicated with a solid red bar at the side of the page. Checking in on how confident you feel in each of these areas will help you to focus your exam preparation. The 'Show it' prompts will allow you to test your rating. You should revisit any areas that you rate 'Needs more work' or 'Almost there'.

Now I can	Show it	Needs more work	Almost there	Confident to move on

Increasing your ability to recognise the signs of exam-related stress and working through some techniques for how to cope with it will help to make your exam preparation manageable. The **Exam skills chapter** will support you with this.

Digital questions

Extra digital questions, in the form of **Multiple choice** and **Flip cards**, for all chapters can be found online at Cambridge GO. For more information on how to access and use your digital resource, please see inside the front cover.

- Provides lots of additional practice to reinforce knowledge and understanding
- Gives instant feedback to support autonomy over your own learning
- Encourages self-assessment to understand your strengths and weaknesses
- User-friendly design to help with easy navigation

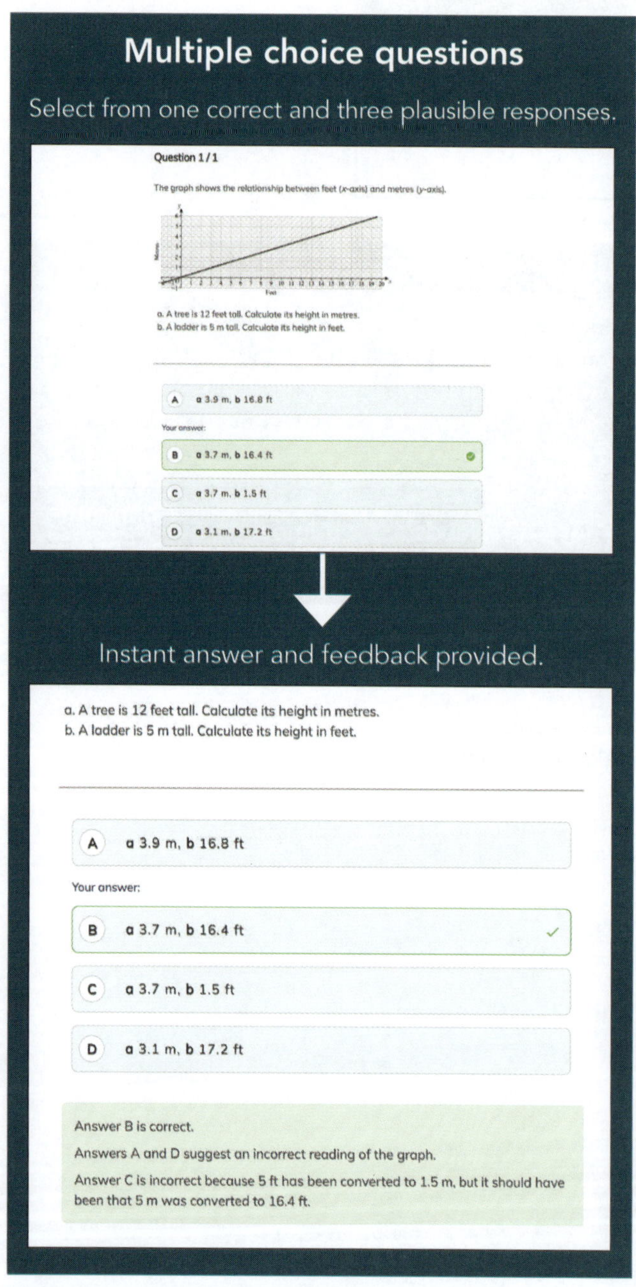

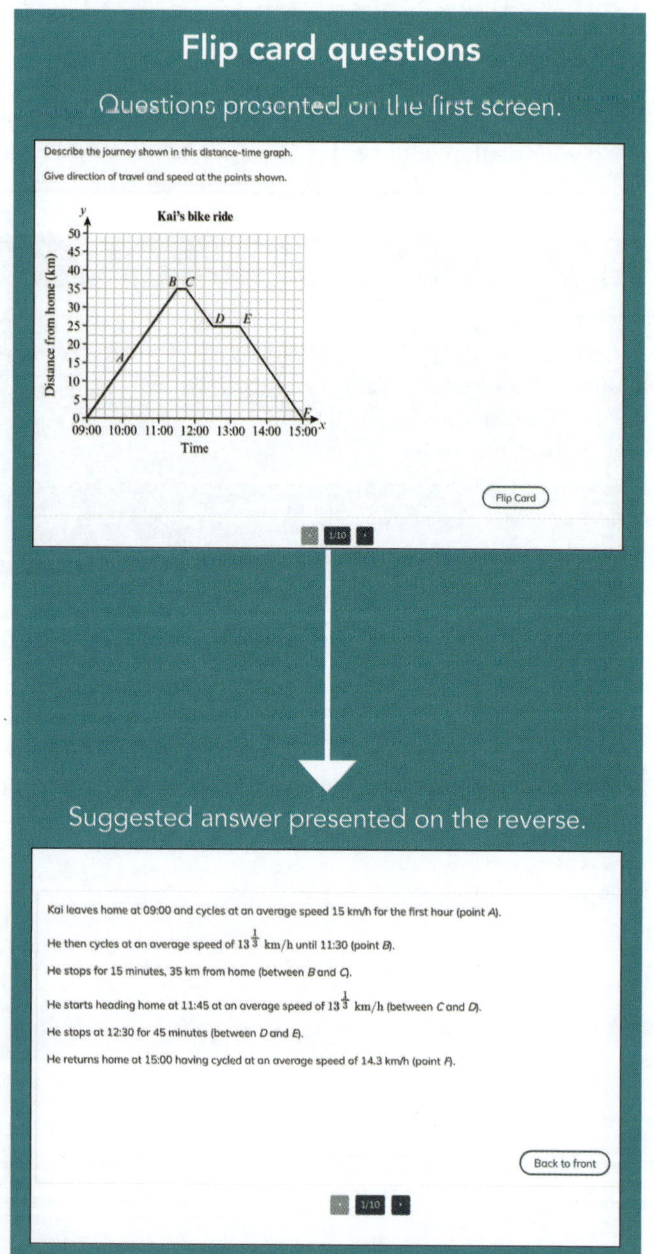

Syllabus assessment objectives for IGCSE Extended Mathematics

You should be familiar with the Assessment Objectives from the syllabus, as you will need to show evidence of these requirements in your responses.

The assessment objectives for this syllabus are:

Assessment objective	IGCSE weighting
AO1: Knowledge and understanding of mathematical techniques	40–50%
AO2: Analyse, interpret and communicate mathematically	50–60%

If a question asks you to complete a diagram/table/graph, you can find a printable copy of this in the Past Paper Practice Questions Resource Sheets, which are available to download from Cambridge GO.

Exam skills

by Lucy Parsons

What's the point of this book?

Most students make one really basic mistake when they're preparing for exams. What is it? It's focusing far too much on learning 'stuff' – that's facts, figures, ideas, information – and not nearly enough time practising exam skills.

The students who work really, really hard but are disappointed with their results are nearly always students who focus on memorising stuff. They think to themselves, 'I'll do practice papers once I've revised everything.' The trouble is, they start doing practice papers too late to really develop and improve how they communicate what they know.

What could they do differently?

When your final exam script is assessed, it should contain specific language, information and thinking skills in your answers. If you read a question in an exam and you have no idea what you need to do to give a good answer, the likelihood is that your answer won't be as brilliant as it could be. That means your grade won't reflect the hard work you've put into revising for the exam.

There are different types of question used in exams to assess different skills. You need to know how to recognise these question types and understand what you need to show in your answers.

So, how do you understand what to do in each question type?

That's what this book is all about. But first a little background.

Meet Benjamin Bloom

The psychologist Benjamin Bloom developed a way of classifying and valuing different skills we use when we learn, such as analysis and recalling information. We call these thinking skills. It's known as Bloom's Taxonomy and it's what most exam questions are based around.

If you understand Bloom's Taxonomy, you can understand what any type of question requires you to do. So, what does it look like?

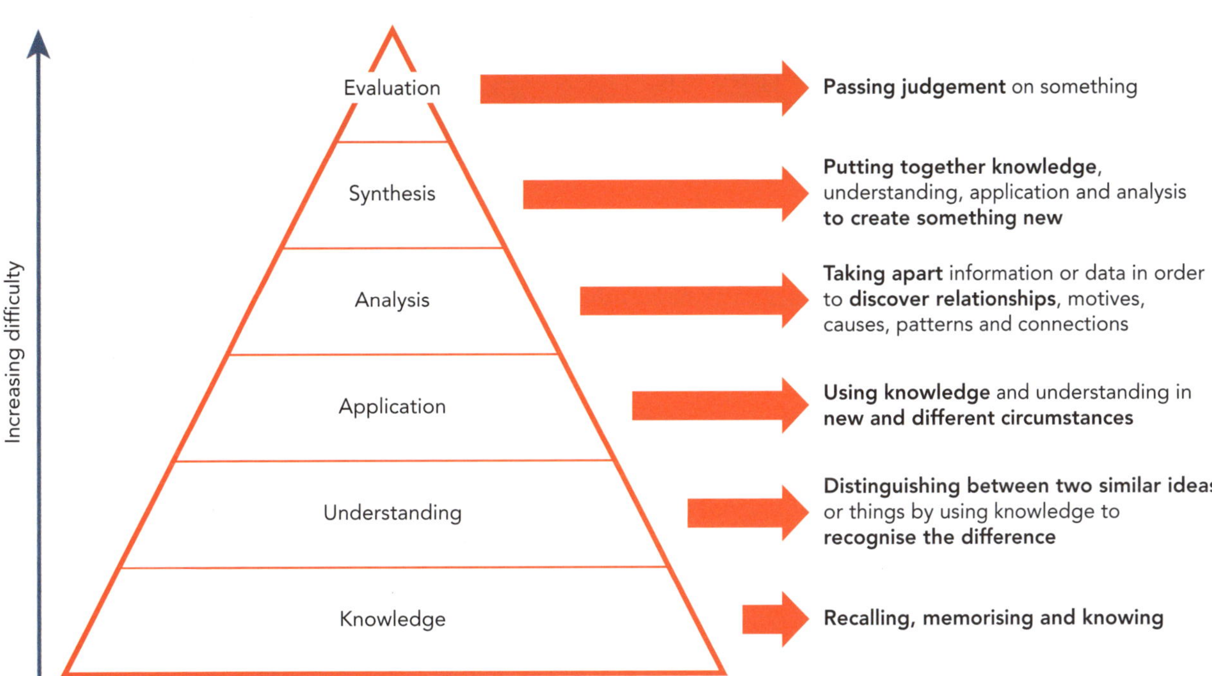

The key things to take away from this diagram are:

- Knowledge and understanding are known as lower-level thinking skills. They are less difficult than the other thinking skills. Exam questions that just test you on what you know are usually worth the lowest number of marks.
- All the other thinking skills are worth higher numbers of marks in exam questions. These questions require you to have some foundational knowledge and understanding but are far more about how you think than what you know. They involve:
  - Taking what you know and using it in unfamiliar situations (application).
  - Going deeper into information to discover relationships, motives, causes, patterns and connections (analysis).
  - Using what you know and think to create something new – whether that's an essay, long-answer exam question a solution to a maths problem, or a piece of art (synthesis).
  - Assessing the value of something, e.g., the reliability of the results of a scientific experiment (evaluation).

In this introductory chapter, you'll be shown how to develop the skills that enable you to communicate what you know and how you think. This will help you achieve to the best of your abilities. In the rest of the book, you'll have a chance to practise these exam skills by understanding how questions work and understanding what you need to show in your answers.

Every time you pick up this book and do a few questions, you're getting closer to achieving your dream results. So, let's get started!

Exam preparation and revision skills

What is revision?

If you think about it, the word 'revision' has two parts to it:

- re – which means 'again'
- vision – which is about seeing.

So, revision is literally about 'seeing again'. This means you're looking at something that you've already learned.

Typically, a teacher will teach you something in class. You may then do some questions on it, write about it in some way, or even do a presentation. You might then have an end-of-topic test sometime later. To prepare for this test, you need to 'look again' or revise what you were originally taught.

Step 1: Making knowledge stick

Every time you come back to something you've learned or revised you're improving your understanding and memory of that particular piece of knowledge. This is called **spaced retrieval**. This is how human memory works. If you don't use a piece of knowledge by recalling it, you lose it.

Everything we learn has to be physically stored in our brains by creating neural connections – joining brain cells together. The more often we 'retrieve' or recall a particular piece of knowledge, the stronger the neural connection gets. It's like lifting weights – the more often you lift, the stronger you get.

However, if you don't use a piece of knowledge for a long time, your brain wants to recycle the brain cells and use them for another purpose. The neural connections get weaker until they finally break, and the memory has gone. This is why it's really important to return often to things that you've learned in the past.

Great ways of doing this in your revision include:

- Testing yourself using flip cards – use the ones available in the digital resources for this book.
- Testing yourself (or getting someone else to test you) using questions you've created about the topic.
- Checking your recall of previous topics by answering the Recall and connect questions in this book.
- Blurting – writing everything you can remember about a topic on a piece of paper in one colour. Then, checking what you missed out and filling it in with another colour. You can do this over and over again until you feel confident that you remember everything.
- Answering practice questions – use the ones in this book.
- Getting a good night's sleep to help consolidate your learning.

The importance of sleep and creating long-term memory

When you go to sleep at night, your brain goes through an important process of taking information from your short-term memory and storing it in your long-term memory.

This means that getting a good night's sleep is a very important part of revision. If you don't get enough good quality sleep, you'll actually be making your revision much, much harder.

Step 2: Developing your exam skills

We've already talked about the importance of exam skills, and how many students neglect them because they're worried about covering all the knowledge.

What actually works best is developing your exam skills at the same time as learning the knowledge.

What does this look like in your studies?

- Learning something at school and your teacher setting you questions from this book or from past papers. This tests your recall as well as developing your exam skills.
- Choosing a topic to revise, learning the content and then choosing some questions from this book to test yourself at the same time as developing your exam skills.

The reason why practising your exam skills is so important is that it helps you to get good at communicating what you know and what you think. The more often you do that, the more fluent you'll become in showing what you know in your answers.

Step 3: Getting feedback

The final step is to get feedback on your work.

If you're testing yourself, the feedback is what you got wrong or what you forgot. This means you then need to go back to those things to remind yourself or improve your understanding. Then, you can test yourself again and get more feedback. You can also congratulate yourself for the things you got right – it's important to celebrate any success, big or small.

If you're doing past paper questions or the practice questions in this book, you will need to mark your work. Marking your work is one of the most important things you can do to improve. It's possible to make significant improvements in your marks in a very short space of time when you start marking your work.

Why is marking your own work so powerful? It's because it teaches you to identify the strengths and weaknesses of your own work. When you look at the mark scheme and see how it's structured, you will understand what is needed in your answers to get the results you want.

This doesn't just apply to the knowledge you demonstrate in your answers. It also applies to the language you use and whether it's appropriately subject-specific, the structure of your answer, how you present it on the page and many other factors. Understanding, practising and improving on these things are transformative for your results.

The most important thing about revision

The most important way to make your revision successful is to make it active.

Sometimes, students say they're revising when they sit staring at their textbook or notes for hours at a time. However, this is a really ineffective way to revise because it's passive. In order to make knowledge and skills stick, you need to be doing something like the suggestions in the following diagram. That's why testing yourself and pushing yourself to answer questions that test higher-level thinking skills are so effective. At times, you might actually be able to feel the physical changes happening in your brain as you develop this new knowledge and these new skills. That doesn't come about without effort.

The important thing to remember is that while active revision feels much more like hard work than passive revision, you don't actually need to do nearly as much of it. That's because you remember knowledge and skills when you use active revision. When you use passive revision, it is much, much harder for the knowledge and skills to stick in your memory.

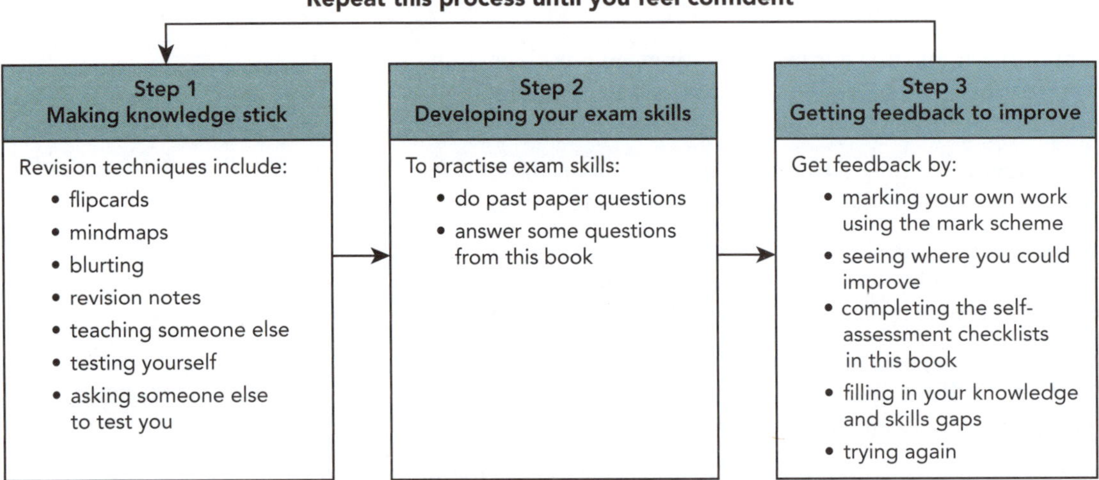

How to improve your exam skills

This book helps you to improve in eight different areas of exam skills, which are divided across three categories. These skills are highlighted in this book in the Exam skills focus at the start of each chapter and developed throughout the book using targeted questions, advice and reflections.

1 **Understand the questions: what are you being asked to do?**

- Know your question types.
- Understand command words.
- Work with mark scheme awareness.

2 **How to answer questions brilliantly**

- Understand connections between concepts.
- Keep to time.
- Know what a good answer looks like.

3 **Give yourself the best chance of success**

- Reflection on progress.
- How to manage test anxiety.

Understand the questions: what are you being asked to do?

Know your question types

In any exam, there will be a range of different question types. These different question types will test different types of thinking skills from Bloom's Taxonomy.

It is very important that you learn to recognise different question types. If you do lots of past papers, over time you will begin to recognise the structure of the paper for each of your subjects. You will know which types of question may come first and which ones are more likely to come at the end of the paper. You can also complete past paper questions in the Exam practice sections in this book for additional practice.

You will also recognise the differences between questions worth a lower number of marks and questions worth more marks. The key differences are:

- how much you will need to write in your answer
- how sophisticated your answer needs to be in terms of the detail you give and the depth of thinking you show.

Types of question

1 Multiple-choice questions

Multiple-choice questions are generally worth smaller numbers of marks. You will be given several possible answers to the question, and you will have to work out which one is correct using your knowledge and skills.

There is a chance of you getting the right answer with multiple-choice questions even if you don't know the answer. This is why you must **always give an answer for multiple-choice questions** as it means there is a chance you will earn the mark.

Multiple-choice questions are often harder than they appear. The possible answers can be very similar to each other. This means you must be confident in how you work out answers or have a high level of understanding to tell the difference between the possible answers.

Being confident in your subject knowledge and doing lots of practice multiple-choice questions will set you up for success. Use the resources in this book and the accompanying online resources to build your confidence.

The following example of a multiple-choice question is worth one mark. You can see that all the answers have one part in common with at least one other answer. For example, palisade cells is included in three of the possible answers. That's why you have to really know the detail of your content knowledge to do well with multiple-choice questions.

Which two types of cells are found in plant leaves?

A Palisade mesophyll and stomata

B Palisade mesophyll and root hair

C Stomata and chloroplast

D Chloroplast and palisade mesophyll

2 Questions requiring longer-form answers

Questions requiring longer-form answers need you to write out your answer yourself.

With these questions, take careful note of how many marks are available and how much space you've been given for your answer. These two things will give you a good idea about how much you should say and how much time you should spend on the question.

A rough rule to follow is to write one sentence, or make one point, for each mark that is available. You will get better and better at these longer form questions the more you practise them.

In the history question example below, you can see it is worth four marks. It is not asking for an explanation, just for you to list Lloyd George's aims. Therefore, you need to make four correct points in order to get full marks.

What were Lloyd George's aims during negotiations leading to the Treaty of Versailles? [4]

3 Essay questions

Essay questions are the longest questions you will be asked to answer in an exam. They examine the higher-order thinking skills from Bloom's Taxonomy such as analysis, synthesis and evaluation.

To do well in essay questions, you need to talk about what you know, giving your opinion, comparing one concept or example to another, and evaluating your own ideas or the ones you're discussing in your answer.

You also need to have a strong structure and logical argument that guides the reader through your thought process. This usually means having an introduction, some main body paragraphs that discuss one point at a time, and a conclusion.

Essay questions are usually level-marked. This means that you don't get one mark per point you make. Instead, you're given marks for the quality of the ideas you're sharing as well as how well you present those ideas through the subject-specific language you use and the structure of your essay.

Practising essays and becoming familiar with the mark scheme is the only way to get really good at them.

Understand command words

What are command words?

Command words are the most important words in every exam question. This is because command words tell you what you need to do in your answer. Do you remember Bloom's Taxonomy? Command words tell you which thinking skill you need to demonstrate in the answer to each question.

Two very common command words are **describe** and **explain**.

When you see the command word **describe** in a question, you're being asked to show lower-order thinking skills like knowledge and understanding. The question will either be worth fewer marks, or you will need to make more points if it is worth more marks.

The command word **explain** is asking you to show higher-order thinking skills. When you see the command word explain, you need to be able to say how or why something happens.

You need to understand all of the relevant command words for the subjects you are taking. Ask your teacher where to find them if you are not sure. It's best not to try to memorise the list of command words, but to become familiar with what command words are asking for by doing lots of practice questions and marking your own work.

How to work with command words

When you first see an exam question, read it through once. Then, read it through again and identify the command word(s). Underline the command word(s) to make it clear to yourself which they are every time you refer back to the question.

You may also want to identify the **content** words in the question and underline them with a different colour. Content words tell you which area of knowledge you need to draw on to answer the question.

In this example, command words are shown in red and underlined with content words in **blue and bold**:

1 a Explain **four** reasons why **governments** might **support business start-ups**. [8]

Adapted from Cambridge IGCSE Business Studies (0450) Q1a Paper 21 June 2022

Marking your own work using the mark scheme will help you get even better at understanding command words and knowing how to give good answers for each.

Work with mark scheme awareness

The most transformative thing that any student can do to improve their marks is to work with mark schemes. This means using mark schemes to mark your own work at every opportunity.

Many students are very nervous about marking their own work as they do not feel experienced or qualified enough. However, being brave enough to try to mark your own work and taking the time to get good at it will improve your marks hugely.

Why marking your own work makes such a big difference

Marking your own work can help you to improve your answers in the following ways:

1 **Answering the question**

Having a deep and detailed understanding of what is required by the question enables you to answer the question more clearly and more accurately.

It can also help you to give the required information using fewer words and in less time, as you can avoid including unrelated points or topics in your answer.

2 **Using subject-specific vocabulary**

Every subject has subject-specific vocabulary. This includes technical terms for objects or concepts in a subject, such as mitosis and meiosis in biology. It also includes how you talk about the subject, using appropriate vocabulary that may differ from everyday language. For example, in any science subject you might be asked to describe the trend on a graph.

Your answer could say it 'goes up fast' or your answer could say it 'increases rapidly'. You would not get marks for saying 'it goes up fast', but you would for saying it 'increases rapidly'. This is the difference between everyday language and formal, scientific language.

When you answer lots of practice questions, you become fluent in the language specific to your subject.

3 **Knowing how much to write**

It's very common for students to either write too much or too little to answer questions. Becoming familiar with the mark schemes for many different questions will help you to gain a better understanding of how much you need to write in order to get a good mark.

4 **Structuring your answer**

There are often clues in questions about how to structure your answer. However, mark schemes give you an even stronger idea of the structure you hould use in your answers.

For example, if a question says:

'Describe and explain two reasons why...'

You can give a clear answer by:

- describing reason 1
- explaining reason 1
- describing reason 2
- explaining reason 2

Having a very clear structure will also make it easier to identify where you have earned marks. This means that you're more likely to be awarded the number of marks you deserve.

5 **Keeping to time**

Answering the question, using subject-specific vocabulary, knowing how much to write and giving a clear structure to your answer will all help you to keep to time in an exam. You will not waste time by writing too much for any answer. Therefore, you will have sufficient time to give a good answer to every question.

How to answer exam questions brilliantly

Understand connections between concepts

One of the higher-level thinking skills in Bloom's Taxonomy is **synthesis**. Synthesis means making connections between different areas of knowledge. You may have heard about synoptic links. Making synoptic links is the same as showing the thinking skill of synthesis.

Exam questions that ask you to show your synthesis skills are usually worth the highest number of marks on an exam paper. To write good answers to these questions, you need to spend time thinking about the links between the topics you've studied before you arrive in your exam. A great way of doing this is using mind maps.

How to create a mind map

To create a mind map:

1 Use a large piece of paper and several different coloured pens.
2 Write the name of your subject in the middle. Then, write the key topic areas evenly spaced around the edge, each with a different colour.
3 Then, around each topic area, start to write the detail of what you can remember. If you find something that is connected with something you studied in another topic, you can draw a line linking the two things together.

This is a good way of practising your retrieval of information as well as linking topics together.

Answering synoptic exam questions

You will recognise questions that require you to make links between concepts because they have a higher number of marks. You will have practised them using this book and the accompanying resources.

To answer a synoptic exam question:

1 **Identify the command and content words**. You are more likely to find command words like **discuss** and **explain** in these questions. They might also have phrases like 'the connection between'.
2 **Make a plan for your answer**. It is worth taking a short amount of time to think about what you're going to write in your answer. Think carefully about what information you're going to put in, the links between the different pieces of information and how you're going to structure your answer to make your ideas clear.
3 **Use linking words and phrases in your answer**. For example, 'therefore', 'because', due to', 'since' or 'this means that'.

Here is an example of an English Literature exam question that requires you to make synoptic links in your answer.

1 Discuss **Carol Ann Duffy's exploration of childhood** in her poetry.

   Refer to **two** poems in your answer. [25]

Content words are shown in blue; command words are shown in red.

This question is asking you to explore the theme of childhood in Duffy's poetry. You need to choose two of her poems to refer to in your answer. This means you need a good knowledge of her poetry, and to be familiar with her exploration of childhood, so that you can easily select two poems that will give you plenty to say in your answer.

Keep to time

Managing your time in exams is really important. Some students do not achieve to the best of their abilities because they run out of time to answer all the questions. However, if you manage your time well, you will be able to attempt every question on the exam paper.

Why is it important to attempt all the questions on an exam paper?

If you attempt every question on a paper, you have the best chance of achieving the highest mark you are capable of.

Students who manage their time poorly in exams will often spend far too long on some questions and not even attempt others. Most students are unlikely to get full marks on many questions, but you will get zero marks for the questions you don't answer. You can maximise your marks by giving an answer to every question.

Minutes per mark

The most important way to keep to time is knowing how many minutes you can spend on each mark.

For example, if your exam paper has 90 marks available and you have 90 minutes, you know there is 1 mark per minute.

Therefore, if you have a 5 mark question, you should spend five minutes on it.

Sometimes, you can give a good answer in less time than you have budgeted using the minutes per mark technique. If this happens, you will have more time to spend on questions that use higher-order thinking skills, or more time on checking your work.

How to get faster at answering exam questions

The best way to get faster at answering exam questions is to do lots of practice. You should practise each question type that will be in your exam, marking your own work, so that you know precisely how that question works and what is required by the question. Use the questions in this book to get better and better at answering each question type.

Use the 'Slow, Slow, Quick' technique to get faster.

Take your time answering questions when you first start practising them. You may answer them with the support of the textbook, your notes or the mark scheme. These things will support you with your content knowledge, the language you use in your answer and the structure of your answer.

Every time you practise this question type, you will get more confident and faster. You will become experienced with this question type, so that it is easy for you to recall the subject knowledge and write it down using the correct language and a good structure.

Calculating marks per minute

Use this calculation to work out how long you have for each mark:

Total time in the exam / Number of marks available = Minutes per mark

Calculate how long you have for a question worth more than one mark like this:

Minutes per mark × Marks available for this question
= Number of minutes for this question

What about time to check your work?

It is a very good idea to check your work at the end of an exam. You need to work out if this is feasible with the minutes per mark available to you. If you're always rushing to finish the questions, you shouldn't budget checking time. However, if you usually have time to spare, then you can budget checking time.

To include checking time in your minutes per mark calculation:

(Total time in the exam – Checking time) / Number of marks available
= Minutes per mark

Know what a good answer looks like

It is much easier to give a good answer if you know what a good answer looks like.

Use these methods to know what a good answer looks like.

1 **Sample answers** – you can find sample answers in these places:
   - from your teacher
   - written by your friends or other members of your class
   - in this book.
2 **Look at mark schemes** – mark schemes are full of information about what you should include in your answers. Get familiar with mark schemes to gain a better understanding of the type of things a good answer would contain.
3 **Feedback from your teacher** – if you are finding it difficult to improve your exam skills for a particular type of question, ask your teacher for detailed feedback. You should also look at their comments on your work in detail.

Give yourself the best chance of success

Reflection on progress

As you prepare for your exam, it's important to reflect on your progress. Taking time to think about what you're doing well and what could be improved brings more focus to your revision. Reflecting on progress also helps you to continuously improve your knowledge and exam skills.

How do you reflect on progress?

Use the 'reflection' feature in this book to help you reflect on your progress during your exam preparation. Then, at the end of each revision session, take a few minutes to think about the following:

	What went well? What would you do the same next time?	What didn't go well? What would you do differently next time?
Your subject knowledge		
How you revised your subject knowledge – did you use active retrieval techniques?		
Your use of subject-specific and academic language		
Understanding the question by identifying command words and content words		
Giving a clear structure to your answer		
Keeping to time		
Marking your own work		

Remember to check for silly mistakes – things like missing out the units after you carefully calculated your answer.

Use the mark scheme to mark your own work. Every time you mark your own work, you will be recognising the good and bad aspects of your work, so that you can progressively give better answers over time.

When do you need to come back to this topic or skill?

Earlier in this section of the book, we talked about revision skills and the importance of spaced retrieval. When you reflect on your progress, you need to think about how soon you need to return to the topic or skill you've just been focusing on.

For example, if you were really disappointed with your subject knowledge, it would be a good idea to do some more active retrieval and practice questions on this topic tomorrow. However, if you did really well you can feel confident you know this topic and come back to it again in three weeks' or a month's time.

The same goes for exam skills. If you were disappointed with how you answered the question, you should look at some sample answers and try this type of question again soon. However, if you did well, you can move on to other types of exam questions.

Improving your memory of subject knowledge

Sometimes students slip back into using passive revision techniques, such as only reading the coursebook or their notes, rather than also using active revision techniques, like testing themselves using flip cards or blurting.

You can avoid this mistake by observing how well your learning is working as you revise. You should be thinking to yourself, 'Am I remembering this? Am I understanding this? Is this revision working?'

If the answer to any of those questions is 'no', then you need to change what you're doing to revise this particular topic. For example, if you don't understand, you could look up your topic in a different textbook in the school library to see if a different explanation helps. Or you could see if you can find a video online that brings the idea to life.

You are in control

When you're studying for exams it's easy to think that your teachers are in charge. However, you have to remember that you are studying for your exams and the results you get will be yours and no one else's.

That means you have to take responsibility for all your exam preparation. You have the power to change how you're preparing if what you're doing isn't working. You also have control over what you revise and when: you can make sure you focus on your weaker topics and skills to improve your achievement in the subject.

This isn't always easy to do. Sometimes you have to find an inner ability that you have not used before. But, if you are determined enough to do well, you can find what it takes to focus, improve and keep going.

What is test anxiety?

Do you get worried or anxious about exams? Does your worry or anxiety impact how well you do in tests and exams?

Test anxiety is part of your natural stress response.

The stress response evolved in animals and humans many thousands of years ago to help keep them alive. Let's look at an example.

The stress response in the wild

Imagine an impala grazing in the grasslands of east Africa. It's happily and calmly eating grass in its herd in what we would call the parasympathetic state of rest and repair.

Then the impala sees a lion. The impala suddenly panics because its life is in danger. This state of panic is also known as the stressed or sympathetic state. The sympathetic state presents itself in three forms: flight, fight and freeze.

The impala starts to run away from the lion. Running away is known as the flight stress response.

The impala might not be fast enough to run away from the lion. The lion catches it but has a loose grip. The impala struggles to try to get away. This struggle is the fight stress response.

However, the lion gets an even stronger grip on the impala. Now the only chance of the impala surviving is playing dead. The impala goes limp, its heart rate and breathing slows. This is called the freeze stress response. The lion believes that it has killed the impala so it drops the impala to the ground. Now the impala can switch back into the flight response and run away.

The impala is now safe – the different stages of the stress response have saved its life.

What has the impala got to do with your exams?

When you feel test anxiety, you have the same physiological stress responses as an impala being hunted by a lion. Unfortunately, the human nervous system cannot tell the difference between a life-threatening situation, such as being chased by a lion, and the stress of taking an exam.

If you understand how the stress response works in the human nervous system, you will be able to learn techniques to reduce test anxiety.

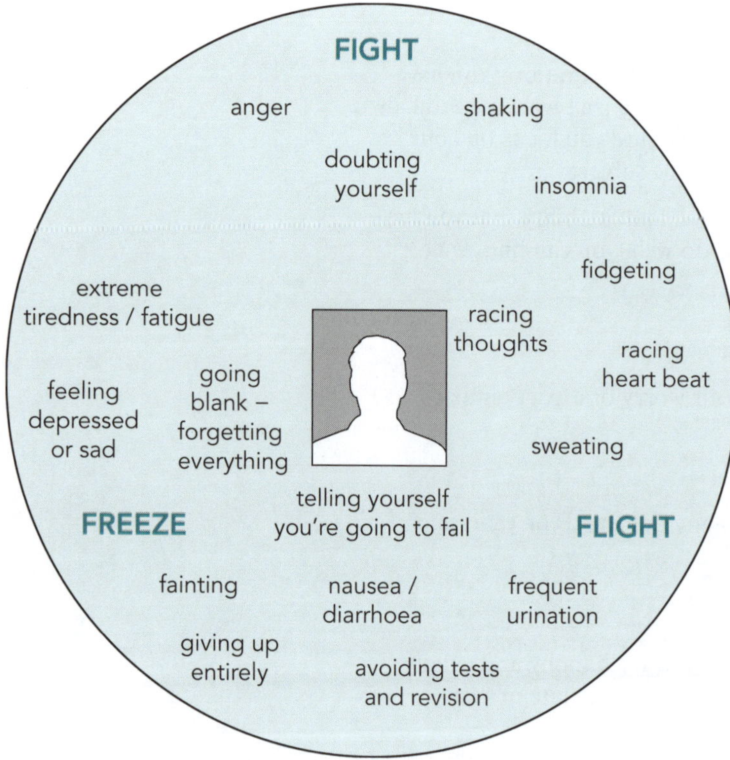

The role of the vagus nerve in test anxiety

The vagus nerve is the part of your nervous system that determines your stress response. Vagus means 'wandering' in Latin, so the vagus nerve is also known as the 'wandering nerve'. The vagus nerve wanders from your brain, down each side of your body, to nearly all your organs, including your lungs, heart, kidneys, liver, digestive system and bladder.

If you are in a stressful situation, like an exam, your vagus nerve sends a message to all these different organs to activate their stress response. Here are some common examples:

- **Heart** beats faster.
- **Kidneys** produce more adrenaline so that you can run, making you fidgety and distracted.
- **Digestive system** and **bladder** want to eliminate all waste products so that energy can be used for fight or flight.

If you want to feel calmer about your revision and exams, you need to do two things to help you move into the parasympathetic, or rest and repair, state:

1 Work with your vagus nerve to send messages of safety through your body.
2 Change your perception of the test so that you see it as safe and not dangerous.

How to cope with test anxiety

1 Be well prepared

Good preparation is the most important part of managing test anxiety. The better your preparation, the more confident you will be. If you are confident, you will not perceive the test or exam as dangerous, so the sympathetic nervous system responses of fight, flight and freeze are less likely to happen.

This book is all about helping you to be well prepared and building your confidence in your knowledge and ability to answer exam questions well. Working through the knowledge recall questions will help you to become more confident in your knowledge of the subject. The practice questions and exam skills questions will help you to become more confident in communicating your knowledge in an exam.

To be well prepared, look at the advice in the rest of this chapter and use it as you work through the questions in this book.

2 Work with your vagus nerve

The easiest way to work with your vagus nerve to tell it that you're in a safe situation is through your breathing. This means breathing deeply into the bottom of your lungs, so that your stomach expands, and then breathing out for longer than you breathed in. You can do this with counting.

Breathe in deeply, expanding your abdomen, for the count of four; breathe out drawing your navel back towards your spine for the count of five, six or seven. Repeat this at least three times. However, you can do it for as long as it takes for you to feel calm.

The important thing is that you breathe out for longer than you breathe in. This is because when you breathe in, your heart rate increases slightly, and when you breathe out, your heart rate decreases slightly. If you're spending more time breathing out overall, you will be decreasing your heart rate over time.

3 Feel it

Anxiety is an uncomfortable, difficult thing to feel. That means that many people try to run away from anxious feelings. However, this means the stress just gets stored in your body for you to feel later.

When you feel anxious, follow these four steps:

1 Pause.
2 Place one hand on your heart and one hand on your stomach.
3 Notice what you're feeling.
4 Stay with your feelings.

What you will find is that if you are willing to experience what you feel for a minute or two, the feeling of anxiety will usually pass very quickly.

4 Write or talk it out

If your thoughts are moving very quickly, it is often better to get them out of your mind and on to paper.

You could take a few minutes to write down everything that comes through your mind, then rip up your paper and throw it away. If you don't like writing, you can speak aloud alone or to someone you trust.

Other ways to break the stress cycle

Exercise and movement • Run or walk. • Dance. • Lift weights. • Yoga. Anything that involves moving your body is helpful.	**Being friendly** • Chat to someone in your study break. • Talk to the cashier when you buy your lunch.	**Laughter** • Watch or listen to a funny show on TV or online. • Talk with someone who makes you laugh. • Look at photos of fun times.
Have a hug • Hug a friend or relative. • Cuddle a pet e.g. a cat. Hug for 20 seconds or until you feel calm and relaxed.	**Releasing emotions** It is healthy to release negative or sad emotions. Crying is often a quick way to get rid of these difficult feelings so if you feel like you need to cry, allow it.	**Creativity** • Paint, draw or sketch. • Sew, knit or crochet. • Cook, build something.

If you have long-term symptoms of anxiety, it is important to tell someone you trust and ask for help.

Your perfect revision session

1 Intention

What do you want to achieve in this revision session?

- Choose an area of knowledge or an exam skill that you want to focus on.
- Choose some questions from this book that focus on this knowledge area or skill.
- Gather any other resources you will need e.g. pen, paper, flashcards, coursebook.

2 Focus

Set your focus for the session

- Remove distractions from your study area e.g. leave your phone in another room.
- Write down on a piece of paper or sticky note the knowledge area or skill you're intending to focus on.
- Close your eyes and take three deep breaths, with the exhale longer than the inhale.

3 Revision

Revise your knowledge and understanding

- To improve your knowledge and understanding of the topic, use your coursebook, notes or flashcards, including active learning techniques.
- To improve your exam skills, look at previous answers, teacher feedback, mark schemes, sample answers or examiners' reports.

4 Practice

Answer practice questions

- Use the questions in this book, or in the additional online resources, to practise your exam skills.
- If the exam is soon, do this in timed conditions without the support of the coursebook or your notes.
- If the exam is a long time away, you can use your notes and resources to help you.

5 Feedback

Mark your answers

- Use mark schemes to mark your work.
- Reflect on what you've done well and what you could do to improve next time.

6 Next steps

What have you learned about your progress from this revision session? What do you need to do next?

- What did you do well? Feel good about these things, and know it's safe to set these things aside for a while.
- What do you need to work on? How are you going to improve? Make a plan to get better at the things you didn't do well or didn't know.

7 Rest

Take a break

- Do something completely different to rest: get up, move or do something creative or practical.
- Remember that rest is an important part of studying, as it gives your brain a chance to integrate your learning.

1 Review of number concepts

KNOWLEDGE FOCUS

In this chapter, you will answer questions on:

- identifying and classifying different types of numbers
- finding common factors and common multiples of numbers
- writing numbers as products of their prime factors
- working with integers used in real-life situations
- calculating with powers and roots of numbers
- understanding the meaning of indices
- using the rules of indices
- revising the basic rules for operating with numbers
- performing basic calculations using mental methods and with a calculator
- rounding numbers in different ways to estimate and approximate answers.

EXAM SKILLS FOCUS

In this chapter you will:

- show that you understand the command word 'give' and can successfully answer 'give' questions
- show that you can use a calculator to work out answers using several operations at once.

In this chapter you will focus on the command word 'give'. It is important that you recognise how to answer a question that has this command word.

Give	produce an answer from a given source or recall/memory.

'Give' is used when you are asked to produce an answer from a given source or from your own recall or memory. For example, you may be asked to 'give three different factors of the number 36', or you may be asked to 'give a clear reason why Juan is incorrect'.

You will also focus on how to complete questions which require you to use several calculator operations at once. For example, you may be asked to estimate the value of an expression such as $\sqrt{\frac{3.2^2 + 3.9^2}{5.1}}$ and then calculate its exact value for comparison with your estimate. The combination of squares, roots and fractions requires care when using your calculator.

1.1 Different types of numbers

UNDERSTAND THESE TERMS

- Odd number
- Even number
- Integer
- Square number
- Cube number

1 List the following.

- **a** Four consecutive odd numbers between 10 and 20.
- **b** All even numbers between 121 and 129.
- **c** All prime numbers between 10 and 20.
- **d** Four integers greater than or equal to 10 **and** less than or equal to 13.
- **e** Three negative integers less than -5.
- **f** Three positive decimals that are less than 0.8.
- **g** Three cube numbers between 5 and 100.

2 State whether the following are odd or even.

- **a** The sum of three odd numbers.
- **b** The product of two even numbers.
- **c** The difference between 18 and 11.
- **d** The difference between two even numbers.
- **e** The product of an even number with an odd number.
- **f** The square of an odd number.

3 Write down three positive decimals that are greater than 100 but less than 100.5.

4 Here is a set of numbers: $\{-7, -6, -3, -1, 0, 2, 4, 6, 7, 13, 17, 49\}$.

- **a** Give two square numbers included in the set. [2]
- **b** Give two prime numbers included in the set. [2]
- **c** Give the smallest integer that is larger than the product of the two smallest numbers included in the set. [2]

[Total: 6]

5 Juan says that he is thinking of a number and that the square of his number is 9.

- **a** Give two possible values of Juan's number. [2]

Juan now says that his number is also less than 2.

- **b** Find Juan's number and give a clear reason for your answer. [2]

[Total: 4]

1.2 Multiples and factors

UNDERSTAND THESE TERMS

- Multiple
- Lowest common multiple (LCM)
- Factor
- Highest common factor (HCF)

1 List the first five multiples of each of the following.

a 7 b 2 c 11

2 Use your calculator to find and list the first six multiples of each of the following.

a 17 b 8 c 12

3 List all multiples of 4 between 61 and 73.

4 Find the lowest common multiple of each of the following.

a 3 and 7 b 5 and 6 c 6 and 8
d 7 and 21 e 24 and 26 f 100 and 125

5 List all the factors of each of the following.

a 3 b 15 c 16
d 25 e 20 f 108

6 Find the highest common factor of each of the following.

a 12 and 15 b 18 and 20 c 20 and 36
d 33 and 66 e 84 and 14 f 36 and 48

7 Estelle and Jotin stand next to each other, facing in the same direction. At the same time, Estelle and Jotin start to spin around on the spot. Estelle takes 5 seconds to complete a single turn and Jotin completes a single turn in 3 seconds.

a Give the first five multiples of 5. [1]

b Give the first five multiples of 3. [1]

Estelle and Jotin stop spinning when they are both facing in the same direction again.

c After how many seconds will Estelle and Jotin stop spinning? [2]

Estelle and Jotin decide to start spinning again, but slower this time.

It now takes Estelle 6 seconds to complete a single turn and Jotin completes a single turn in 9 seconds.

d After how many seconds of spinning at new speeds will Estelle and Jotin both be facing in the same direction again? [2]

[Total: 6]

« RECALL AND CONNECT 1 «

Explain why both the HCF and LCM of any two even numbers will be even.

1.3 Prime numbers

1 List all the prime numbers that are:

a between 10 and 20

b less than 15

c even

d multiples of 7

REFLECTION

How did you know you had written down all the correct answers? What method or checks did you use to feel confident that you hadn't missed any? What might help you do this more efficiently next time?

2 Express the following numbers as a product of their prime factors.

a 36

b 80

c 480

d 1024

e 3072

f 2025

3 Copy and complete the table. For each pair of numbers:

- express each number as the product of prime factors
- find the highest common factor (HCF)
- find the lowest common multiple (LCM).

Pair of numbers	Product of prime factors		HCF	LCM
48 and 36	48 =	36 =		
120 and 125	120 =	125 =		
162 and 18	162 =	18 =		

4 Khaleel completes an assault course every 60 seconds and immediately starts the course again. Shauri does the same but only takes 45 seconds to complete the course.

a Find the lowest common multiple of 45 and 60. [2]

b Find the time it will take for Khaleel and Shauri to reach the finish line at the same time. Give your answer in minutes and seconds. [2]

[Total: 4]

« RECALL AND CONNECT 2 «

Explain why it is not possible to write a prime number as a product of prime factors.

1.4 Working with directed numbers

1 Arrange each of the following lists of numbers in descending order.

a $-6; 3; 8; -9; -11; 12; 15$

b $-8; 8; -9; -7; 6; -10$

c $(-6 + 6); (-12 + 18); (2 \times -6); (18 \div -9); (-3 \times -3 \times -3); (-3 - -4)$

2 The water in a lake starts to freeze if the surface temperature falls below freezing point, which is at 0 °C. On Monday, at 6.00 am, the surface temperature is 5 degrees below freezing point.

a Give the temperature on Monday at 6.00 am as a directed number. [1]

During Monday, the surface temperature of the lake increases by 6 °C and then falls by 18 °C by midnight.

b Give the temperature at midnight as a directed number. [2]

[Total: 3]

≪ RECALL AND CONNECT 3 ≪

Rewrite each of these statements using mathematical symbols.

You may choose from any of $=, \neq, <, \leqslant, >, \geqslant$.

a 7.2 is bigger than 7.1.

b −2 multiplied by −3 is not equal to −6.

c The number of cars, C, in a car park is greater than or equal to 17.

d 10.01 is greater than 10.005.

e The square of 6 is bigger than 27.

f 4 is greater than 20 divided by 6.

REFLECTION

How did you remember which symbol was appropriate for each question?
Did the shape or structure of the symbol help you recall its meaning?
How might you remember the difference more easily next time?

1.5 Powers, roots and laws of indices

1 Work out the following.

a 5^2 b 8^2 c 2^3 d 10^5

e 100^3 f 13^2 g 1^{17} h 0^{84}

2 Work out the following, using a calculator if you need to.

a 11^3 b 13^3 c 17^4 d 40^4

3 Find a value of x to make each of the following statements true.

a $x^4 = 625$ **b** $3x = 81$ **c** $x^{18} = 1$

d $\sqrt{x} = 13$ **e** $\sqrt[3]{x} = 3$ **f** $\sqrt{x \times x} = 5$

4 Find the square root of each of the following numbers.

a $2 \times 2 \times 2 \times 2 \times 3 \times 3 \times 3 \times 3 \times 3 \times 3 \times 5 \times 5$

b $3 \times 3 \times 3 \times 3 \times 7 \times 7 \times 7 \times 7 \times 13 \times 13$

5 Find the cube root of
$3 \times 3 \times 3 \times 3 \times 3 \times 3 \times 4 \times 4 \times 4 \times 5 \times 5 \times 5 \times 5 \times 5 \times 5 \times 5 \times 5 \times 5$

6 Calculate each of the following.

a $\sqrt{25} + \sqrt{100}$ **b** $\sqrt{100 + 44}$ **c** $\sqrt{100 - 64}$

d $\sqrt{36} - \sqrt{100}$ **e** $\sqrt{8} \times \sqrt{50}$ **f** $\sqrt{6} \times \sqrt{6}$

g $\sqrt{\dfrac{75}{3}}$ **h** $\sqrt{(4^3)}$

7 Write the following numbers in ascending order.

7^3; 9^0; 8^2; 5^3; 2^7

8 Evaluate each of the following.

a $3^2 \times 2^3$ **b** $\sqrt[3]{27} \times \sqrt{9}$ **c** $\dfrac{3^4}{\sqrt[4]{81}}$ **d** $\sqrt[3]{1000} + \sqrt[3]{64}$

9 Express the following as products of prime factors. Give your answers in index notation.

a 32 **b** 40 **c** 54 **d** 108

e 2500 **f** 72 **g** 12 580 **h** 450 450

10 Simplify each of the following, using the laws of indices.

a $8^4 \times 8^5$ **b** $7^6 \div 7^4$ **c** $(5^3)^4$ **d** $5^{-3} \div 5^{-7}$

e 17^0 **f** $(8^{-1})^{-1}$ **g** $18^0 \times 63^0$ **h** $4^{-8} \times 4^8$

11 Evaluate the following, giving your answers as fractions.

a 5^{-1} **b** 7^{-2} **c** 2^{-7} **d** $(4^{-6})^0$

e $\left(\dfrac{2}{3}\right)^3$ **f** $\left(\dfrac{3}{4}\right)^{-2}$ **g** $(-3)^{-2}$ **h** $\dfrac{(20 - 4)^3}{(2^2)^2}$

12 Rewrite each of these using the root symbol.

a $48^{\frac{1}{2}}$ **b** $13^{\frac{1}{3}}$ **c** $5^{\frac{3}{4}}$ **d** $20^{\frac{1}{5}}$

13 Use a calculator to evaluate the following. Give your answers to 3 decimal places.

a $48^{\frac{1}{2}}$ **b** $13^{\frac{1}{3}}$ **c** $5^{\frac{3}{4}}$ **d** $20^{\frac{1}{5}}$

14 You are given that $a = 3^6 \times 5^8 \times 7^2$.

a Give a reason why you know that a is a square number. [1]

b Find the square root of a. Give your answer as the product of powers of prime numbers. [2]

[Total: 3]

≪ RECALL AND CONNECT 4 ≪

Find the HCF and LCM for the two numbers shown. Give your answers as products of powers of prime factors.

$a = 3^4 \times 5^7 \times 11^3$

$b = 2^5 \times 3^6 \times 5^4 \times 11 \times 13$

1.6 Order of operations

1 Work out each of the following, showing all steps in your calculations.

a $(4 + 3) \times 6$ **b** $(16 - 12) \times 3$

c $25 \div (24 - 19)$ **d** $18 - (14 - 3)$

e $(48 - 16)(48 - 16) \div (16 - 12)$ **f** $(13 - 8) \times (12 - 7)$

2 Work out each of the following, showing all steps in your calculations.

a $13 - 4 \times 6 + 12$ **b** $300 + (40 - 12 + 6)$

c $\sqrt{(40 - 36)} + 4 \times 3$ **d** $\dfrac{38 \div 2}{19 \times 5}$

e $\dfrac{25}{\sqrt{3 \times 8 - 19 \times 1 + 4 \times 5}}$ **f** $\sqrt{\dfrac{48 - 24}{5 \times 6 - 24}}$

3 Use your calculator to find each of the following.

a $12 - 4 \times 2$ **b** $(8 + 4) - 9 + 3$ **c** $48 - 3(2 - 7)$

d $36 \div (8 + 4) \times 3$ **e** $\dfrac{3 \times \sqrt{25}}{2^2 + 3^2 + 8 - 6}$ **f** $\dfrac{40 - 2 \times 4^2}{2 \times \sqrt[3]{8}}$

g $\sqrt{3^4 \times 5^8 \times 7^2}$ **h** $\sqrt[3]{2^6 \times 3^3 \times 5^6}$

REFLECTION

When you used your calculator, how did you make sure the operations were done in the right order? Did you break the question into steps or check your working to avoid mistakes? What part of the process could you improve?

4 $a = 3$; $b = 2.5$; $c = -4.23$

Use your calculator to find $\dfrac{\sqrt{a^2 + b^2 - c}}{2 \times a \times b \times c}$

Give the full answer as shown on your calculator. [2]

[Total: 2]

1.7 Rounding and estimating

UNDERSTAND THIS TERM

- Estimate

1 Round each number to the nearest 10.

a	44	**b**	36	**c**	108	**d**	4
e	55	**f**	125.1	**g**	123.49	**h**	3.2^2

2 Round each number to the nearest 1000.

a	12 450	**b**	501	**c**	500
d	2499	**e**	10	**f**	2 342 345

3 Round the number 4.567 75.

a to 1 significant figure

b to 2 significant figures

c to 5 significant figures.

4 Estimate the value of each of the following. Show the rounded values you use in your working.

a $\dfrac{22.1}{5.2}$ **b** $\dfrac{13.2}{0.091 \times 19.8}$

c $\dfrac{\sqrt{35}}{17.8 - 8.4}$ **d** $0.0987 \times 328.54 + 2.7^2$

e $\sqrt{4.1 \times 9.63}$ **f** $3.2^5 - 2.3^5$

g $\dfrac{\sqrt{3.1^2 + 3.9^2}}{\sqrt{5.2^2 + 11.8^2}}$ **h** $\dfrac{\sqrt{63.2}}{\sqrt{6.1 \times 4.4}}$

REFLECTION

How did you use estimation to check that the answer showing on your calculator made sense? How does this help you feel more confident that your answer is close to being correct?

5 Janice is trying to find an approximation to $\dfrac{5.5^2 - 2.34^2}{\sqrt{8.67}}$.

a Calculate the value of $\dfrac{5.5^2 - 2.34^2}{\sqrt{8.67}}$. Give your answer to 5 decimal places. [2]

b Janice finds her approximation by rounding all of the numbers in the question to 1 significant figure and leaves her answer as a fraction in its lowest term. Find the fraction Janice calculated. [2]

c Use your calculator to find the value of Janice's approximation. Give your answer to 5 decimal places. [1]

d State whether Janice's approximation is an underestimate or an overestimate. [1]

[Total: 6]

≪ RECALL AND CONNECT 5 ≪

Use your calculator to evaluate $\dfrac{3.6-\sqrt{2.1}}{1.3^2-\sqrt{2}}$ and round your answer:

a to the nearest whole number

b to the nearest 10

c to 1 decimal place

d to 3 significant figures.

REFLECTION

How can you use estimation to check the answer shown on your calculator is sensible? How can this make you feel confident that you are at least close to the correct answer?

SELF-ASSESSMENT CHECKLIST

Let's revisit the Knowledge and Exam skills focus for this chapter.
Decide how confident you are with each statement.

	Now I can	Show it	Needs more work	Almost there	Confident to move on
1	identify and classify different types of numbers	List all the even, odd, square, cube and prime numbers from 1 to 30.			
2	find common factors and common multiples of numbers	Complete Question 6 in section 1.2. Then write your own HCF/LCM question and swap with a partner to solve and mark.			
3	write numbers as products of their prime factors	Create sets of flashcards with a number, its prime factorisation and with a factor tree.			
4	work with integers used in real-life situations	A room starts at 10 °C. Find the temperature if the room cools by 19 degrees. Now write your own real-life example involving negative numbers.			
5	calculate with powers and roots of numbers	Complete Q1 and Q4 in section 1.5. Then explain the difference between a square root and a cube root to someone else.			

CONTINUED

	Now I can	Show it	Needs more work	Almost there	Confident to move on
6	understand the meaning of indices	Work out 4^5. Write a sentence to explain what the index means.			
7	use the rules of indices	Simplify $3^8 \times 3^9$, writing your answer as a power of 3.			
8	revise the basic rules for operating with numbers	Evaluate $3 \times (4 + 7) + 52$. Now write down three number sentences and identify which operation comes first in each.			
9	perform basic calculations using mental methods and with a calculator	Mentally work out 25×4 and $150 \div 6$. Then use a calculator to work out $(6.5 \times 4.3) \div 2$ and explain each step to a friend.			
10	round numbers in different ways to estimate and approximate answers	Round 4.2567 to 2 significant figures. Then estimate the value of $\sqrt{51 \times 9}$ by rounding and comparing it with your calculator result.			
11	answer questions that include the command work 'give'	Explain to a partner how to answer a 'give' question clearly and completely.			
12	use a calculator to work out answers using several operations at once.	Calculate $\frac{3.2^7 - 2.3^8}{3.6 \times 7.1}$. Give your answer to 3 significant figures. Then reflect on how you checked the steps were in the right order.			

2 Making sense of algebra

KNOWLEDGE FOCUS

In this chapter, you will answer questions on:

- using letters to represent numbers
- writing expressions to represent mathematical information
- substituting numbers for words and letters in expressions
- adding and subtracting like terms to simplify expressions
- multiplying and dividing to simplify expressions
- expanding expressions by removing grouping symbols
- using index notation in algebra
- learning and applying the laws of indices to simplify expressions
- working with fractional indices.

EXAM SKILLS FOCUS

In this chapter you will:

- show that you understand the command 'write down' and can successfully answer 'write down' questions
- make connections between different maths concepts.

In this chapter you will focus on the command 'write down'. It is important that you recognise how to answer a question that includes this command.

Write down	give an answer without significant working.

When asked to 'write down' an answer, you just need to give an answer without significant working. There is no expectation that you would take time setting out your reasoning; only the answer is required. For example, if you are asked to write down all the prime numbers between 15 and 20, you just list them '17 and 19' and do not need to explain anything about your answer. You do not need to show that these numbers are prime, you just need to recall them.

You will also look at making connections in this chapter. Index notation is a good example of how algebra and basic number work connect. Indices and roots are used in the same way for both numbers and algebra.

2.1 Using letters to represent unknown values

UNDERSTAND THIS TERM

- Expression

1 Write each expression in its simplest form, using algebraic notation.

a $8 \times x$

b $3 \times c \times c$

c $x \times y \times y$

d $3x \div 5z$

e $y \times (2 \times x - 4)$

f $7 \times a + 4 \times b$

g $(5 \times y) \div (4 \times y - 3 \times z)$

h $(y \times y + z \times z) \div (z \times z + t \times t)$

2 Let an unknown number be x. Write expressions for each of the following.

a The sum of the unknown number and 18.

b A number that is 6 greater than the unknown number.

c Three less than one third of the unknown number.

d Seven lots of the unknown number taken away from the square of the unknown number.

e The sum of −6 and the unknown number.

f The fraction obtained when 5 more than the unknown number is divided by 7 more than the unknown number.

g Three times the unknown number, subtracted from 12.

h Seven times the answer you get when the unknown number is subtracted from 5.

3 The bill for a meal is $$p$. Three friends decide to share the cost between them equally. How much does each person pay?

4 The prize money for a competition is $$d$. A group of n friends enter the competition together and win. They decide to share the prize money equally.

a Write down an expression for the prize money each of the friends will receive. [1]

An anonymous person decides to add $$p$ to the total prize.

b Write down an expression for the prize money each of the friends will receive in total. [1]

[Total: 2]

5 A group of friends decide to hire boats to sail on a lake. The boat owner charges $$x$ per boat and a group charge of $$y$ on top of the total hire charge. The cost is then shared equally amongst the n friends in the group.

Write down an expression for the amount paid by each of the friends. [2]

[Total: 2]

REFLECTION

How did you know your answers to Questions 4 and 5 were correct? Do you know how to use numerical examples to check?

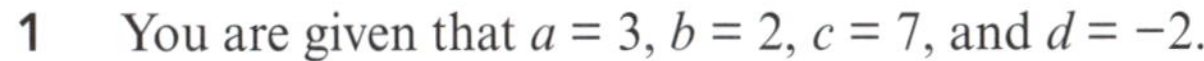

2.2 Substitution

1 You are given that $a = 3$, $b = 2$, $c = 7$, and $d = -2$.

Work out the value of each of the following expressions.

a	$4a$	b	$3b^2$	c	$c^2 + d^2$
d	$(a + b)(c + d)$	e	$a(bc)^2$	f	$\frac{5c^2}{bd}$
g	$\frac{300}{ab^2}$	h	$\frac{1}{4}bdc$	i	$\frac{a^2 + b^2}{5b^2}$
j	$\frac{a}{b} - \frac{c}{d}$	k	$(abc)^3$	l	$b^3 - d^3$

2 A clock pendulum has length l metres. If the pendulum is pulled to one side, released and allowed to swing, the time, in seconds, taken to return to the starting position is approximately $2a\sqrt{\frac{l}{g}}$.

It is known that the value of a is approximately 3.14 and the value of g is approximately 9.81.

Find the approximate time taken for the pendulum to complete a full swing if the length of the pendulum is 0.65 metres.

« RECALL AND CONNECT 1 «

Round your answer for Question 2 to 3 significant figures.

REFLECTION

Although this is only the second chapter of the book, have you noticed how key ideas from the previous chapter keep returning? Each time a connection between chapters comes up, do you spend time thinking about and discussing why those connections might be important? Learning how to understand connections will help you get even better at problem solving.

3 The volume of a cone is given by the expression $\frac{1}{3}ah$, where a is the area of the base and h is the height of the cone.

a Find the volume of the cone if the base area is 11 cm^2 and the height of the cone is 18 cm. [2]

You are given instead that the height of the cone is 6 times the area of the base.

b Write down an expression for the height of the cone in terms of a. [1]

c Write down an expression for the volume of the cone in terms of a only, using index notation where appropriate. [2]

[Total: 5]

2.3 Simplifying expressions

UNDERSTAND THIS TERM

- Simplify

1 Simplify each of the following expressions by adding or subtracting like terms.

a $8p + 10p$

b $15t - 8t$

c $4k - 7k$

d $9m + 9m$

e $9m - 9m$

f $3x + 2y + 5y$

g $4pqr + 2xyz - 3pqr - xyz$

h $5mn + 6nm$

i $3p^2 + 4q - 6p^2 + 11q$

j $12p^3q + 3p^2q^2 - 8p^3q$

k $4(x + y) + 6(x^2 + y^2) - 2(x + y) + 8(x^2 + y^2)$

l $3xy + 6xy + 6yz + 12xz$

m $4x + 6y + 8x + 12$

n $7c - 8d + 3 - 9c - 8d - 17$

2 Multiply each of the following.

a $4 \times 6x$

b $8y \times 9$

c $3x \times 4x$

d $4xy \times 3x$

e $3 \times 4x \times 5y$

f $2a \times 3ab \times 4ab^2$

g $7 \times -3 \times 4p \times 5pq$

h $12xy \times 2xz \times 6yz$

i $xyz \times xyz \times xyz$

3 Simplify each of the following.

a $\frac{8r}{4}$

b $\frac{24y^2}{12y^2}$

c $\frac{5mn}{15mn}$

d $\frac{17pqr}{3pq}$

e $\frac{65xy^2}{15y^2}$

f $4x \times \frac{6}{12x}$

g $\frac{a}{3} \times \frac{b}{6}$

h $\frac{15uv}{7} \times \frac{14}{3u}$

4 Joachim is painting lines on a playground. He paints the lines in stages, walking in a straight line, but in a different direction for each stage. Here are the distances Joachim walks in each stage.

Stage 1: $4d$ metres.

Stage 2: Three times the distance he walked in Stage 1.

Stage 3: 4 metres more than he walked in Stage 1

Stage 4: $3d$ metres less than he walked in Stage 2.

a Write down expressions for the distances Joachim walked in each of Stages 2, 3 and 4. [3]

b Write down an expression for the total distance walked across all four stages and simplify your answer as far as possible. [2]

[Total: 5]

REFLECTION

Why do you think algebra is important for problems like this? Think about how your answer compares to the words given in each stage. What are the benefits of using algebra for problems like this?

2.4 Working with brackets

UNDERSTAND THIS TERM

- Expand

1 Expand each of the following.

a	$3(x + 6)$	**b**	$8(p + 4)$	**c**	$5(u - 3)$
d	$6(2 + 6a)$	**e**	$4m(m + n)$	**f**	$3pq(4 - p)$
g	$6x^2(x + y)$	**h**	$5p^2q(2q + 3)$	**i**	$12xyz(2x + 3y + 4z)$

2 Expand and simplify each of the following.

a	$4(x + 5) + x + 2$	**b**	$5p + 4(p - 7)$
c	$4x(x - 3) + x^2 - 5$	**d**	$4mn(4 + m) + 5m^2n - 7mn^2$
e	$3(x + 4) + 5(x + 6)$	**f**	$5(g - 4) + 3(g + 6)$
g	$4(2h - 4) + 5(5h - 3)$	**h**	$4(xy - 3) + x(y - 4)$
i	$9(8k - 7) + 9(8k - 7)$		

3 Expand and simplify each of the following.

a	$-3(x + 6) + x - 32$	**b**	$-2p + 4(p - 7)$
c	$-7x(x - 2) + 3x^2 - 4$	**d**	$-2mn(5 - m) + 8m^2n - 11mn^2$
e	$-7(x + 3) + 5(x + 6)$	**f**	$-5(g - 4) - 3(g + 7)$
g	$4(3h - 5) - 5(5h - 3)$	**h**	$-3(xy - 7) - x(y - 2)$
i	$-6(3k - 7) - 9(4k - 7)$		

4 The diagram shows a garden with a pond cut from the corner.
The lengths of some of the edges of the garden are shown.

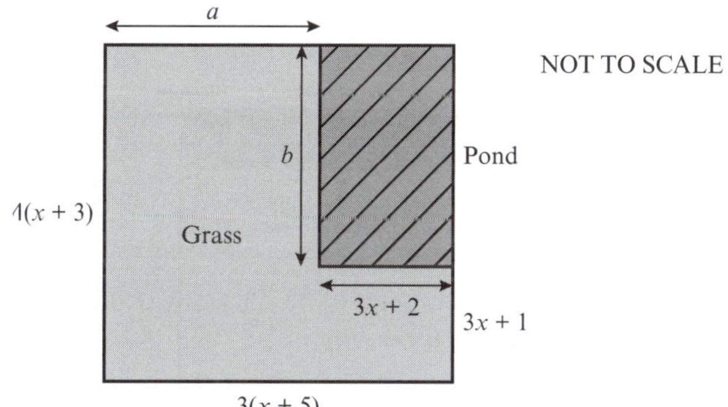

a Write down an expression for a. Expand and simplify your answer. [2]

b Write down an expression for b. Expand and simplify your answer. [2]

c Write down an expression for the total perimeter of the grass. [1]

d Simplify your answer to part **c**. [1]

[Total: 6]

REFLECTION

How do you know if you have simplified an answer completely?

2.5 Indices

UNDERSTAND THESE TERMS

- Index
- Indices

1 Simplify each of the following.

a $y^3 \times y^4$ b $a^3 \times a^0$ c $4g^3 \times 5g^7$

d $8n \times 4n^2$ e $c^3 \times c^5 \times c$ f $b^5 \div b^3$

g $h^7 \div h^2$ h $\frac{t^8}{t}$ i $\frac{10k^6}{2k^4}$

j $\frac{6p^{12}}{12p^6}$ k $\frac{728y^{456}}{728y^{456}}$ l $\frac{32xyz^4}{12xz^2}$

2 Simplify each of the following.

a $(p^3)^2$ b $(2x)^4$ c $(4m^2)^2$

d $(j^2k^2)^3$ e $(5m^3n^4)^3$ f $\left(\frac{x}{y}\right)^4$

g $\frac{(h^3)^4}{h^8}$ h $(745c^{45})^0$ i $\frac{(3x^2y^4)^3}{(2xy)^2}$

3 Write each of the following as a fraction, using positive indices only.

a 5^{-4} b 7^{-6} c 3^{-2}

d x^{-3} e p^{-8} f q^{-7}

g $4 \times t^{-6}$ h $3p \times h^{-4}$ i $5c^{-3}d^{-5}$

« RECALL AND CONNECT 2 «

Simplify each of the following. Write your answers using positive indices only.

a $y^{-2} \times y^{-5}$ b $z^5 \div z^{-6}$ c $t^{-3} \div t^{-8}$

d $\frac{k^{-3}}{k^2}$ e $\frac{w^{-7}}{w^{-9}}$ f $12h^{-4} \div 9h^{-7}$

g $(g^2h)^{-3}$ h $(3d^{-3}e^{-2})^{-5}$ i $\frac{5g^{-3}}{14g^{-3}} \times \frac{21g^{-8}}{10g^4}$

4 Find the value of x that will make each of the following true.

a $3^x = 27$ b $2^x = 16$ c $5^{x+3} = 25$

d $4^x = \frac{1}{256}$ e $10^{x-4} = \frac{1}{10\,000}$ f $8^x + 7 = 71$

g $(3^x)^2 = 81$ h $2(2^x)^4 = 32$ i $34\,563^x = 1$

≪ RECALL AND CONNECT 3 ≪

Simplify each of the following.

a $y^{\frac{1}{4}} \times y^{\frac{3}{4}}$ b $x^{\frac{2}{3}} \times x^{\frac{4}{3}}$ c $\left(\frac{x^{\frac{4}{5}}}{x^{\frac{3}{5}}}\right)^0$

d $\frac{4h^{\frac{1}{2}}}{12h}$ e $\frac{3}{4}b^{\frac{1}{3}} \times \frac{1}{4}b^{\frac{1}{6}}$ f $-\frac{4}{5}k^{\frac{1}{4}} \div \frac{2}{5}k^{-\frac{3}{4}}$

g $(16h^{\frac{1}{2}})^{\frac{1}{2}}$ h $(36p^{-\frac{2}{3}})^{\frac{3}{2}}$ i $(x^2y^3)^{\frac{1}{4}} \div (x^2y^3)^{\frac{3}{8}}$

5 Write down these expressions in fully simplified form.

a x^0 [1]

b $(x^{\frac{1}{2}})^2$ [1]

c $\left(\frac{x}{y}\right)^{-2}$ [2]

[Total: 4]

REFLECTION

How confident do you feel when following the instruction to 'write down' an answer? Have you ever wasted time by giving too much explanation or writing too much working? Remember that 'write down' does not require anything other than an answer, which you do not need to simplify unless asked to.

SELF-ASSESSMENT CHECKLIST

Let's revisit the Knowledge and Exam skills focus for this chapter.
Decide how confident you are with each statement.

	Now I can	Show it	Needs more work	Almost there	Confident to move on
1	use letters to represent numbers	Explain to a partner why letters are used in algebra. Write an example.			
2	write expressions to represent mathematical information	If n people each pay \$$a$ to take part in a competition, how much money is paid in total?			
3	substitute numbers for words and letters in expressions	If $a = 3$ and $b = 7$, find the value of $a^2 + b^2$. Make flashcards with an expression, values and the substituted answer.			
4	add and subtract like terms to simplify expressions	Simplify $7x + 4y - 3x - 10y$			

CONTINUED

	Now I can	Show it	Needs more work	Almost there	Confident to move on
5	multiply and divide to simplify expressions	Simplify $\frac{3x^2}{5y} \times \frac{15y^2}{9x}$ Make a two-step problem and swap it with a friend to solve.			
6	expand expressions by removing grouping symbols	Expand and simplify $-4x(x - 3) + 2(x + 5)$			
7	use index notation in algebra	Understand that $x^5 = x \times x \times x \times x \times x$			
8	learn and apply the laws of indices to simplify expressions	Simplify $5x^2 \times 4y^3 \times 3xy$ Write and solve your own question using at least two laws of indices.			
9	work with fractional indices	Simplify $3x^{\frac{1}{2}} \times 5x^{\frac{3}{4}}$ Create a table comparing fractional indices with their root forms.			
10	work with the 'write down' command word.	A rectangle has sides of length $3x + 2y - 4z$ and $5x - 4y + 6z$. Write down an expression for the perimeter of the rectangle. Look back at question 2.1 Q4. What made this a 'write down' question? How did you know what to do?			

3 Lines, angles and shapes

KNOWLEDGE FOCUS

In this chapter, you will answer questions on:

- using the correct terms to talk about points, lines, angles and shapes
- classifying, measuring and constructing angles
- calculating unknown angles using angle relationships
- talking about the properties of triangles, quadrilaterals, circles and polygons
- constructing triangles using a ruler and a pair of compasses.

EXAM SKILLS FOCUS

In this chapter you will:

- learn to answer questions involving the command word 'construct'
- think carefully about how you can help yourself keep to time in an examination.

A very important part of understanding examination questions is recognising command words and knowing what they mean in a mathematics examination. In this chapter you will focus on the command word 'construct'.

Construct	make an accurate drawing.

When asked to 'construct' an object in an examination, you are being asked to use mathematical instruments to draw accurately. It is likely the instruments you are expected to use will be set out in the question, so you will always need to make sure you take all the required items to an examination. When constructing with compasses and a straight edge, you will need to make sure all arcs and lines you use to make the construction are clear.

3.1 Lines and angles

UNDERSTAND THESE TERMS

- Reflex angle
- Obtuse angle
- Acute angle
- Alternate angles
- Co-interior angles
- Complementary angles
- Corresponding angles
- Parallel
- Perpendicular
- Supplementary angles
- Vertically opposite angles

1 For each angle listed:

i state if it is acute, obtuse or reflex

ii estimate the size of the angle in degrees

iii measure the angle to the nearest degree.

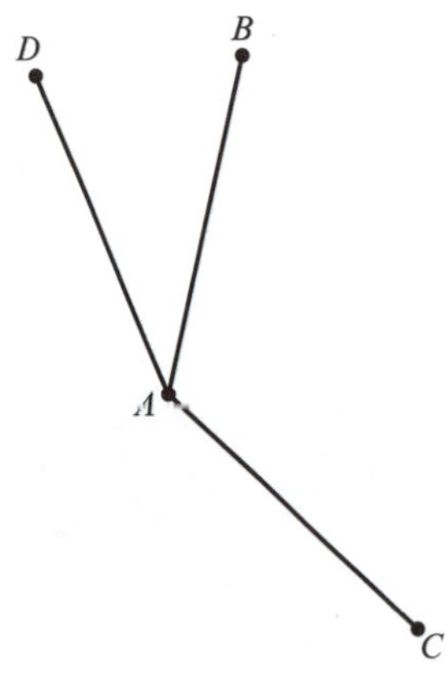

a *BAC* **b** *BAD* **c** *CAD*

2 Using a protractor and a straight edge, construct a triangle *ABC* where $\angle ABC = 40°$. [3]

[Total: 3]

3 For each diagram, find each angle marked with a letter.

a

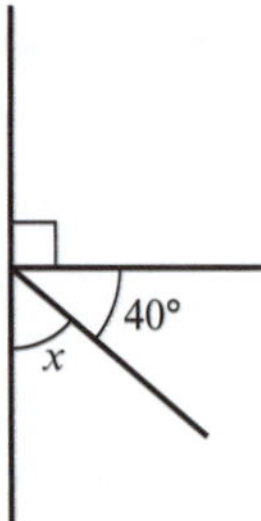

b

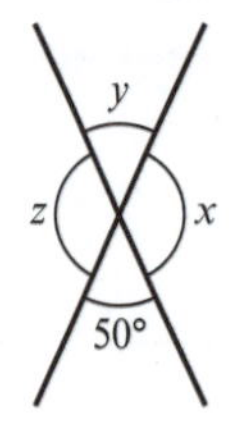

c

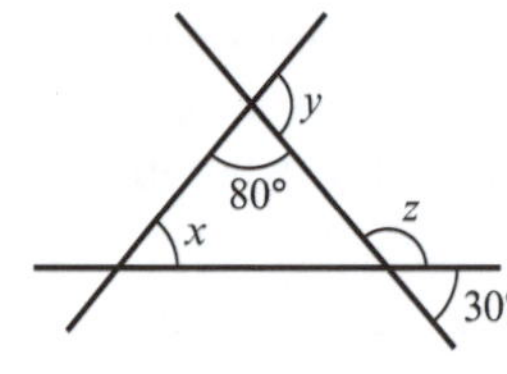

d

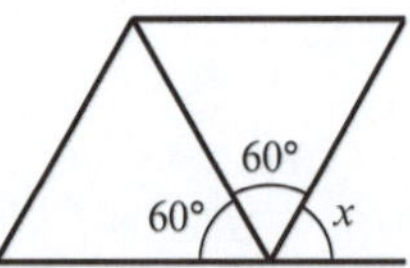

e

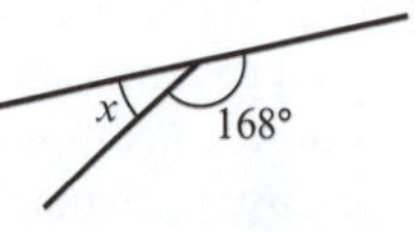

f

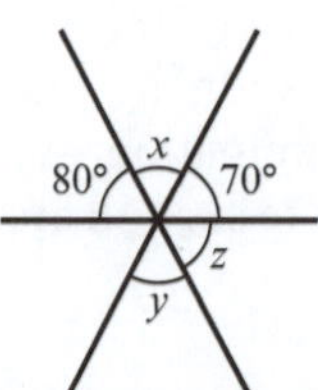

g

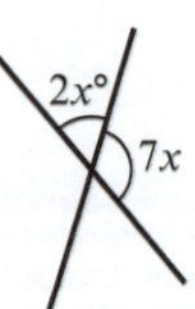

h

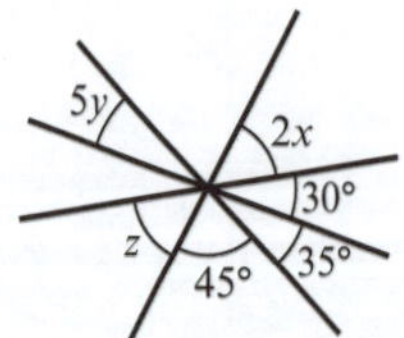

i

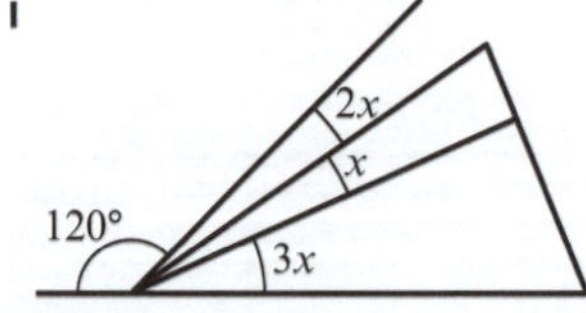

4 For each diagram, find each angle marked with a letter.

a

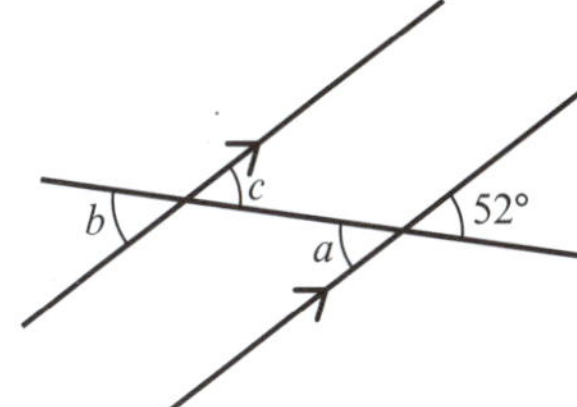

b

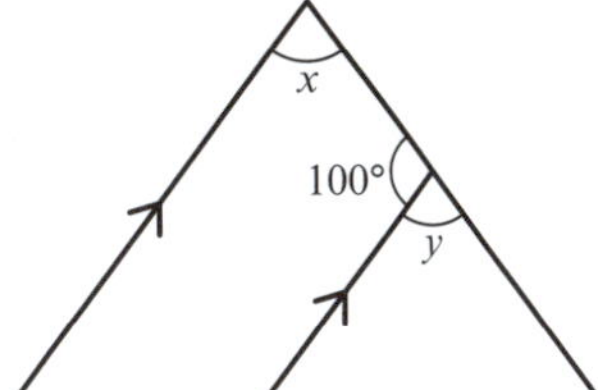

c

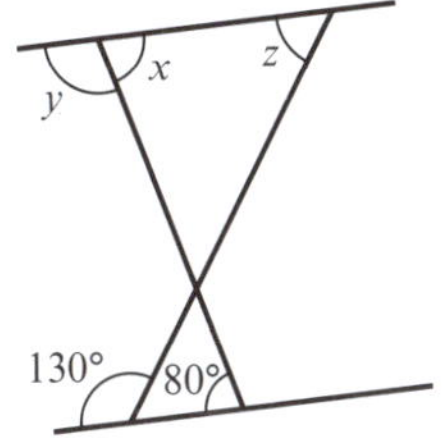

5 Look at the diagram.

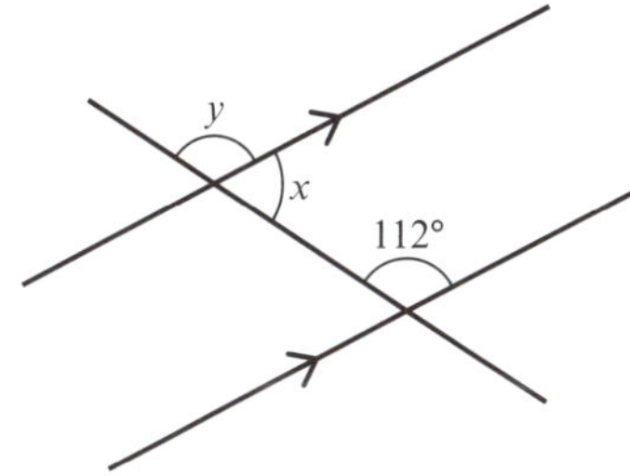

a Find the value of y. Explain your answer by giving the geometric property you have used. [2]

b Find the value of x. Explain your answer by giving the geometric property you have used. [2]

[Total: 4]

REFLECTION

How do you know that two lines are parallel? Have you ever assumed two lines are parallel without being told that they are? How can you be sure to avoid doing this?

REFLECTION

How much do you need to write when asked to 'explain' an answer? It is important to make your point, but not to write too much. You will run out of time if you write too many words.

3.2 Triangles

《 RECALL AND CONNECT 1 《

From memory, draw:

a an equilateral triangle

b an isosceles triangle

c a right-angled triangle

d a scalene triangle.

1 For each diagram, find each angle marked with a letter.

a

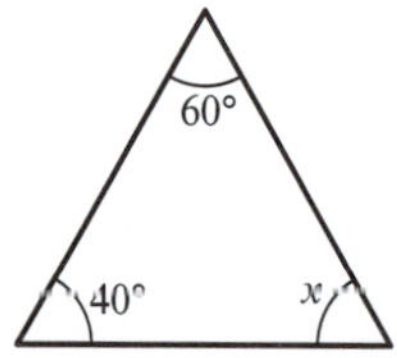

b

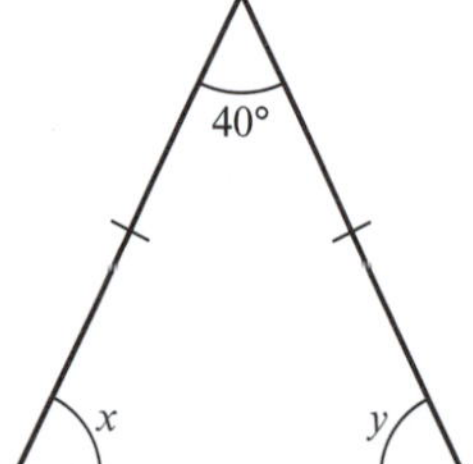

c

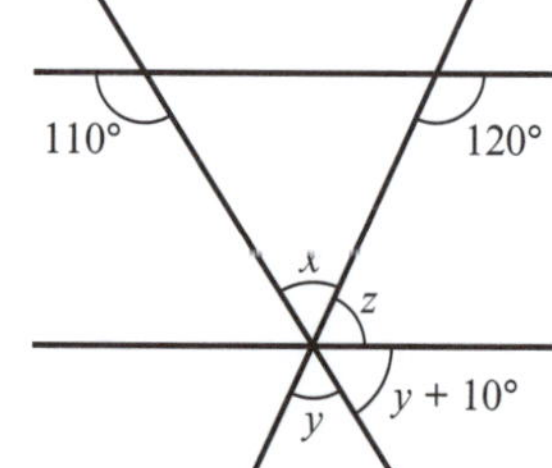

2 For each diagram, find each angle marked with a letter and explain your reasons fully.

a

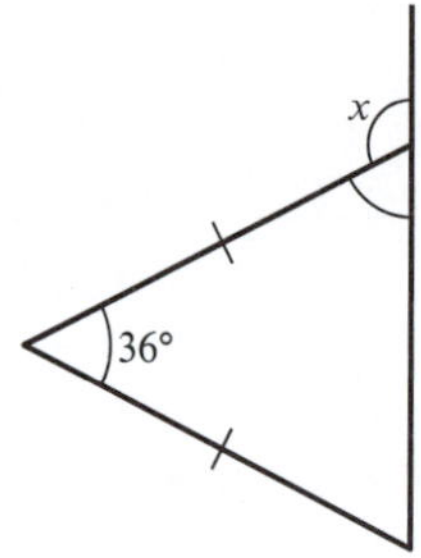

b

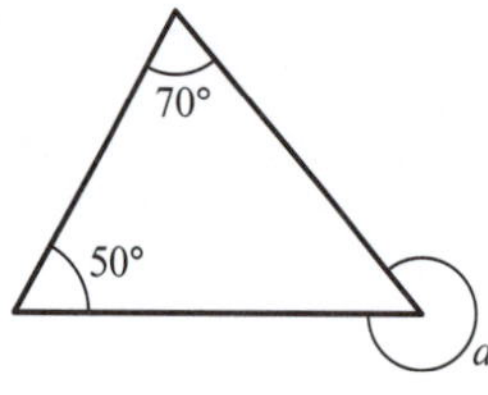

c

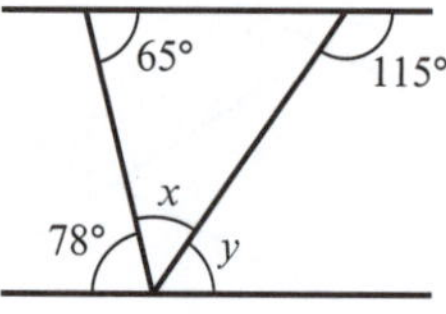

3 The triangle has exterior angles $a°$, $b°$ and $c°$.

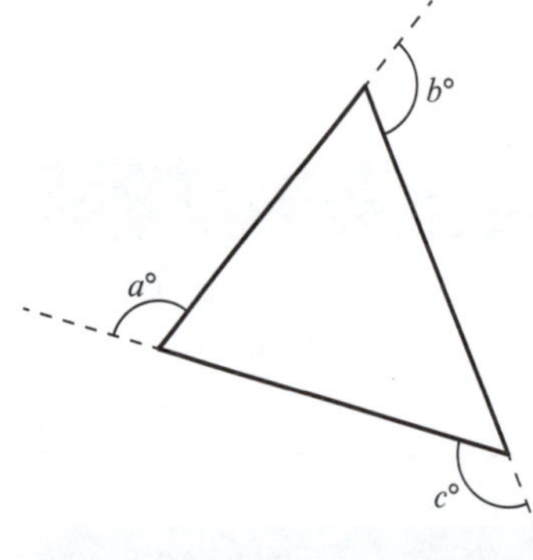

a Write down expressions for the three interior angles. [1]

b Write down and simplify an expression for the sum of the interior angles. [2]

c Write down the sum of the interior angles in *any* triangle. [1]

d Use your answers to parts **b** and **c** to explain why $a + b + c = 360$. [2]

[Total: 6]

3.3 Quadrilaterals

1 For each diagram, find each angle marked with a letter.

a

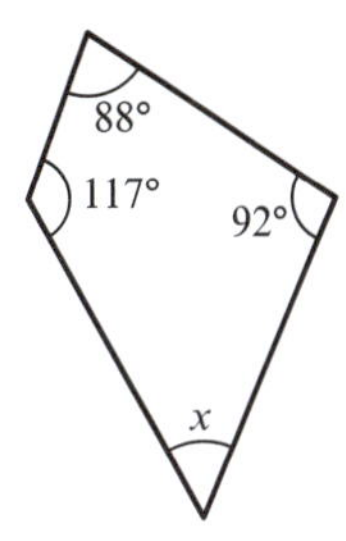

b

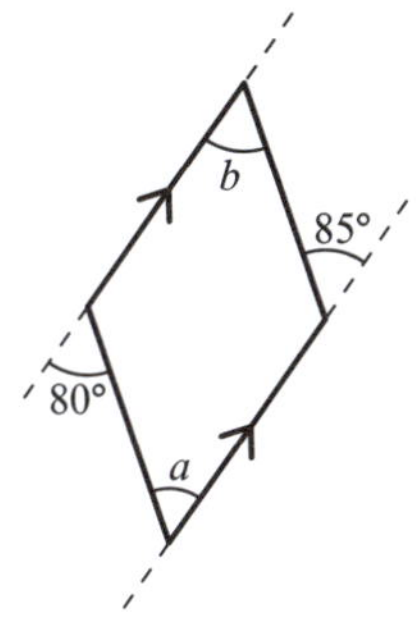

c

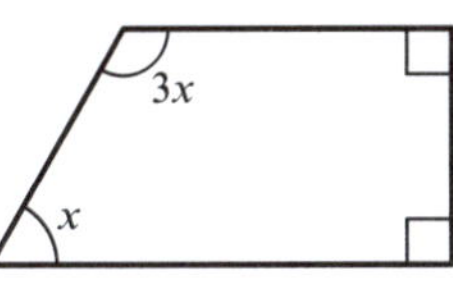

d

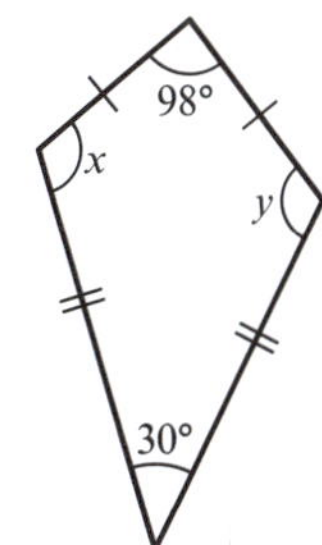

e

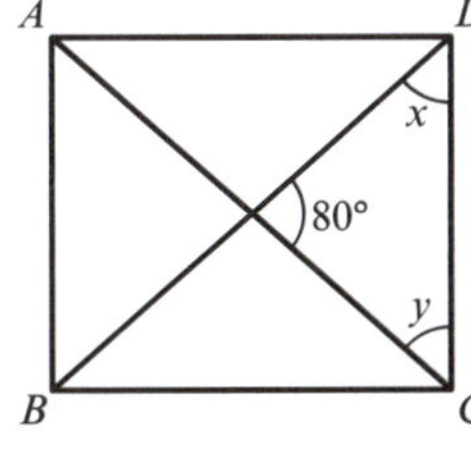

f

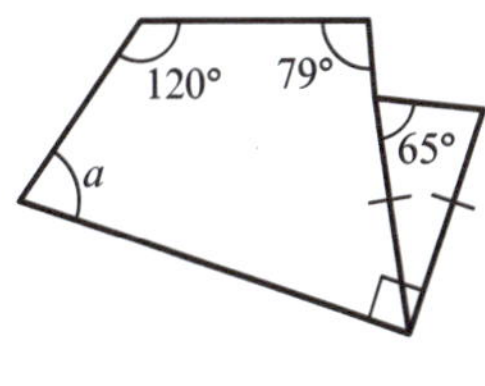

2 Look at the following quadrilateral.

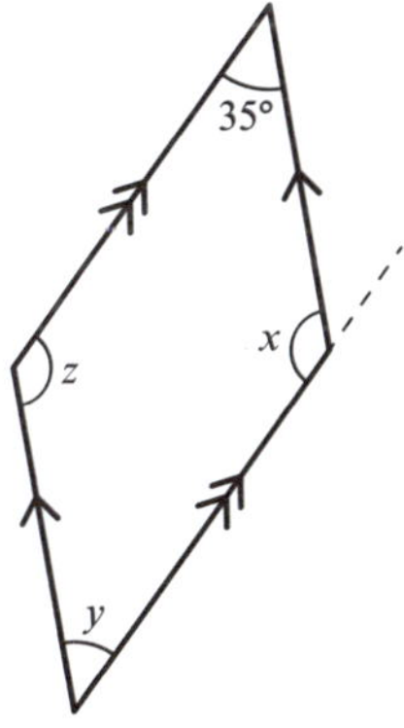

a Find the value of x, giving the geometric property you have used. [2]

b Find the value of y, giving the geometric property you have used. [2]

c Find the value of z, giving the geometric property you have used. [2]

[Total: 6]

3.4 Polygons

UNDERSTAND THESE TERMS

- Interior angle
- Exterior angle

《 RECALL AND CONNECT 2 《

What is the sum of the angles in:

a a triangle?

b a quadrilateral?

1 Find the angle marked x in each of the following diagrams.

a

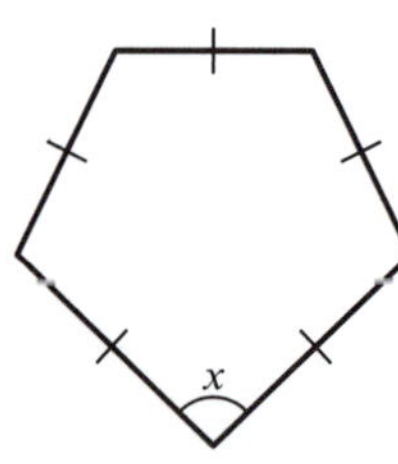

b

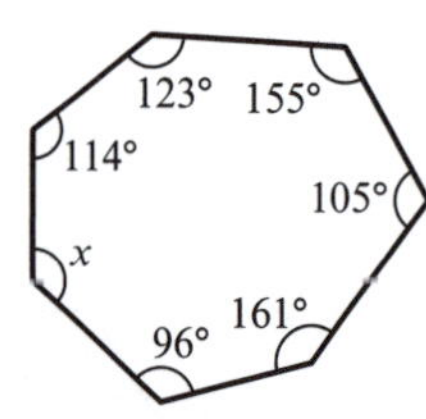

c

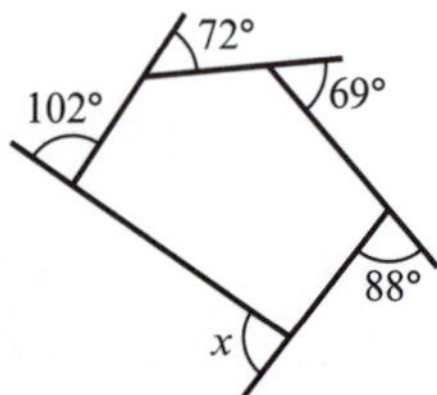

d

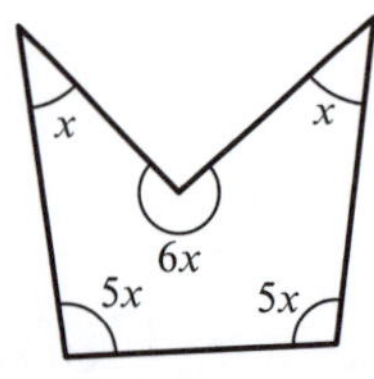

2 Find the interior angle of a regular polygon with 15 sides. [3]

[Total: 3]

3 Each interior angle of a regular polygon measures 160°.

Find the number of sides of the polygon, showing your working clearly. [3]

[Total: 3]

3.5 Circles

1 Draw six different circles and label them **a**–**f**. Use each circle to show the meaning of the following terms.

a diameter	**b** circumference	**c** chord
d major segment	**e** radius	**f** sector

2 Draw a circle and add three chords to form a triangle inside the circle.

3 **a** Draw a circle.

b Draw two chords, AB and CD, with both chords intersecting inside the circle at the point X.

c Measure the distances AX, BX, CX and DX.

d Calculate $AX \times BX$ and $CX \times DX$. What do you notice?

e Repeat parts **a**–**d** for some different circles and chords. What do you notice?

4 a Draw a circle with radius 8 cm. [1]

b Draw a chord inside the circle by joining any two points on the circumference. [1]

c Draw a second chord that crosses the first chord. [1]

d Use a ruler to extend both chords until they meet. Mark the intersection point. [1]

e Explain what you notice about the position of this intersection point. [1]

[Total: 5]

3.6 Construction

UNDERSTAND THESE TERMS

- Radius
- Circumference
- Diameter
- Chord
- Tangent

« RECALL AND CONNECT 3 «

a What tools do you need for geometric constructions?

b Explain the following.

i How to draw a perpendicular line from a point.

ii How to construct a triangle with three known sides.

1 Accurately construct these triangles.

a 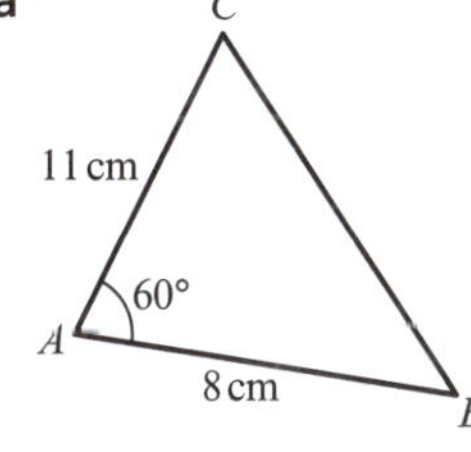

b 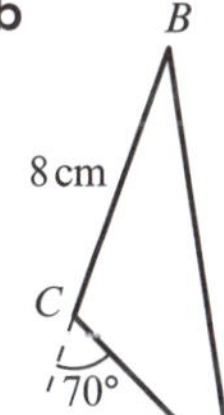

c 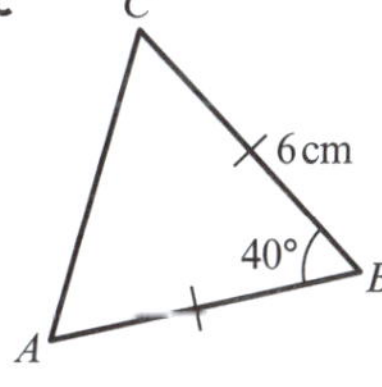

d 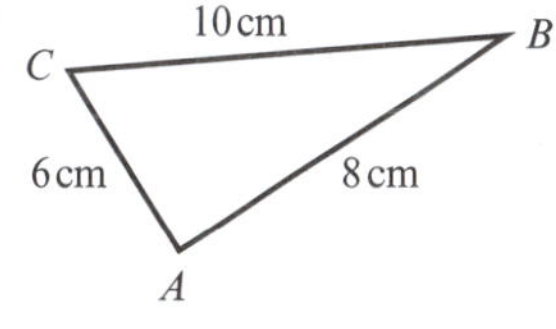

REFLECTION

How did you make sure your constructions were accurate? What steps did you take to make sure you kept things accurate?

How did the construction lines and arc(s) you leave on each diagram help you to check you have drawn the diagrams correctly?

2 Construct a triangle with sides 5.6 cm, 4.7 cm and 6.3 cm. [3]

[Total: 3]

SELF-ASSESSMENT CHECKLIST

Let's revisit the Knowledge and Exam skills focus for this chapter.
Decide how confident you are with each statement.

	Now I can	Show it	Needs more work	Almost there	Confident to move on
1	use the correct terms to talk about points, lines, angles and shapes	Create a glossary of key terms, each with a diagram and your own example.			
2	classify, measure and construct angles	Draw a diagram you would use to explain to a friend how to measure and classify angles.			
3	calculate unknown angles using angle relationships	Try to complete Questions 6–9 in Unit 1 Exam Practice section.			
4	talk about the properties of triangles, quadrilaterals, circles and polygons	Read through your answers to Question 1 in Section 3.5 and write a definition for each feature of a circle.			
5	construct triangles using a ruler and a pair of compasses	Write a paragraph to explain how you construct a triangle when you know the lengths of all three sides.			
6	use the command word 'construct'	Write a list of the things you need to remember to have and to do when constructing a diagram.			
7	think carefully about how you can help yourself keep to time in an examination.	Set a timer and complete Question 2 from Section 3.6. What strategies helped you stay within time?			

4 Collecting, organising and displaying data

KNOWLEDGE FOCUS

In this chapter, you will answer questions on:

- collecting data and classifying different types of data
- organising data using tally tables, frequency tables, stem-and-leaf diagrams and two-way tables
- drawing pictograms, bar charts and pie charts to display data and answering questions about it.

EXAM SKILLS FOCUS

In this chapter you will:

- show that you understand the command word 'explain' and can successfully answer 'explain' questions.

In this chapter you will focus on the command word 'explain'. It is important that you recognise how to answer a question that has this command word.

Explain	set out purposes or reasons, make the relationships between things clear, or say why and/or how and support with relevant evidence.

When answering an 'explain' question, you are expected to set out purposes or reasons for something, make the relationships between things clear or say why or how something works, supporting your ideas with relevant evidence. For example, you may be presented with a solution produced by someone else and be asked to explain why it is incorrect. When that happens, you need to work through the solution line by line and identify where there are mistakes. You then need to explain how to correct those mistakes.

4.1 Collecting and classifying data

UNDERSTAND THESE TERMS

- Quantitative
- Qualitative
- Categorical
- Numerical
- Discrete
- Continuous

1 State whether each of the following is *qualitative/categorical* or *quantitative/numerical* data.

- **a** The age of a cat in years.
- **b** The number of seats in a theatre.
- **c** The colour of a fence.
- **d** The name of a movie.
- **e** The age of a cat in months.
- **f** The temperature at the summit of Mount Everest.
- **g** The first digit of a telephone number.

2 State whether each of the following numerical data is *discrete* or *continuous*.

- **a** The height of Cotopaxi Volcano in metres.
- **b** The shoe sizes of children in a Year 11 class.
- **c** The number of plums growing on a tree.
- **d** The age of the Sun in years.
- **e** The depth of the ocean.
- **f** The speed of a car.
- **g** The length of a river.

3 Helga is recording the masses in grams of Hyacinth Macaws as part of a conservation project in southern Brazil. The masses of two birds, Jessica and Avril, are both measured to be 145 g. Helga says that this does not mean the birds have exactly the same mass.

- **a** Explain why Helga is correct. [2]
- **b** Work out the biggest possible difference between the masses of Jessica and Avril. [2]

[Total: 4]

REFLECTION

Do your explanations use the correct mathematical terminology?
How can you be even better at choosing the right words?

4.2 Organising data

UNDERSTAND THESE TERMS

- Tally
- Frequency
- Stem-and-leaf diagram
- Total

1 Mr Rafi runs a public library. Over a period of three days he notes how many books have been borrowed during each hour. His records are shown below.

3	2	4	3	8	7	9	3	10	2
4	6	8	4	12	10	8	5	6	4
3	2	6	9	4	5	7	6	5	7

a Construct a tally and frequency table for this data.

b What was the largest number of books borrowed in any hour?

c What was the smallest number of books borrowed in any hour?

d What was the most common number of books borrowed in any hour?

2 Sapna asked each of 40 friends how many minutes they took to travel to get to work. The table shows some information about her results. Some of the data is missing.

Time taken (m minutes)	Frequency
$0 < m \leqslant 10$	3
$10 < m \leqslant 20$	8
$20 < m \leqslant 30$	11
$30 < m \leqslant 40$	
$40 < m \leqslant 50$	

a Work out how many people take 20 minutes or less to travel to work.

b It turns out that the last two classes have the same frequency.
Calculate the number of people who take 40 minutes or less to get to work.

3 Thirty people are asked to record the number of books they had read during the year 2024. The results are listed below.

42	31	29	38	24	17	9	18	28	27
34	35	38	40	40	19	32	39	22	11
11	9	2	17	32	19	22	29	31	33

Illustrate this data using an ordered stem-and-leaf diagram.

4 A wool farm in Peru has 79 guanacos and 74 alpacas. The guanacos and alpacas are a mixture of adult and juvenile. There are 28 adult guanacos and a total of 93 juveniles.

a Copy and complete the following table to show the number of adult and juvenile guanacos and alpacas.

	Guanaco	Alpaca	Total
Juvenile			
Adult			
Total			

b Comment on the proportion of adult and juvenile alpacas.

5 The following data gives the number of days of sunshine in one year for 17 Cornish towns and 15 Kentish towns.

Cornish	139	169	184	143	167	156	149	176	154
Kentish	176	155	165	165	156	157	165	154	147

Cornish	166	186	155	178	130	177	189	155
Kentish	176	146	152	140	143	152		

a Construct a back-to-back stem-and-leaf diagram to represent these data sets. [3]

b Explain how the diagram could help you decide where to build a new open-air cinema. [3]

[Total: 6]

4.3 Using charts to display data

UNDERSTAND THESE TERMS

- Pie chart
- Line graph

1 The students in a class were asked how they got to school that day. Here are the results.

Method of travel	Tally	Frequency
Walk	𝍸 ||||	9
Bike	|||	3
Car	𝍸 |	6
Bus	𝍸 𝍸 ||	12
	Total	30

Draw a pictogram to show the results.

2 The table below shows the stopping distances for cars, under perfect conditions. At each speed, the stopping distance is split into 'thinking distance' and 'braking distance'.

Thinking distance is the distance the car travels from the moment a driver notices the need to stop, to before the brakes are applied (reaction time).

Braking distance is the distance travelled from the moment the brakes are applied, until the car stops.

Speed (km/h)	Thinking distance (m)	Braking distance (m)	Total stopping distance (m)
32	6	6	12
48	8	14	22
64	11	23	34
80	15	38	**Y**
96	18	**X**	72
112	21	73	94

a Work out the missing distances labelled **X** and **Y**.

b Draw a bar chart to show this information, using shading within each bar to show both the thinking time and the braking time.

« RECALL AND CONNECT 1 «

The students in Mr Free-Quincy's class take a Geography test and receive scores out of 10, which are listed below.

3	7	6	2	5	9	10	8	7	1
8	4	3	6	5	7	8	7	6	5
3	6	9	8	7	5	9	6	7	8

a Illustrate the results in a tally chart and work out the frequency for each test result.

b Illustrate the results in a pie chart.

3 As part of a science project, the height of a plant is measured every 3 days. The readings are listed in the table below.

Day	0	3	6	9	12	15	18
Height (cm)	4	7	9	14	16	19	24

a Draw a line graph to show how the height of the plant changes with time.

b Estimate the height of the plant after 14 days.

c Estimate the age of the plant when the height was 11 cm.

4 The pie charts below show some information about the ages of people in two different hotels in the same town.

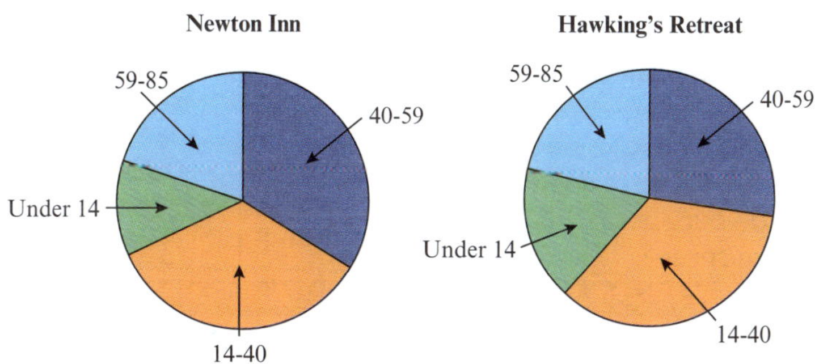

a Estimate the percentage of people staying in Newton Inn that are aged 40–59. [1]

b There are 250 guests staying in the Newton Inn. Use your answer to part **a** to work out how many people staying there are aged 40–59. [2]

c Justin says: *'These charts show there are more people under 14 staying at Hawking's Retreat than at Newton Inn.'*

Justin is incorrect. Explain why the charts do not show this. [1]

[Total: 4]

REFLECTION

Have you thought carefully about *why* each of the different data display methods are used? They are all designed for different purposes. Do you know what those purposes are?

SELF-ASSESSMENT CHECKLIST

Let's revisit the Knowledge and Exam skills focus for this chapter. Decide how confident you are with each statement.

	Now I can	Show it	Needs more work	Almost there	Confident to move on
1	collect data and classify different types of data	Explain which data is continuous.			
2	organise data using tally tables, frequency tables, stem-and-leaf diagrams and two-way tables	Construct a frequency table from the data provided.			
3	draw pictograms, bar charts and pie charts to display data and answer questions about it	Construct a pie chart to show the different instruments in an orchestra.			
4	use the command word 'explain' and answer examination questions that use the word	Explain why an answer is correct, using appropriate mathematical terms.			
5	work with the command word 'explain'.	Now you have completed this chapter, go back to each question in which you attempted to 'explain' and read your answers. Do they make sense?			

Exam practice 1

This section contains past paper questions from previous Cambridge exams, which draw together your knowledge on a range of topics that you have covered up to this point. These questions give you the opportunity to test your knowledge and understanding.

The following question has an example student response and commentary provided. Work through the question first, then compare your answer to the sample response and commentary. Are your answers different to the sample responses?

1 $234 = 2 \times 3^2 \times 13$

$1872 = 2^4 \times 3^2 \times 13$

$234 \times 1872 = 438\,048$

Use this information to write 438 048 as a product of its prime factors. [1]

Cambridge IGCSE Mathematics (0580) Paper 21 Q7 June 2020 **[Total: 1]**

Example student response	Commentary
$438\,048 = 234 \times 1872$ $= 2 \times 2^4 \times 3^2 \times 13 \times 3^2 \times 13$	The student has correctly worked out how to use the information provided and has written an answer that is correct, but it should be simplified. ***This answer scores 0 out of 1 mark.***

Now that you have read the commentary to the previous question, here is a similar question that you should attempt. Use the information from the previous response and commentary to guide you as you answer.

2 $P = 2^5 \times 3^3 \times 7$

$Q = 540$

a Find the highest common factor (HCF) of P and Q. [2]

b Find the lowest common multiple (LCM) of P and Q. [2]

c $P \times R$ is a cube number, where R is an integer. [2]

Find the smallest possible value of R.

Cambridge IGCSE Mathematics (0580) Paper 42 Q3c June 2021 **[Total: 6]**

The following question has an example student response and commentary provided. Work through the question first, then compare your answer to the sample response and commentary. Are your answers different to the sample responses?

3 **a** Simplify, giving your answer as a single power of 7.

i $7^5 \times 7^6$ [1]

ii $7^{15} \div 7^5$ [1]

iii $42 + 7$ [1]

b Simplify

$(5x^2 \times 2xy^4)^3$ [3]

Cambridge IGCSE Mathematics (0580) Paper 42 Q3a & b June 2021 **[Total: 6]**

Example student response	Commentary
a i $7^5 \times 7^6 = 49^{11}$	The student attempted to multiply powers but did not apply the correct index law. The exponent in their answer was correct, but they changed the base incorrectly, which makes the overall answer wrong. ***This answer scores 0 out of 1 mark.***
a ii $7^{15} \div 7^5 = 7^{\frac{15}{5}}$	The student has not applied the relevant index rule correctly. While they kept the base the same, they incorrectly combined the indices. ***This answer scores 0 out of 1 mark.***
a iii $42 + 7 = 49$ $= 7^2$	This is correct. The student was right to work out the sum and then noticed that 49 is a power of 7. ***This answer scores 1 out of 1 mark.***
b $(5x^2 \times 2xy^4)^3$ $= (10 \times x^2 \times xy^4)^3$ $= (10x^3y^4)^3$ $= 10^3(x^3)^3(y^4)^3$ $= 1000x^6y^7$	The student achieves 1 mark for simplifying the inside of the bracket correctly. However, they have not simplified two of the terms to achieve a second mark, and the final answer is wrong. ***This answer scores 1 out of 3 marks.***

4 Now that you have gone through the commentary, try to write an improved answer for your own solution and edit the sample student response to improve their answer to each part.

5 **a** $3^{3p} \times 3^{2p} = 729$

Find the value of p. [2]

b Simplify $(32x^{10})^{\frac{1}{5}}$ [2]

Cambridge IGCSE Mathematics (0580) Paper 22 Q13 November 2023 **[Total: 4]**

The following question has an example student response and commentary provided. Work through the question first, then compare your answer to the sample response and commentary. Are your answers different to the sample responses?

6 **a** The diagram shows an isosceles triangle with the base extended.

Find the value of x.

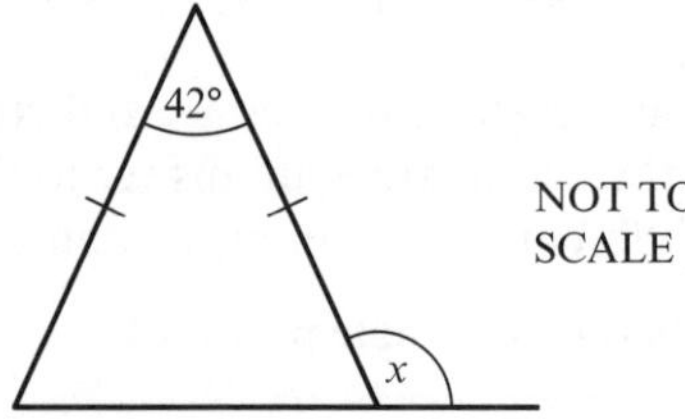

[3]

b The diagram shows three lines meeting at a point.

The ratio a:b:c = 3:4:5.

Find the value of c.

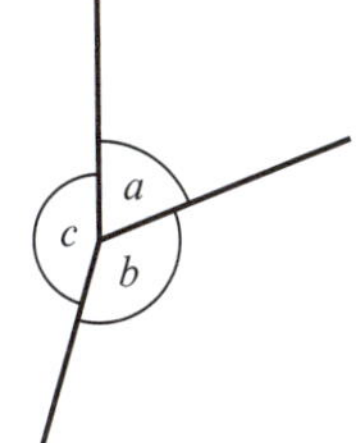

NOT TO SCALE

[3]

c A regular pentagon has an exterior angle, d.

A regular hexagon has an interior angle, h.

Find the fraction $\frac{d}{h}$.

Give your answer in its simplest form. [4]

Cambridge IGCSE Mathematics (0580) Paper 42 Q1 June 2023 **[Total: 10]**

Example student response	Commentary
a The two base angles are the same, so each will be $\frac{180-42}{2} = 69$ One of the base angles and the angle marked x form a straight line, so $x + 69 = 180$. $x = 180 - 69 = 111$	The student scores a perfect 3 out of 3: 1 mark for $\frac{180-42}{2} = 69$, 1 mark for 180 − 69, and the final mark for the correct answer, 111. ***This answer scores 3 out of 3 marks.***
b $c = 90$	The student has worked out a rather than c. Because no working is shown, it is not possible to award any of the marks, even though the student is likely to have understood what to do. Always show working! ***This answer scores 0 out of 3 marks.***
c $d = \frac{360}{5} = 72$ $h = 180 - \frac{360}{6} = 180 - 60 = 120$ $\frac{d}{h} = \frac{120}{72} = \frac{5}{3}$	1 mark for correct methods for calculating either d or h. 1 mark for each of the correct values of d and h. 0 marks for final, correctly simplified answer. The student has not substituted the values of d and h correctly. ***This answer scores 3 out of 4 marks.***

7 Find the interior angle of a regular polygon with 24 sides. [2]

Cambridge IGCSE Mathematics (0580) Paper 22 Q4 March 2020 **[Total: 2]**

8 The diagram shows two straight lines intersecting two parallel lines.

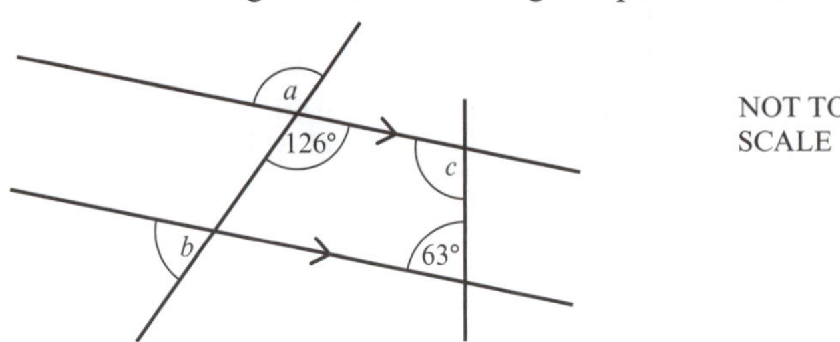

Find the values of a, b and c. [3]

Cambridge IGCSE Mathematics (0580) Paper 42 Q3a March 2021 **[Total: 3]**

9 The diagram shows an isosceles triangle.

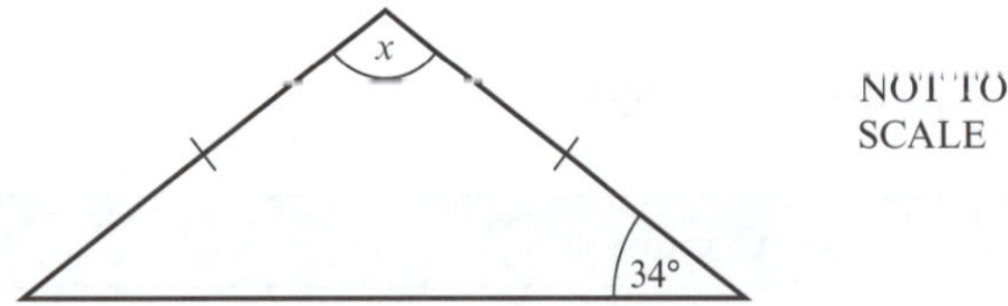

Find the value of x. [2]

Cambridge IGCSE Mathematics (0580) Paper 22 Q1 November 2022 **[Total: 2]**

The following question has an example student response and commentary provided. Work through the question first, then compare your answer to the sample response and commentary. Are your answers different to the sample responses?

10 Thibault records the number of cars of each colour in a car park.

Colour	Black	White	Silver	Red
Number of cars	8	5	4	3

He draws a pie chart to show this information.

Calculate the sector angle for the red cars. [2]

Cambridge IGCSE Mathematics (0580) Paper 22 Q2 June 2022 **[Total: 2]**

Example student response	Commentary
The fraction of cars that are red = $\frac{3}{20}$ We need this fraction of a full circle = $\frac{3}{20} \times 360° = 54°$ Sector area for the red cars = 54°	The student has the correct answer and all the working provided is correct, but they should have showed where 20 came from. 2/2 is still awarded, but if the student miscalculated the final answer, the examiner may have been required to remove both marks. ***This answer scores 2 out of 2 marks.***

11 There are 18 birds in a tree. 5 of the birds are blue, 7 are orange, 2 are green and the rest are yellow.

James wants to draw a pie chart to show this information.

Find the angle of the sector for the orange birds in this pie chart. [2]

[Total: 2]

5 Fractions, percentages and standard form

KNOWLEDGE FOCUS

In this chapter, you will answer questions on:

- finding equivalent fractions
- simplifying fractions
- adding, subtracting, multiplying and dividing fractions and mixed numbers
- finding fractions of numbers
- finding a percentage of a number
- finding one number as a percentage of another
- calculating percentage increases and decreases
- increasing and decreasing by a given percentage
- calculating reverse percentages (undoing increases and decreases)
- using standard form
- calculating with values in standard form.

EXAM SKILLS FOCUS

In this chapter you will:

- show that you understand the command word 'write' and can successfully answer 'write' questions
- show that you can make connections between different topics and combine them in answering exam questions.

In this chapter you will focus on the command word 'write'. It is important that you recognise how to answer a question that has this command word.

Write	give an answer in a specific form.

'Write' is used when you are expected to give your answer in a specific form.

For example, you may be asked to 'write the fraction $\frac{1}{5}$ as a decimal' or to 'write \$1.45 as a percentage of \$2.50'.

Examination questions often test several mathematics topics within one question. Try to make the connections between different topics when you are preparing for examinations. For example, a lot of percentage calculations involve fractions and decimals.

5.1 Revisiting fractions and 5.2 Operations on fractions

UNDERSTAND THESE TERMS

- Denominator
- Common denominator
- Numerator
- Equivalent fractions
- Mixed number

1 Express each of these fractions in their simplest form.

a $\frac{24}{36}$ b $\frac{12a}{32}$ c $\frac{15}{5x}$ d $\frac{6n}{39n}$

e $\frac{18y}{45xy}$ f $\frac{2.1}{3.6}$ g $\frac{0.02}{0.5}$

2 Evaluate the following, giving each answer in its simplest form.

a $\frac{3}{4}\times\frac{5}{9}$ b $2\frac{1}{4}\times 2\frac{3}{5}$ c $\frac{2x}{3}\times\frac{6}{4x}$

d $\frac{2}{3}+\frac{2}{7}$ e $3\frac{5}{7}+4\frac{4}{5}$ f $\frac{2}{x}+\frac{3}{x+1}$

g $\frac{7}{12}-\frac{2}{3}$ h $5\frac{5}{9}-2\frac{4}{5}$ i $\frac{2x}{7}-\frac{7}{x}$

j $\frac{6}{7}\div\frac{6}{5}$ k $2\frac{1}{5}\div 1\frac{2}{3}$ l $\frac{x+1}{2}\div\frac{6}{x-1}$

3 Write $\frac{3x^2y}{9x}$ in its simplest form. [1]

[Total: 1]

4 Write $\frac{4.5}{210}$ in its simplest form. [1]

[Total: 1]

5  Write $0.6\dot{8}$ as a fraction in its simplest form.

You must show all your working. [3]

[Total: 3]

« RECALL AND CONNECT 1 «

Write down the prime numbers between 70 and 100.

REFLECTION

Reflect on your confidence in using algebraic expressions in fractions. What strategies help you feel more certain about your understanding?

When answering Question **3**, how did you check that you had simplified correctly?

Question **5** asked you to 'Write $0.6\dot{8}$ as a fraction in its simplest form'; how did you determine that you had simplified it to its simplest form? What method did you use to confirm this?

5.3 Percentages

1 Find each of the following.

a 5% of 250
b 30% of $125
c 14% of $45.50
d 32% of $58.50
e 2.5% of 40
f 17.2% of $255
g 120% of 450
h 115% of $32

2 Express

a 15 as a percentage of 60
b 2.6 as a percentage of 40
c 27 as a percentage of 72

3 A football stadium has 32 150 seats. The owners plan to rearrange the seats so that there is room for 6% more. How many seats will there be after the rearrangement?

4 Muniz makes 340 pots in a year. The following year he makes 15% fewer pots. How many pots does Muniz make in the second year?

5 The population of the UK increased from 58 789 154 in 2001 to 63 182 178 in 2011.

What was the percentage increase in the population between 2001 and 2011?

6 The number of people buying cars in Italy in 2020 was 1 381 496. This was a decrease of 27.9% from the previous year.

How many people bought cars in Italy in 2019?

7 A shop reduces its prices by 10% for one day. By what percentage does it need to increase its prices the following day to be charging the original price?

8 Write the following percentages as fractions in their simplest form.

a 25% [1]
b 24% [1]
c 7.5% [1]
d 127.5% [1]

[Total: 4]

9 The value of a new car decreases by 15% every year.

The value today is $12 750.

a Calculate the value of the car after one year. [2]
b Calculate the value of the car one year ago. [2]

[Total: 4]

10 Priya had 35% more hits on her website in July than June.

She had 351 hits in July.

Work out how many more hits she received in July than June. [3]

[Total: 3]

11 Ranjeev buys a new car.

a The price is \$25 750.

He gets a 12.5% discount.

Calculate the amount he pays. [2]

b The range on a full charge is 410 miles.

This is 82% of the range on his previous car.

Calculate the range of his previous car. [2]

[Total: 4]

« RECALL AND CONNECT 2 «

Write 31 752 as the product of its prime factors in index notation.

5.4 Standard form

1 Convert each of the following numbers into standard form.

a	12 000	**b**	145 000 000	**c**	45 800 000 000
d	8	**e**	0.0015	**f**	0.000 045 8
g	0.000 000 000 000 24	**h**	1.000 000 5		

2 Use your calculator to find the following. Give your answers to 4 significant figures.

a	2356^7	**b**	$175\,300 \times 759\,800$	**c**	256^{16}
d	0.0009^8	**e**	$745\,000\,000 \div 0.004\,5$	**f**	$(27 \times 719)^5$
g	$\dfrac{6754}{(0.006)^3}$	**h**	$(5.34 \times 10^{-3})^4$	**i**	$(4.56 \times 10^8) + (8.7 \times 10^9)$

3 Lake Nasser is a reservoir in Egypt. The average volume of the reservoir is 1.32×10^{14} litres.

The average volume of a raindrop is 5×10^{-2} millilitres.

How many raindrops would it take to fill Lake Nasser?

4 Evaluate the following.

a	$(4 \times 10^4) \times (5.3 \times 10^5)$	**b**	$(2.4 \times 10^{10})^2$
c	$(3.2 \times 10^{-3}) \div (1.6 \times 10^{-5})$	**d**	$(4 \times 10^5) + (6 \times 10^3)$
e	$(0.3 \times 10^6) \times (34 \times 10^5)$	**f**	$(4.5 \times 10^5) \div (3.6 \times 10^{-3})$

5 $4.8 \times 10^{17} \times n = 7.2 \times 10^{25}$

Calculate the value of n.

Give your answer in standard form. [2]

[Total: 2]

6 a Write the number 0.00507 in standard form. [1]

b Calculate $(3.67 \times 10^9) \times (9.24 \times 10^{-3})$.

Give your answer in standard form. [1]

[Total: 2]

7 Calculate $(6 \times 10^{-4})^4$.

Give your answer in standard form. [1]

[Total: 1]

« RECALL AND CONNECT 3 «

How does standard form relate to place value?

REFLECTION

How will you approach questions that use the command word 'write' in exams?

Think about how you have learned to respond to these types of question. What strategies help you recognise when you need to present an answer in a specific form (like standard form or a fraction in simplest terms), or follow a rounding instruction (such as to a set number of significant figures)?

SELF-ASSESSMENT CHECKLIST

Let's revisit the Knowledge and Exam skills focus for this chapter.
Decide how confident you are with each statement.

	Now I can	Show it	Needs more work	Almost there	Confident to move on
1	find equivalent fractions	Create a set of at least four equivalent fractions using different numerators and denominators. Explain how you know they are equivalent.			
2	simplify fractions	Make flashcards with unsimplified fractions on one side and simplest form on the other. Test yourself or a partner.			

CONTINUED

	Now I can	Show it	Needs more work	Almost there	Confident to move on
3	add, subtract, multiply and divide fractions and mixed numbers	Write a multi-step word problem that involves two different fraction operations. Solve it and include a mark scheme.			
4	find fractions of numbers	Write a question that asks for a fraction of a quantity (e.g. 'What is 5/6 of 72?'). Swap with a friend and solve each other's.			
5	find a percentage of a number	Explain how to find 10%, 25%, and 1% of a number and how to build other percentages from them.			
6	find one number as a percentage of another	Choose any two numbers and write a sentence explaining how to find one as a percentage of the other. Show your steps.			
7	calculate percentage increases and decreases	Work out how much a quantity has increased or decreased as a percentage of the original quantity. For example: Priya's gas bill has increased from \$45 to \$60. What is the percentage increase?			
8	increase and decrease by a given percentage	Solve a problem like: 'A jacket costs \$80 and is increased by 15%. What is the new price?' Then write your own version.			
9	calculate reverse percentages (undoing increases and decreases)	Work out the original quantity given the new quantity and the percentage increase or decrease. For example, if a coat has been reduced by 15% in a sale and now costs \$102, what was the original price?			

CONTINUED

	Now I can	Show it	Needs more work	Almost there	Confident to move on
10	use standard form	Write and understand numbers in standard form. For example, answer Question 6a in Section 5.4.			
11	calculate with values in standard form	Choose one calculator and one non-calculator question from Section 5.4. Explain your method in full sentences or a worked example.			
12	show that you understand the command word 'write' and can successfully answer 'write' questions	Choose two 'write' questions from this chapter. Describe what made you notice the command and how you chose your answer format.			
13	show that you can make connections between different topics and combine them in answering exam questions.	Pick one question that involves both standard form and percentages, or fractions and decimals. Write a few sentences explaining how the topics were linked and how you approached the problem.			

6 Equations, factors and formulae

KNOWLEDGE FOCUS

In this chapter, you will answer questions on:

- solving a linear equation
- solving equations where the unknown is a power
- factorising algebraic expressions
- rearranging a formula to change the subject.

EXAM SKILLS FOCUS

In this chapter you will:

- show that you understand the command words 'work out' and can successfully answer 'work out' questions
- show that you can distinguish between calculator and non-calculator questions.

You will be familiar with the instruction to 'work out' from your previous learning in mathematics.

Work out	calculate from given facts, figures or information, with or without the use of a calculator.

Typical examination questions that use the command 'work out' usually involve carrying out some calculations, such as 'work out the probability …' or 'work out the difference …'.

In any examination, look to see how many marks are allocated to a 'work out' question. If there are more than 1, you should make sure that you write down the steps in your calculations so that you can access method marks.

You will also see the instructions 'solve' when working with equations, and 'factorise' when manipulating expressions and equations. Although these are not command words, they do appear in examinations. When asked to 'solve', you should find the value(s) that satisfy the equation(s). When asked to 'factorise' (or 'factorise fully'), you should rewrite the expression or equation as the product of its factors.

Some questions require formulae to be rearranged. Usually, you will be asked to 'rearrange' or to 'make (a term) the subject of the formula'.

The mathematics examinations are divided into calculator and non-calculator papers. On the calculator paper, examiners are looking for evidence that you use your calculator efficiently and are able to interpret the display properly. For example, some calculator questions will test your ability to round the answer at the end of the calculation, not rounding values within the calculation.

The non-calculator assessment tests your ability to work without a calculator. It is important to be able to carry out simple calculations without relying on the calculator.

6.1 Solving equations

UNDERSTAND THESE TERMS

- Equation
- Factorise
- Product
- Unknown
- Variable

1 Solve the following equations.

a $5x + 7 = 42$ b $9x - 11 = 7$

c $13x - 13 = -52$ d $4x + 3 = 12x - 53$

e $6x - 4 = 68 - 2x$ f $5x - 4 = 35$

g $63x - 4 = 8x - 9$ h $6x + 2 = 8(x - 1)$

i $6x + 5 - 3x - 4 = 10$ j $-2x - 11 + 3x + 2 = 2(x + 16)$

2 Solve the following equations.

a $\frac{5x+4}{9} = 6$ b $\frac{4x}{5} - 7 = 5$

c $\frac{4}{x} - 2 = \frac{1}{2} + \frac{1}{x}$ d $\frac{4}{x} + \frac{7}{2x} = 3\frac{3}{4}$

e $\frac{7x+1}{x} = \frac{3(x+7)}{x}$ f $\frac{3}{2x} + \frac{2}{5} = \frac{1}{2} + \frac{1}{x}$

g $4^x = 64$ h $5^{2x+1} = 3125$

i $37^{2x-1} = 1$ j $4^{2x+1} = 64^{x-1}$

3 Work out the value of x that satisfies this equation.

$$\frac{2x}{4x-1} = \frac{1}{5}$$

[3]

[Total: 3]

4 Work out the value of x that satisfies this equation.

$3^{3x-1} = 243$ [3]

[Total: 3]

<< RECALL AND CONNECT 1 <<

What is a simple way of checking whether your solution for the unknown in an equation is correct?

6.2 Factorising algebraic expressions

1 Factorise the following expressions.

a $5x + 15$ b $16m - 64$ c $16x - 24y$

d $3a + 6b - 12c$ e $6x^2 + 2xy$

2 Factorise the following as completely as possible.

a $4x + 8y + 6x + 12y$ b $2x - 7y + 4x - 14y$

c $7mx + 9my + 9mx + 6my$ d $12x^5 - 16x^3 + 6x^2 - 8$

e $15ac + 18ad + 20bc + 24bd$ f $-2mx - 6my + 2x + 6y$

3 Factorise the following expressions completely.

a $16xy - 12x$ [2]

b $2ax - b - a + 2bx$ [2]

[Total: 4]

4 In an isosceles triangle, there are two sides of length $x + 12$ and one of length $x + 6$.

Work out the perimeter of the triangle and simplify your answer as completely as possible. [2]

[Total: 2]

5 Factorise completely

$2x^3 + 3x^2y + 6x + 9y$ [3]

[Total: 3]

<< RECALL AND CONNECT 2 <<

What is the reverse operation of factorising?

6.3 Rearranging formulae

UNDERSTAND THESE TERMS

- Formula
- Coefficient
- Expression
- Term
- Variable

1 Rearrange each equation so that x is the subject.

a $a + x = b$ b $a - x = b$ c $bx = c$

d $\frac{a}{x} = d$ e $ex - d = f$ f $\frac{gx}{a} = b$

g $a(x - b) = c$ h $\frac{a - x}{b} = d$ i $\frac{x}{m} = \frac{a}{b}$

j $ax^2 = b$

2 Rearrange each equation so that a is the subject.

a $2a^2 = bc$ **b** $(ac)^2 = bc$ **c** $\sqrt{a} = b$

d $\sqrt{ax} = d$ **e** $x\sqrt{a} = e$ **f** $\sqrt{a - b} = c$

g $\sqrt{b - a} = c$ **h** $\frac{b}{\sqrt{a}} = 2c$

3 The formula $s = ut + \frac{1}{2}at^2$ is used in physics to find displacement (s).

Rearrange the formula so that

a u is the subject [2]

b a is the subject. [3]

[Total: 5]

4 Rearrange $6ax = b(2 - x)$ to make x the subject. [4]

[Total: 4]

5 The formula for simple harmonic motion is $v = w\sqrt{A^2 - x^2}$.

Make A the subject of the formula. [3]

[Total: 3]

REFLECTION

When you see a 'work out' question, how does your approach differ on a calculator paper compared to a non-calculator paper? What helps you decide what to write down, especially when more than one mark is available?
How do you make sure your working is clear enough to get method marks?

‹‹ RECALL AND CONNECT 3 ‹‹

a What symbol do we use to mean 'implies that'?

b How is rearranging formulae similar to solving equations?

SELF-ASSESSMENT CHECKLIST

Let's revisit the Knowledge and Exam skills focus for this chapter.
Decide how confident you are with each statement.

	Now I can	Show it	Needs more work	Almost there	Confident to move on
1	solve a linear equation	Write your own one-step and two-step linear equation. Swap with a friend to solve and explain your method.			
2	solve equations where the unknown is a power	Make a flashcard set: one side shows an exponential equation, the other shows the simplified solution steps.			
3	factorise algebraic expressions	Choose an expression and write three multiple-choice options for its factorised form (only one correct). Justify the answer.			
4	rearrange a formula to change the subject	Choose one formula from this chapter and write a step-by-step explanation to teach it to someone else.			
5	show that you understand the command words 'work out' and can successfully answer 'work out' questions	Look at three 'work out' questions. How did you know what working to show? Annotate one with method marks.			
6	show that you can distinguish between calculator and non-calculator questions.	Compare two similar examination questions – one from a calculator paper and one from a non-calculator paper. What did you do differently and why?			

7 Perimeter, area and volume

KNOWLEDGE FOCUS

In this chapter, you will answer questions on:

- calculating areas and perimeters of two-dimensional shapes
- calculating areas and perimeters of shapes that can be separated into two or more simpler shapes
- calculating areas and circumferences of circles
- calculating areas and perimeters of circular sectors
- using nets for three-dimensional solids
- calculating volumes and surface areas of solids
- calculating volumes and surface area of pyramids, cones and spheres.

EXAM SKILLS FOCUS

In this chapter you will:

- show that you understand the command word 'calculate' and can successfully answer 'calculate' questions
- show that you are aware of how marks are allocated for examination questions.

The word 'calculate' has a very similar meaning to 'work out'. The general rule is to use the calculator when asked to calculate.

Calculate	work out from given facts, figures or information.

Examples of where you might see the use of the word calculate in this chapter are 'calculate the perimeter', 'calculate the surface area' and 'calculate the volume'.

When practising examination questions, it is a good idea to check where the marks are allocated. This may give you clues about how many stages there are in the calculation. Always show your working out, as examiners will look to award method marks and will allow an incorrect answer to an early part of the question to be used in a later part.

7.1 Perimeter and area in two dimensions

UNDERSTAND THESE TERMS

- Denominator
- Common denominator
- Numerator
- Equivalent fractions
- Mixed number

1 Calculate the perimeter of the following shapes.

a
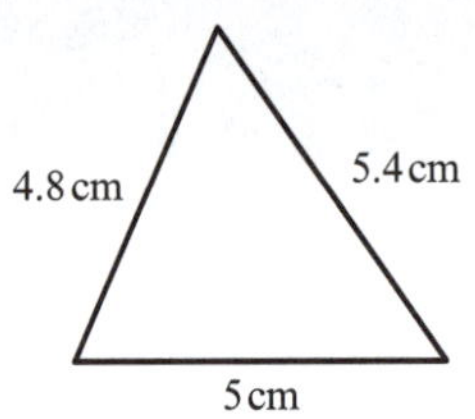

b
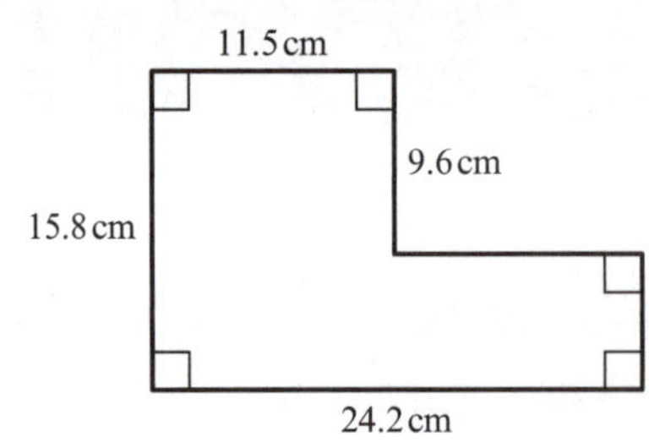

c
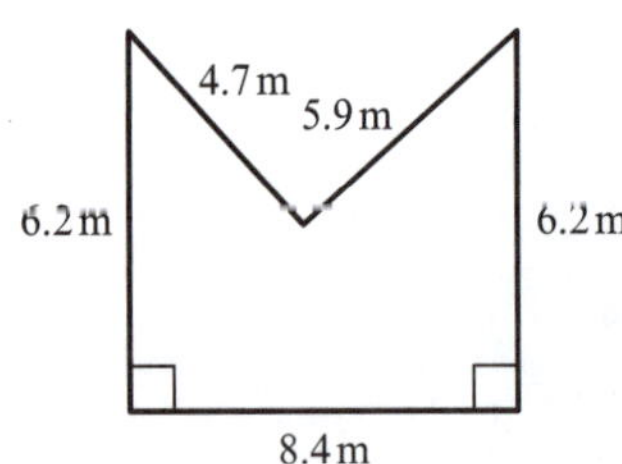

d
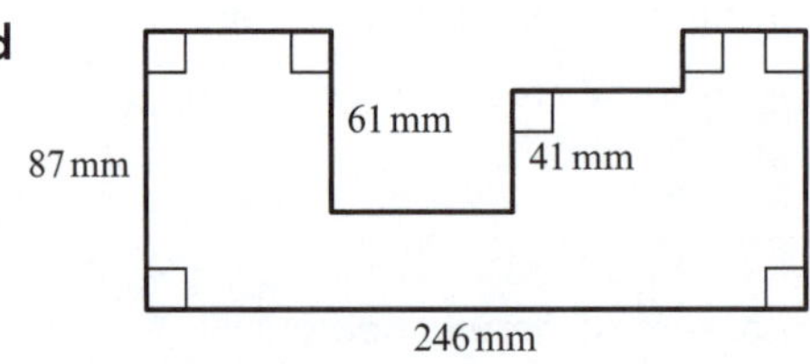

2 Calculate the area of the following shapes.

a
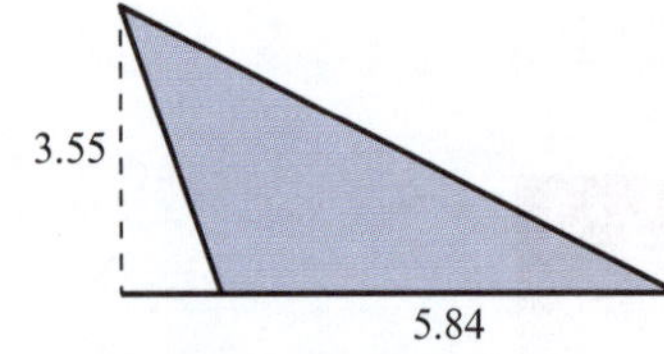

b
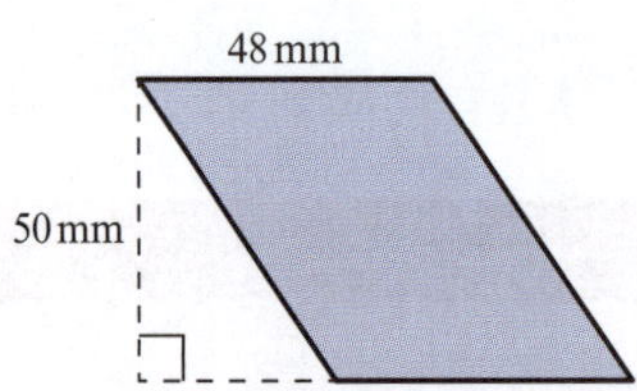

c
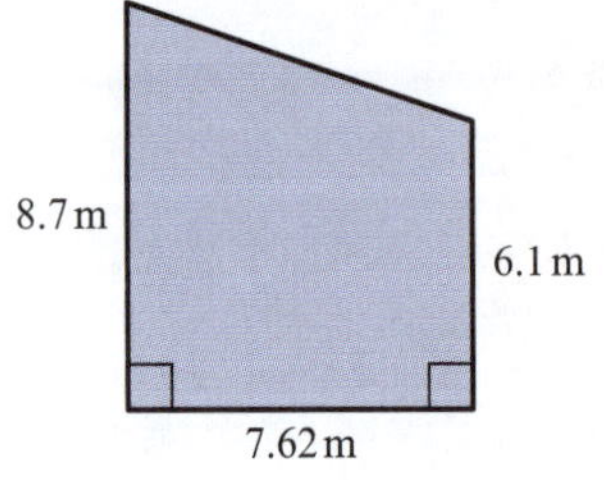

d
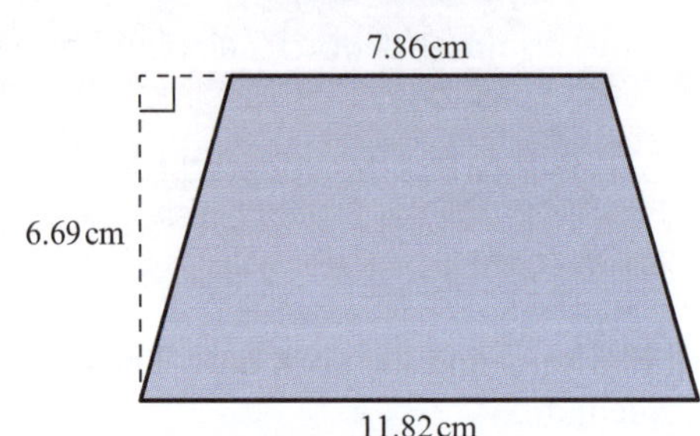

e
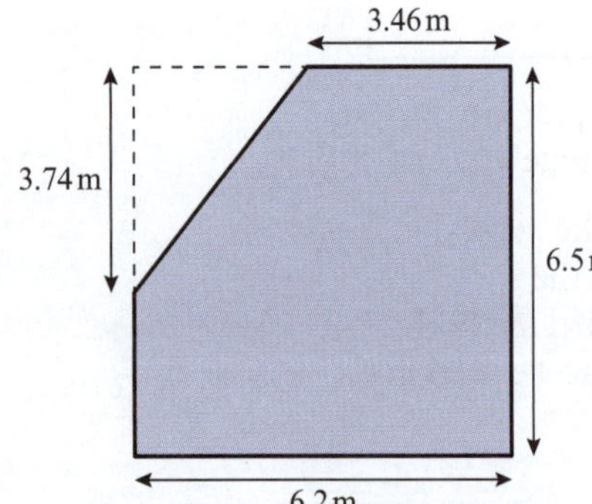

f
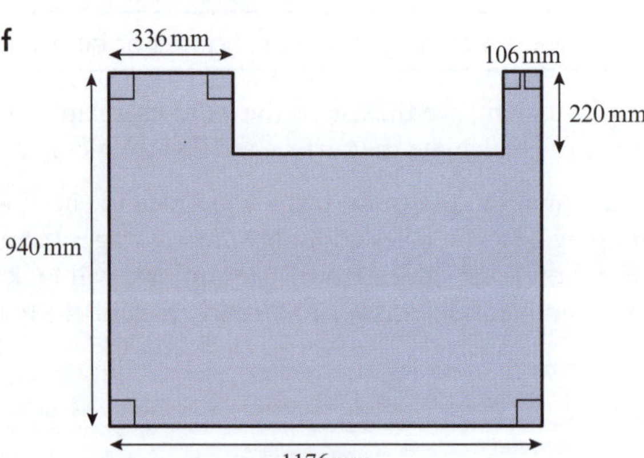

3 Calculate the area and circumference of the following circles.

a Radius = 5 cm

b Diameter = 12.4 m

c Diameter = $\sqrt{5}$ m

d Radius = $\frac{3}{\pi}$ km

4 Calculate the area of the shaded region in each diagram.

a

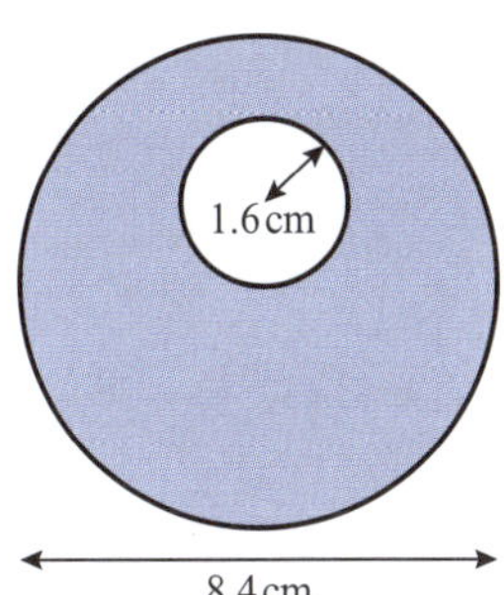

b

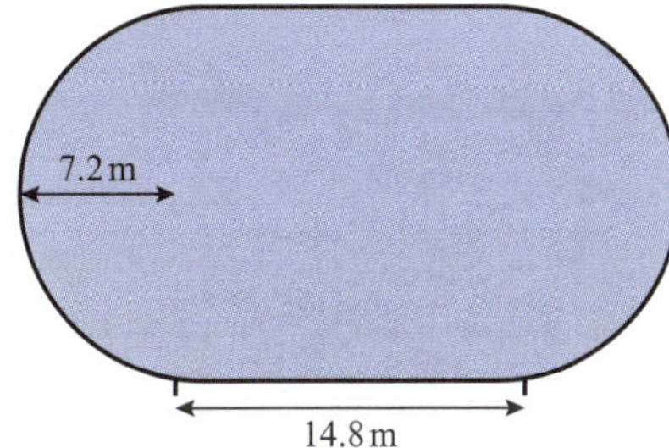

c

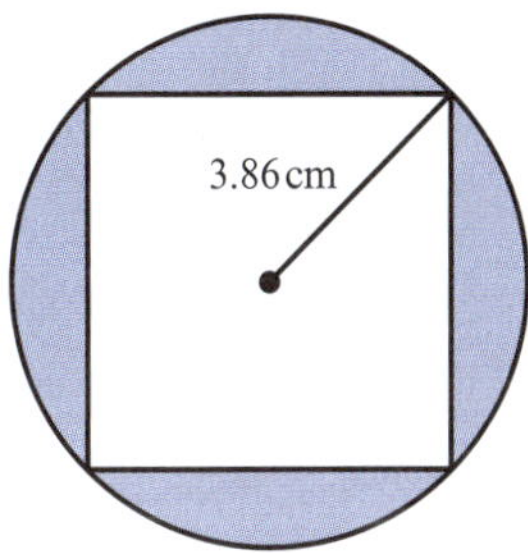

d

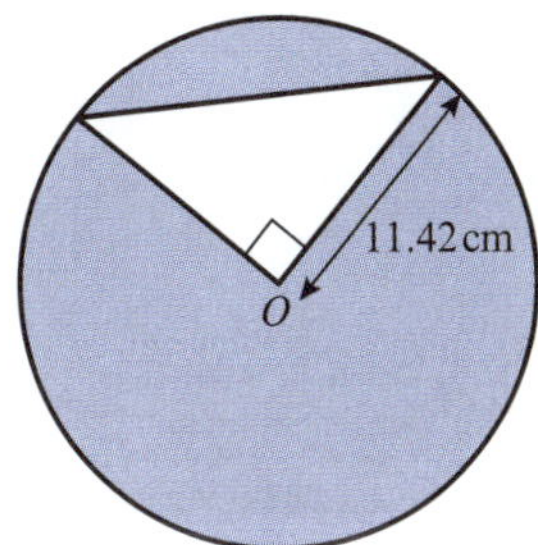

5 Calculate the area and perimeter of each of the following shapes.

a

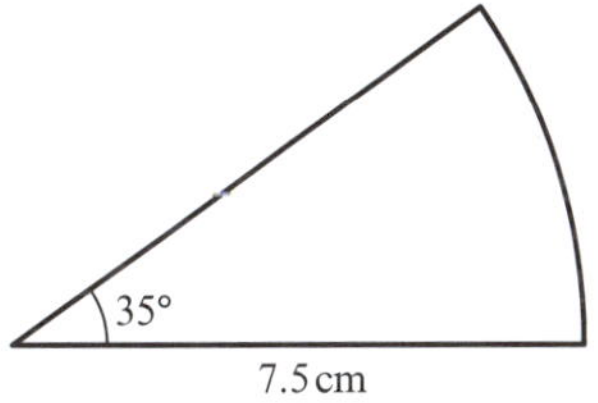

b

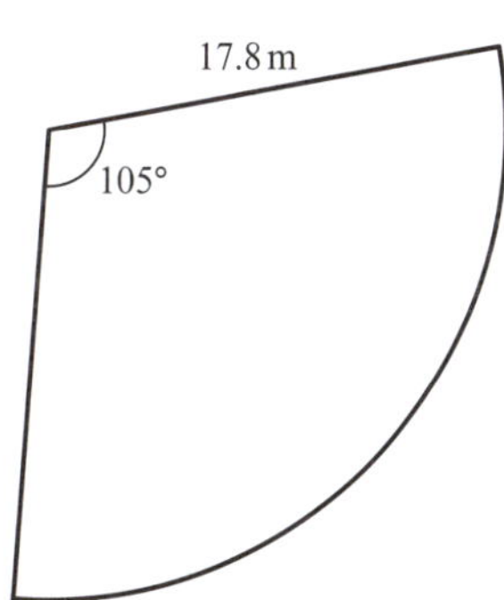

6 Calculate the area and perimeter of the shaded part of this shape.

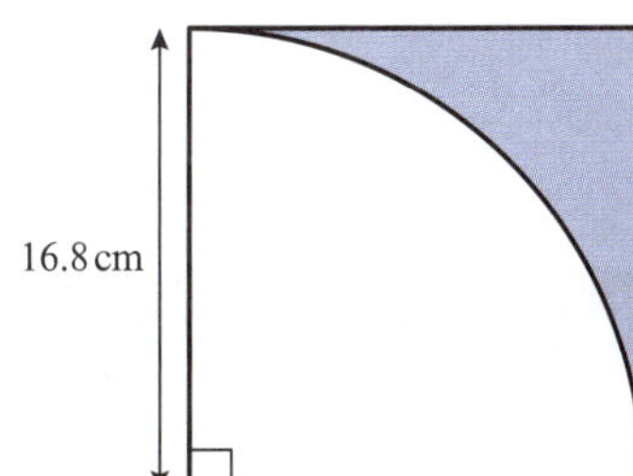

7 This shape is made from a triangle and three semicircles.
Calculate the area and perimeter.

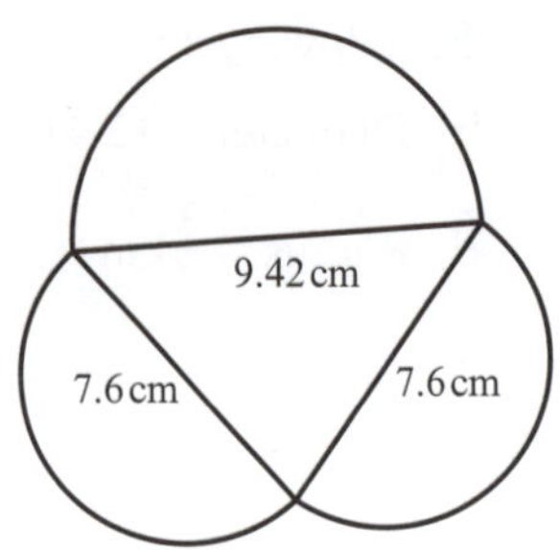

8 A football (soccer) pitch has the dimensions given below.

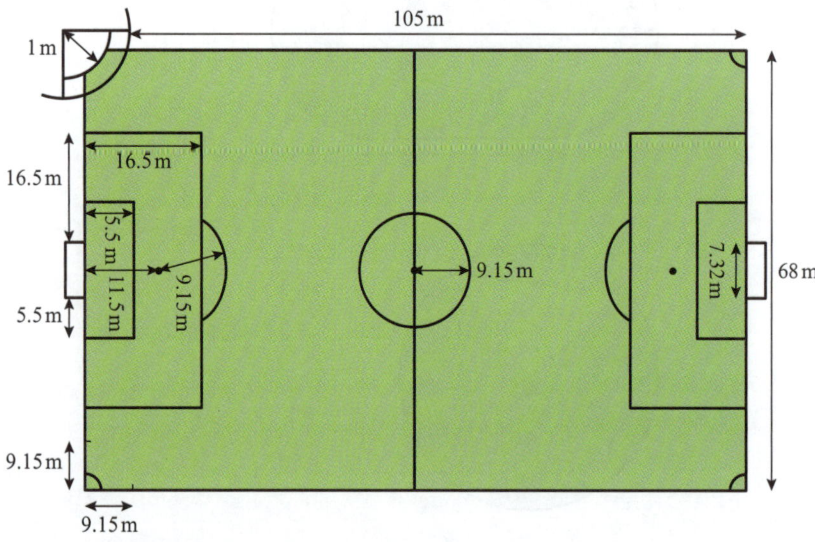

Find the area of the pitch, not including the centre circle.

Give your answer to 3 significant figures. [4]

[Total: 4]

9 The length of one side of a rectangle is 15 cm.

The length of the diagonal of the rectangle is 17 cm.

Find the area of the rectangle. [3]

[Total: 3]

10 A plate of metal measuring 23.4 cm long × 12.6 cm wide has two circular holes drilled into it.

Each hole has a diameter of 4.2 cm.

Find the area of metal that is left after the holes have been drilled.

Give your answer to 3 significant figures. [3]

[Total: 3]

⟪ RECALL AND CONNECT 1 ⟪

What is the area of a triangle with base 6 cm and height 4 cm?

7.2 Three-dimensional objects

1 a Sketch a net of a cuboid that has dimensions 25.2 cm, 14.6 cm and 7.4 cm.

b Calculate the surface area and volume of the cuboid.

2 The diagram shows the net of a cuboid.

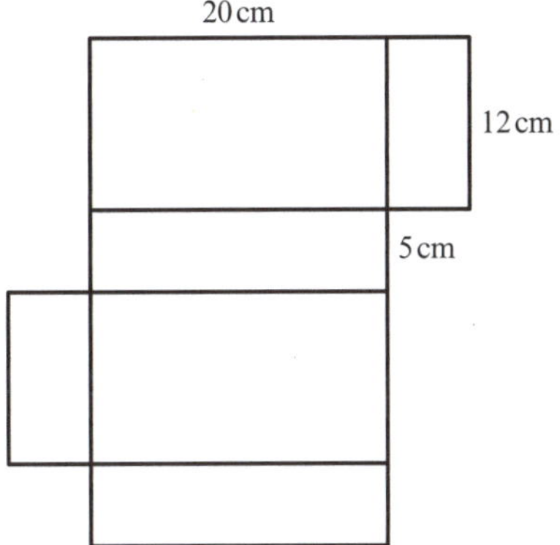

a Calculate the volume of the cuboid. [2]

b Calculate the surface area of the cuboid. [2]

c Show that the total length of the edges of the cuboid is 148 cm. [2]

[Total: 6]

《 RECALL AND CONNECT 2 《

Sketch the net of a cube and label the lengths. What is the total surface area if one edge is 5 cm?

7.3 Surface areas and volumes of solids

1 Copy and complete these formulae.

a surface area of a prism = 2 × area of cross-section + perimeter of cross-section × ______________________

b volume of a prism = ______________________ × length

c curved surface area of a cylinder = ________

d volume of a cylinder = ________

2 The diagram shows a cuboid.

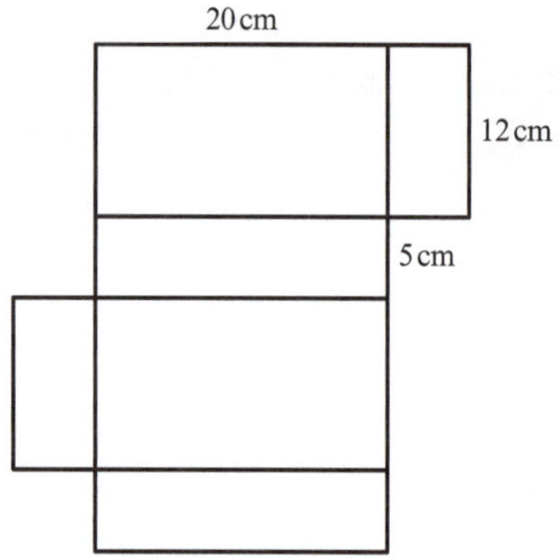

a Find the surface area of the cuboid to 2 significant figures.

b Find the volume of the cuboid to 2 significant figures.

3 A cylindrical glass beaker is 12.6 cm tall and has a base of radius 5.6 cm.

a Find the maximum amount of water that would fit in the beaker (to 4 significant figures).

A different cylindrical beaker has the same capacity but is 18 cm tall.

b Find the radius of the base of the second beaker.

4 A chocolate box is in the shape of a triangular prism.

The cross-section of the prism is a triangle with a base of 6 cm and a perpendicular height of 4 cm.

The length of the box is 12 cm.

a Find the surface area of the box.

b Find the volume of the box.

5 A football has an internal radius of 11.2 cm.

a Find the internal volume of the football.

The skin of the football is 4 mm thick.

b Find the surface area of the outside of the football.

6 A square-based pyramid has a perpendicular height of 18.6 cm and a volume of 1047.8 cm^3.

Find the side length of the square base.

7 A triangular prism has a cross-section that is an equilateral triangle of side length 12 cm.

The length of the prism is 23 cm.

a Calculate the volume of the prism. [3]

b Calculate the surface area of the prism. [2]

[Total: 5]

8 A sphere of solid metal has a volume of $2145\,cm^3$.

a Calculate the radius of the sphere. [3]

b Calculate the surface area of the sphere. [2]

c The sphere is melted and the metal formed into cubes with volume $3.375\,cm^3$.

i Calculate how many cubes can be made. [2]

ii Find the amount of metal not used. [1]

d Calculate the surface area of one of the cubes. [2]

[Total: 10]

4 A frustum has been made by reducing the perpendicular height of a cone from 18 cm to 12 cm.

The radius of the base of the cone is 6 cm.

Calculate the volume of the frustum. [3]

[Total: 3]

REFLECTION

When a question says 'calculate', how do you decide what steps to write down? How does checking the number of marks help you plan your method and avoid losing marks? What strategies help you keep track of whether you are working with length, area, or volume - and the correct units?

SELF-ASSESSMENT CHECKLIST

Let's revisit the Knowledge and Exam skills focus for this chapter. Decide how confident you are with each statement.

	Now I can	Show it	Needs more work	Almost there	Confident to move on
1	calculate areas and perimeters of two-dimensional shapes	Draw three different quadrilaterals and label their dimensions. Ask a friend to calculate the perimeter and area.			
2	calculate areas and perimeters of shapes that can be separated into two or more simpler shapes	Choose a question from Section 7.1 and explain how you broke it into simpler parts. Then make your own compound shape to calculate.			
3	calculate areas and circumferences of circles	Make a flashcard set for area and circumference formulas. Test yourself on when and how to use each.			

CONTINUED

	Now I can	Show it	Needs more work	Almost there	Confident to move on
4	calculate areas and perimeters of circular sectors	Write a step-by-step guide for finding the arc length and area of a sector. Include diagrams.			
5	use nets for three-dimensional solids	Build a simple net out of card (e.g. a cuboid or a triangular prism). Label all dimensions and calculate the surface area.			
6	calculate volumes and surface areas of solids	Calculate the volume and surface area of a cuboid of side lengths 4, 5 and 6 cm.			
7	calculate volumes and surface area of pyramids, cones and spheres	Compare the surface area of a cylinder and a cuboid that have the same height and volume.			
8	show that you understand the command word 'calculate' and can successfully answer 'calculate' questions	Highlight three questions that use 'calculate' and explain how you decided what steps to show.			
9	show that you are aware of how marks are allocated for exam questions.	Pick one question with three or more marks. Highlight where each mark comes from (e.g. formula, substitution, final answer).			

8 Introduction to probability

KNOWLEDGE FOCUS

In this chapter, you will answer questions on:

- expressing probabilities mathematically
- calculating probabilities associated with simple experiments
- using sample space diagrams to help calculate the probability of combined events.

EXAM SKILLS FOCUS

In this chapter you will:

- show that you understand the command word 'give' and can answer questions that ask you to 'give'
- be aware that the command word 'give' often follows other command words such as 'find'.

In this chapter, you will calculate and describe probabilities using words, numbers and diagrams. You will work with simple events, sample spaces and combined events, and identify when outcomes are independent or mutually exclusive.

You will also practise responding clearly to the command word 'give'.

Give	produce an answer from a given source or recall/memory.

The word 'give' often appears on its own or alongside another instruction such as 'find' or 'explain'. For example, in this chapter you will see 'give' used as an instruction to write a probability in a particular form, such as 'give your answer as a fraction in its simplest form'. You might also see it being used to define the number of decimal places or significant figures (give your answer to …), or when you are being asked for an explanation (give full reasons …).

8.1 Understanding basic probability

UNDERSTAND THESE TERMS

- Sample space
- Relative frequency
- Event
- Bias
- Outcomes

1 What is the sample space when rolling a fair six-sided die?

A (2, 4, 6)   B (1, 2, 3, 4, 5, 6)

C (Even, Odd)   D (0, 1)

2 Select the correct statement about probability.

A A probability can be greater than 1.

B A probability must always be exactly 0.5.

C A probability is always between 0 and 1.

D A probability can be negative if the event is unlikely.

3 What is the term for the number of times an event occurs in a repeated experiment?

A Trial   B Sample space

C Relative frequency   D Event

4 A spinner has 10 equal sectors, each with a different number from 1 to 10.

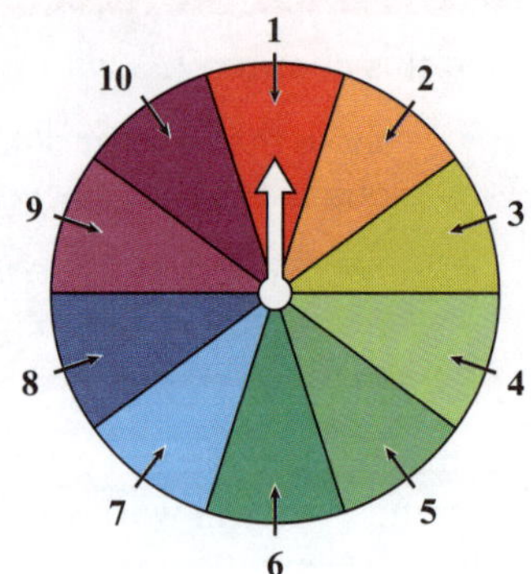

a The spinner is spun once.

Find the probability that the number is:

i an odd number

ii a prime number

iii a multiple of 6

iv an odd multiple of 3.

b Rani spins the spinner 240 times.

How many times should she expect the spinner to land on a multiple of 4?

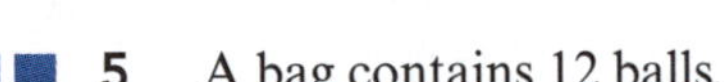

5 A bag contains 12 balls.

Five are blue, four are red and the rest are green.

a Luca selects a ball at random.

Find the probability that the ball selected is:

i red

ii blue

iii not blue

b Luca says that if he picks three balls (and replaces them each time) he is bound to get at least one green. Is Luca correct? Give a reason for your answer.

c Luca goes on to pick and replace 60 times.

How many times is he likely to pick a green ball?

6 Three different dice numbered 1 to 6 are thrown.

The results are shown in the graphs below.

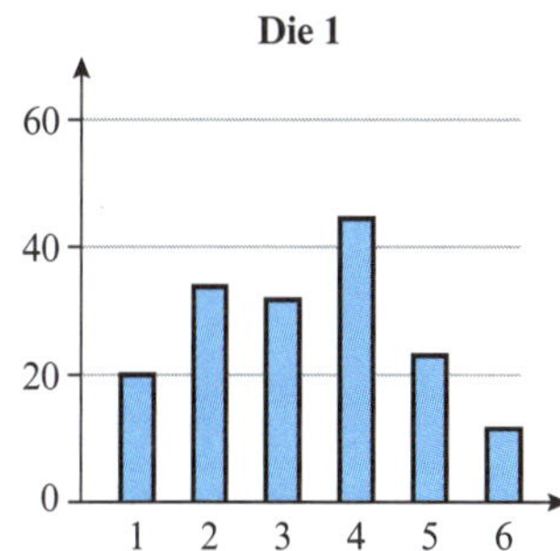

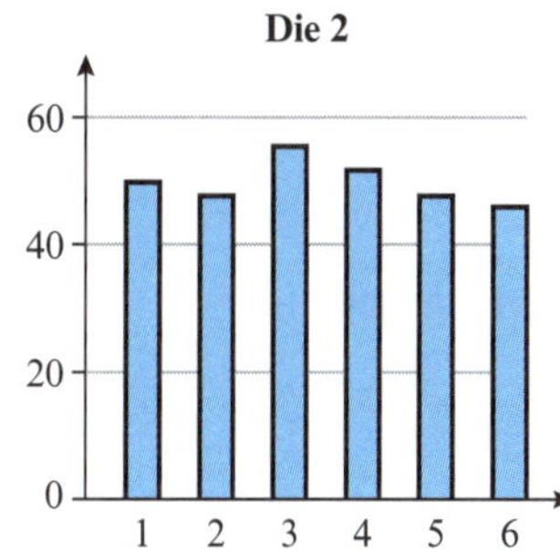

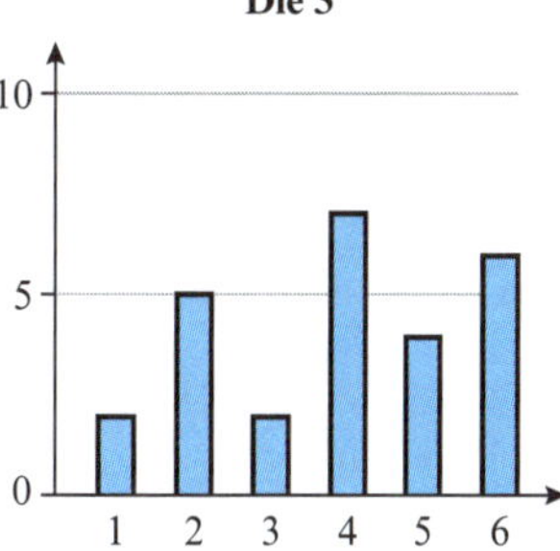

Which of the dice do you think are biased?

Give reasons for your answers. [3]

[Total: 3]

7 A spinner has six equal sectors.

Three are coloured red, one is blue and two are green.

a Find P(Red). Give your answer as a fraction in its simplest form. [1]

b Find P(Green). Give your answer as a fraction in its simplest form. [1]

c The spinner is spun 72 times. Work out how many times you would expect it to land on blue. [1]

[Total: 3]

8 Maggie and Maisie play a game.

The game can end as a win for Maggie, a win for Maisie or a tie.

The probability that Maggie will win is 0.14.

a Maisie is three times more likely to win than Maggie.

Work out the probability that Maisie will win.

Give your answer as a decimal to 2 decimal places. [1]

b Find the probability that the game will end in a tie. [1]

c The game is played 250 times. Work out how many times you would expect Maisie to win. [1]

d Explain why your answer to part **c** may not be precisely correct. [2]

[Total: 5]

≪ RECALL AND CONNECT 1 ≪

Which of the following fractions are equivalent?

A	B	C	D	E	F	G	H
$\frac{2}{5}$	$\frac{6xy}{12x}$	$\frac{x^2y}{2x^2}$	$\frac{12x}{30}$	$\frac{3(2x+3)}{6x+45}$	$\frac{4x^2}{10x}$	$\frac{2x^2}{5y}$	$\frac{y}{2}$

8.2 Sample space diagrams

1 Maria has two spinners. One has four equal sections coloured blue, red, green and yellow.

The other spinner has three equal sections with the numbers 1, 2 and 3.

a Draw a sample space to show all the probabilities.

b Use your sample space to calculate the probability of Maria getting

i a red and a two

ii a three and a colour that is not red

iii an odd number and blue.

2 Dev has a spinner with six equal sectors.

Two are red, one is blue and three are green.

He also has a fair, six-sided die.

He draws the following sample space.

	1	2	3	4	5	6
Red	1R	2R	3R	4R	5R	6R
Green	1G	2G	3G	4G	5G	6G
Blue	1B	2B	3B	4B	5B	6B

a Explain why Dev's sample space is incorrect.

b Draw a correct sample space and use it to find the following probabilities.

i P(2, Red)

ii P(Odd, Green)

iii P(Even, Blue)

iv P(Prime)

3 A red die and a blue die are both rolled and their scores added together.

Both dice are fair.

a Draw a sample space diagram to show all the possible outcomes. [2]

b Work out the following probabilities. Give your answers as fractions in their simplest form.

i P(6) [1]

ii P(11) [1]

iii P(7) [1]

iv P(Odd) [1]

v P(Prime) [1]

c Munira says that the probability of getting a total of 4 is twice the probability of getting a 2.

Explain why Munira is wrong. [2]

[Total: 9]

4 Samir has five coins in her pocket.

He has a \$1 coin, two 50-cent coins, a 25-cent coin and a 5-cent coin.

Mikey has 4 coins in his pocket.

He has a 5-cent coin, two 10-cent coins and a 50-cent coin.

They agree to pull a coin out at random at the same time and to add their values together.

a Draw a sample space diagram to show all the possibilities. [3]

b Find the probability that the value of their two coins is:

i less than 50 cents [1]

ii more than \$1 [1]

iii exactly 55 cents. [1]

c Work out the probability that they will both pull out a coin of the same value.

Give your answer as a fraction in its simplest form. [1]

[Total: 7]

8.3 Combining independent and mutually exclusive events

UNDERSTAND THIS TERM

- Combined events

1 Explain why the probability of getting one head and one tail is 0.25 when the same coin is flipped twice.

2 A bag has four red balls, three blue balls and two yellow balls.

A ball is picked at random then replaced. A second ball is then picked.

Find the probabilities of each of these events.

a Two reds

b One red and one blue

c One yellow and one other that is not red

3 Every day, Bo picks a piece of fruit and a snack bar at random from his cupboard.

On a given day he has three bananas, two apples and four mangoes; four Whizzo bars, three Riceos and one Snacko.

a Calculate the following probabilities.

Give each answer as a fraction in its simplest form.

i An apple and a Riceo bar [1]

ii A banana and a Whizzo bar [1]

iii A Mango and a Snacko bar [1]

b i Write down the least likely combination. [1]

ii Work out the probability of it occurring. [1]

[Total: 5]

4 Ahmed plants some rose bushes.

The probability that the rose bush will flower in the first year is 0.72.

The probability that when the rose flowers it will be yellow is 0.4, and the probability that it will be red is 0.35.

a Calculate the probability that a bush will have a red flower in the first year. Give your answer to 2 decimal places. [1]

b Calculate the probability that, in the first year, a bush will have a flower that is neither yellow nor red. [2]

c Ahmed chooses two bushes at random. Calculate the probability that, in the first year, one produces flowers and the other does not. Give your answer to 2 decimal places. [3]

[Total: 6]

REFLECTION

When you answer a probability question, how do you decide what form your answer should take? How do you remember to simplify fractions or check if your answer makes sense? What helps you understand whether two events are independent or mutually exclusive?

SELF-ASSESSMENT CHECKLIST

Let's revisit the Knowledge and Exam skills focus for this chapter. Decide how confident you are with each statement.

	Now I can	Show it	Needs more work	Almost there	Confident to move on
1	express probabilities mathematically	Write a probability in fraction, decimal and percentage forms. Explain which is best to use and why.			
2	calculate probabilities associated with simple experiments	Create your own bag of coloured counters. Write three probability questions and solve them.			
3	use sample space diagrams to help calculate the probability of combined events	Draw a sample space diagram for rolling two dice. Highlight the outcomes that total 6 or 7.			

CONTINUED

	Now I can	Show it	Needs more work	Almost there	Confident to move on
4	show understanding of the command word 'give' and answer questions that ask you to 'give'	Pick two questions with the word 'give' in the command. Write what format the answer should be in and why.			
5	be aware that the command word 'give' often follows other command words, such as 'find'.	Look at two multi-step problems. Identify the point where the instruction 'give' appears and describe what it is asking for.			

Exam practice 2

This section contains past paper questions from previous Cambridge exams, which draw together your knowledge on a range of topics that you have covered up to this point. These questions give you the opportunity to test your knowledge and understanding.

The following question has an example student response and commentary provided. Work through the question first, then compare your answer to the sample response and commentary. Are your answers different to the sample responses?

1 Work out $1\frac{3}{4} + \frac{5}{6}$, giving your answer as a mixed number in its simplest form. [3]

[Total: 3]

Example student response	Commentary
$\frac{7}{4} + \frac{5}{6}$ Lowest common denominator = 12 $\frac{21}{12} + \frac{10}{12} = \frac{31}{12}$	The student has correctly converted the mixed number to an improper fraction for 1 mark. They have found the lowest common denominator and correctly added the fractions for a second mark. But the answer is not given as a mixed number in its simplest form. ***This answer scores 2 out of 3 marks.***

2 Without using a calculator, work out $\frac{1}{3} \div \frac{7}{6} + \frac{1}{5}$, giving your answer as a fraction in its simplest form. [4]

Adapted from Cambridge IGCSE Mathematics (0580) Paper 22 Q6 November 2021 **[Total: 4]**

The following question has an example student response and commentary provided. Work through the question first, then compare your answer to the sample response and commentary. Are your answers different to the sample responses?

3 A company employed 300 workers when it started and now employs 852 workers.

a Calculate the percentage increase in the number of workers. [2]

b Of the 852 workers, the ratio part-time workers : full-time workers = 5 : 7.

Calculate the number of full-time workers. [2]

c The company makes 40 600 headphones in one year.

Write this number

i in words [1]

ii in standard form. [1]

d In one month, the company sells 3000 headphones.

Of these, 48% are exported, $\frac{3}{8}$ are sold to shops and the rest are sold online.

Calculate the number of headphones that are sold online. [3]

e One year, sales increased by 15%.

The following year sales increased by 18%.

Calculate the overall percentage increase in sales. [3]

Cambridge IGCSE Mathematics (0580) Paper 42 Q1 March 2022 **[Total: 12]**

Example student response	Commentary
a $852 \div 300 \times 100 = 284\%$	The student has calculated 852 as a percentage of 300 correctly for 1 mark. But their answer does not reflect the percentage increase from 300. ***This answer scores 1 out of 2 marks.***
b $5 + 7 = 12$ $852 \div 12 = 71$	1 mark for the calculation, but the student has not identified the number of full-time workers so does not achieve the second mark. ***This answer scores 1 out of 2 marks.***
c i 40 thousand and thirty six	This doesn't match the number given. ***This answer scores 0 out of 1 mark.***
c ii 40.6×10^3	Not fully in correct standard form. ***This answer scores 0 out of 1 mark.***
d $48\% = \frac{48}{100}$ $\frac{3}{8} + \frac{48}{100} = \frac{51}{108}$ $1 - \frac{51}{108} = \frac{57}{108}$ $\frac{57}{108} \times 3000 = 1583.3$	The student has correctly found the method to calculate the remainder for 1 mark. But they've confused fractions and added 48/100 + 3/8 incorrectly. ***This answer scores 1 out of 3 marks.***
e $15 + 18 = 33\%$	The student has not combined percentages correctly, not considering that the second year increase is also on additional sales from Year 1. ***This answer scores 0 out of 3 marks.***

4 **a** Divide \$24 in the ratio 7 : 5. [2]

b Write \$24.60 as a fraction of \$2870.

Give your answer in its lowest terms. [2]

c Write \$1.92 as a percentage of \$1.60. [1]

Cambridge IGCSE Mathematics (0580) Paper 42 Q1a June 2020 **[Total: 5]**

The following question has an example student response and commentary provided. Work through the question first, then compare your answer to the sample response and commentary. Are your answers different to the sample responses?

5 **a** Solve $3x - 8 = 6 - 4x$ [2]

b Factorise fully $10a^2 + 5a$ [2]

c Factorise fully $(2x - 3)^2 - 9$ [2]

Cambridge IGCSE Mathematics (0580) Paper 42 Q7a–c June 2024 **[Total: 6]**

Example student response	Commentary
a $3x - 8 = 6 - 4x$ $-x = 14$ $x = -14$	Errors made in manipulating the equation. ***This answer scores 0 out of 2 marks.***
b $10a^2 + 5a$ $5a(2a + 2)$	Correct factor identified. Factorisation incorrect. ***This answer scores 0 out of 2 marks.***
c $(2x - 3)^2 - 9$ $4x^2 - 12x - 9 - 9$ $4x^2 - 12x - 18$ $2(2x^2 - 6x - 9)$	$4x^2 - 12x - 18$ is correct, but the brackets are not expanded correctly, so the student has factorised the incorrect expression. ***This answer scores 0 out of 2 marks.***

6 Now that you have gone through the commentary, try to write an improved answer for your own solution and edit the sample student response to improve their answer to each part.

The following question has an example student response and commentary provided. Work through the question first, then compare your answer to the sample response and commentary. Are your answers different to the sample responses?

7 Factorise.

a $5am + 10ap - bm - 2bp$ [2]

b $15(k + g)^2 - 20(k + g)$ [2]

c $4x^2 - y^4$ [2]

Cambridge IGCSE Mathematics (0580) Paper 42 Q9a March 2021 **[Total: 6]**

Example student response	Commentary
a $5am + 10ap - bm - 2bp$ $5a(m + 2p) - b(m + 2p)$	Partly factorised. Student has correctly taken a factor of $5a$ and b but expression is not completely factorised. 1 mark for $5a(m + 2p) - b(m + 2p)$ ***This answer scores 1 out of 2 marks.***
b $15(k + g)^2 - 20(k + g)$ $(k + g)(15(k + g) - 20)$	Part factorised. Student has correctly taken out a factor of $(k + g)$, but expression has not been completely factorised. 1 mark for $(k + g)(15(k + g) - 20)$ ***This answer scores 1 out of 2 marks.***
c $4x^2 - y^4$ $(2x - y^2)^2$	The student has correctly factorised $4x^2$ but there is an error in the factorisation of $-y^4$ related to directed number. ***This answer scores 0 out of 2 marks.***

8 Factorise the following completely.

a $x^2 - 3x - 28$ [2]

b $7(a + 2b)^2 + 4a(a + 2b)$ [2]

Cambridge IGCSE Mathematics (0580) Paper 42 Q3d June 2021

[Total: 4]

The following question has an example student response and commentary provided. Work through the question first, then compare your answer to the sample response and commentary. Are your answers different to the sample responses?

9 The diagram shows a container for storing grain.

The container is made from a hemisphere, a cylinder and a cone, each with a radius 2 m.

The height of the cylinder is 5.2 m and the height of the cone is h m.

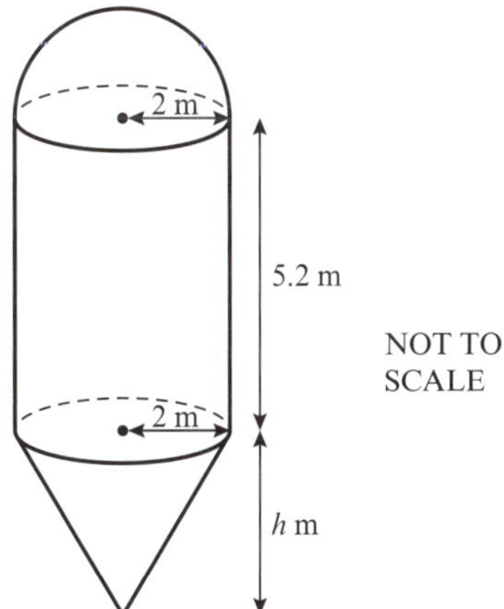

a Calculate the volume of the hemisphere.

Give your answer as a multiple of π.

[The volume, V, of a sphere with radius r is $V = \frac{4}{3}\pi r^3$.] [2]

b The total volume of the container is $\frac{88\pi}{3}$ m^3.

Calculate the value of h.

[The volume, V, of a cone with radius r and height h is $V = \frac{1}{3}\pi r^3 h$.] [4]

c The container is full of grain.

Grain is removed from the container at a rate of 35 000 kg per hour.

1 m^3 of grain has a mass of 620 kg.

Calculate the time taken to empty the container.

Give your answer in hours and minutes. [3]

Cambridge IGCSE Mathematics (0580) Paper 42 Q7a November 2021 **[Total: 9]**

Example student response	Commentary
a $5v = \frac{4}{3}\pi(2)^3$ $= \frac{32\pi}{3}$	Correct formula for 1 mark but student has found volume of whole sphere. ***This answer scores 1 out of 2 marks.***
b $\frac{88}{3}\pi - \frac{32}{3}\pi = \frac{56}{3}\pi$ $\frac{56}{3}\pi - (\pi \times 2^2 \times 5.2) = -\frac{32}{15}\pi$	The student got part **a** wrong, and so part **b** is also incorrect. However, the student still achieves the 3 marks here because they have done everything else correctly in this part of the question. This is called 'error carried forward' (or 'follow-through'). This is why you should always attempt all question parts! ***This answer scores 3 out of 3 marks.***
c $\left(\frac{88\pi}{3} \times 620\right) = 57\,135$ $57\,135 \div 35\,000 = 1.632$ 1 hour and 63 minutes = 2 hours and 3 minutes	The student has correctly found the mass of the grain, for 1 mark, and divided by the rate of extraction for a second mark. But there's an error in interpretation of time in the answer given. ***This answer scores 2 out of 3 marks.***

10 a

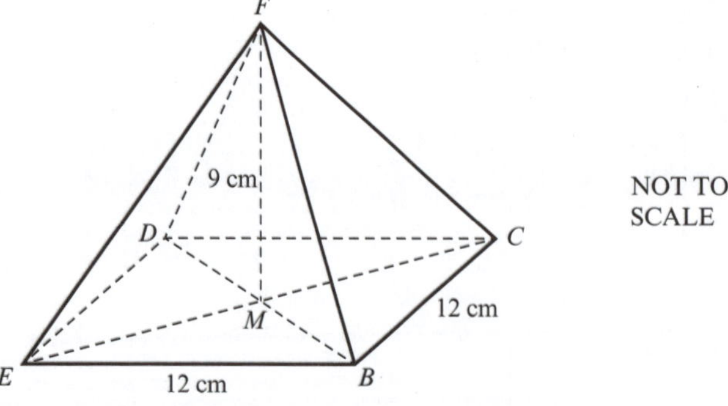

The diagram shows a pyramid with a square base $BCDE$.

The diagonals CE and BD intersect at M, and the vertex F is directly above M.

$BE = 12$ cm and $FM = 9$ cm.

i Calculate the volume of the pyramid.
[The volume, V, of a pyramid with base area A and height h is $V = \frac{1}{3}Ah$.] [2]

ii Calculate the total surface area of the pyramid. [5]

b

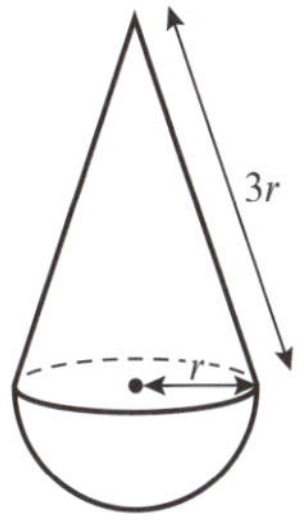

NOT TO SCALE

The diagram shows a toy made from a cone and a hemisphere.

The base radius of the cone and the radius of the hemisphere are both r cm.

The slant height of the cone is $3r$ cm.

The total surface area of the toy is 304 cm^2.

Calculate the value of r.

[The curved surface area, A, of a cone with radius r and slant height l is $A = \pi rl$.]

[The curved surface area, A, of a sphere with radius r is $A = 4\pi r^2$.] [4]

Cambridge IGCSE Mathematics (0580) Paper 42 Q4 March 2024 **[Total: 11]**

The following question has an example student response and commentary provided. Work through the question first, then compare your answer to the sample response and commentary. Are your answers different to the sample responses?

11 A bag contains 7 red discs, 5 green discs and 2 pink discs.

a Helen takes one disc at random, records the colour and replaces it in the bag.

She does this 140 times.

Find how many times she expects to take a green disc. [2]

b Helen adds 9 green discs and some pink discs to the discs already in the bag.

The probability of taking a green disc is now $\frac{2}{7}$.

Find the number of pink discs that Helen added to the bag. [2]

Cambridge IGCSE Mathematics (0580) Paper 23 Q11 November 2020] **[Total: 4]**

Example student response	Commentary
a Probability of green $= \frac{5}{7+2} = \frac{5}{9}$ $\frac{5}{9} \times 140 = 77.8$ She would get 78 green discs	The student has correctly multiplied the number of draws but has incorrectly calculated the probability of getting a green disc. ***This answer scores 0 out of 2 marks.***
b Green is now 14 Green is $\frac{2}{7} = \frac{14}{x}$ $x = 49$	The student has calculated the total number of discs in the bag. The questions asks how many pink discs are added. ***This answer scores 0 out of 2 marks.***

12 Suleika has six cards numbered 1 to 6.

1	2	3	4	5	6

She takes one card at random, records the number and replaces the card.

a Write down the probability that the number is 5 or 6. [1]

b Suleika does this 300 times.

Find how many times she expects the number 5 or 6. [1]

Cambridge IGCSE Mathematics (0580) Paper 42 Q6a March 2020

[Total: 2]

9 Sequences, surds and sets

KNOWLEDGE FOCUS

In this chapter, you will answer questions on:

- describing the rule for continuing a sequence
- finding the nth term of some sequences
- using the nth term to find terms from later in a sequence
- generating and describing sequences from patterns of shapes
- distinguishing rational and irrational numbers
- expressing recurring decimals as fractions
- simplifying, calculating and solving problems with surds
- using set language and notation to describe sets
- finding complements, unions and intersections of sets
- representing sets and solve problems using Venn diagrams.

EXAM SKILLS FOCUS

In this chapter you will:

- show that you understand the command word 'determine' and can answer a 'determine' question
- understand the difference between 'determine' and 'work out'.

In this chapter you will practise answering questions that use the command word 'determine' and other questions that use the command word 'work out'.

Determine	establish with certainty.
Work out	calculate from given facts, figures or information, with or without the use of a calculator.

Whenever you see the command word 'determine', you must establish the answer with certainty. This will often involve using logic or short calculations to work out the answer. For example, you may use the rule for the nth term of a sequence to determine the tenth term.

'Determine' is different to 'work out'. When you are asked to 'work out', you generally need to do more working out than you would if you need to 'determine'. For example, in this chapter you will 'work out' answers to questions that require you to leave your answer as a surd.

9.1 Sequences

UNDERSTAND THESE TERMS

- Sequence
- Term

1 Carry out the following steps for each linear sequence **a**–**k**.

i Work out an expression for the nth term of the sequence, u_n.

ii Use your expression to determine the 30th term of the sequence.

iii Determine whether or not 100 is a term in the sequence.
If 100 is in the sequence, state n, the number of its term.

a $-1, 3, 7, 11, 15, \ldots$

b $10, 7, 4, 1, -2, \ldots$

c $1.5, 3.0, 4.5, 6.0, 7.5, \ldots$

d $2.2, 3.0, 3.8, 4.6, 5.4, \ldots$

e $20, 17, 14, 11, 8, \ldots$

f $0.5, 1.0, 1.5, 2.0, 2.5, \ldots$

g $10.0, 9.6, 9.2, 8.8, 8.4, \ldots$

h $\frac{1}{4}, \frac{1}{2}, \frac{3}{4}, 1, \frac{5}{4}, \ldots$

i $\frac{5}{2}, 2, \frac{3}{2}, 1, \frac{1}{2}, \ldots$

j $1.25, 1.5, 1.75, 2.0, 2.25, \ldots$

k $-2, -5, -8, -11, -14, \ldots$

REFLECTION

In Question 1, step iii, you were asked to 'determine whether'. How did you make sure that you could establish with certainty whether or not 100 was in the sequence?

2 For each of the following quadratic sequences, work out:

i the nth term.

ii the 12th term

a $2, 8, 18, 32, 50, \ldots$

b $1, 10, 25, 46, 73, \ldots$

c $3, 10, 21, 36, 55, \ldots$

d $1, 5, 13, 25, 41, \ldots$

e $10, 1, -10, -23, -38, \ldots$

f $6, -1, -10, -21, -34, \ldots$

g $-5, 2, 13, 28, 47, \ldots$

h $30, 21, 14, 9, 6, \ldots$

3 The diagram shows a growing pattern of triangles made from matchsticks.

Pattern 1
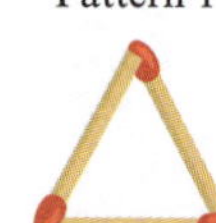

Pattern 2
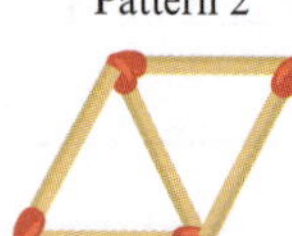

Pattern 3
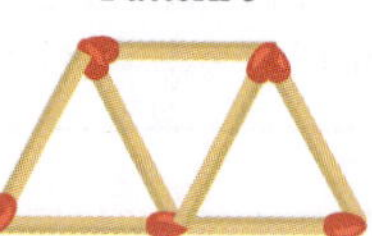

Each new triangle shares a side with the previous one.

a Copy and complete the table.

Pattern number (n)	1	2	3	4	5
Matchsticks used					

b Find a rule for the nth term of the sequence.

c Determine the number of matchsticks needed for the 50th pattern.

d Is 131 a possible total number of matchsticks in any pattern? Justify your answer.

<< RECALL AND CONNECT 1 <<

a Find the value of $\frac{\sqrt{xy^2}}{z + x^3}$ when $x = 2.1$, $y = 3.4$ and $z = 7.89$.

b Expand and simplify $3x(x + 4) - 2x(x + 7)$.

4 The nth triangular number, T_n, is the sum of the first n positive integers.

The nth triangular number can be expressed using the formula

$$T_n = \frac{n(n+1)}{2}$$

a Find the 5th triangular number. [1]

b Determine the value of n for which the triangular number $T_n = 45$. [3]

[Total: 4]

5 A sequence begins

5, 8, 11, 14, 17, …

a Write down the next two terms in the sequence. [1]

b Describe, in words, the rule for continuing the sequence. [1]

c Find an expression, in terms of n, for the nth term of the sequence. [2]

d Use your expression to find the 20th term of the sequence. [2]

[Total: 6]

9.2 Rational and irrational numbers

1 Copy the following table and put a tick in the correct column for each number.

	Rational	Irrational
$\sqrt{2}$		
0.125		
$\frac{3}{7}$		
π		
$\sqrt{25}$		
0.3		

UNDERSTAND THIS TERM

- Recurring decimal

2 Use algebra to write each recurring decimal as a fraction. Simplify your answers as far as possible.

a $0.\dot{6}$	**b** $1.\dot{2}$	**c** $0.\dot{7}\dot{8}$
d $0.\dot{0}\dot{9}$	**e** $0.\dot{3}4\dot{2}$	**f** $0.21\dot{3}\dot{4}$
g $0.00\dot{6}$	**h** $0.\dot{5}1\dot{6}$	**i** $0.45\dot{8}\dot{1}$

≪ RECALL AND CONNECT 2 ≪

Calculate

a $1\frac{2}{5} + 3\frac{1}{4}$

b $2\frac{1}{4} \times 1\frac{3}{5}$

3 Express the recurring decimal $0.1\dot{6}$ as a fraction in its simplest form. [3]

[Total: 3]

4 By first converting each recurring decimal to a fraction, write $2.\dot{4}0\dot{7} + 3.0\dot{5}\dot{9}$ as a fraction in its simplest form. [4]

[Total: 4]

9.3 Surds

UNDERSTAND THIS TERM

- Surd

1 Simplify each expression.

a $\sqrt{48}$	**b** $\sqrt{72}$	**c** $3\sqrt{8}$
d $\sqrt{75}$	**e** $\sqrt{200}$	**f** $2\sqrt{27}$

2 Write each expression as a single surd.

a $\sqrt{18} + \sqrt{32}$	**b** $5\sqrt{2} + 3\sqrt{8}$	**c** $\sqrt{200} - \sqrt{50}$
d $2\sqrt{20} - 3\sqrt{45}$	**e** $5\sqrt{50} + \sqrt{18}$	**f** $4\sqrt{12} - 2\sqrt{27}$
g $6\sqrt{20} - 3\sqrt{80}$	**h** $3\sqrt{48} + 2\sqrt{75}$	**i** $2\sqrt{27} + 5\sqrt{12}$

3 Simplify each expression fully.

a $\frac{\sqrt{5} \times \sqrt{20}}{\sqrt{25}}$	**b** $\frac{\sqrt{32} \times \sqrt{8}}{4\sqrt{2}}$	**c** $\frac{\sqrt{72}}{\sqrt{2}} \times \sqrt{3}$

4 For each expression, rationalise the denominator.

a $\frac{3}{2 + \sqrt{3}}$	**b** $\frac{4}{\sqrt{3} + 1}$	**c** $\frac{2}{\sqrt{7} - 1}$
d $\frac{2\sqrt{7}}{\sqrt{5} - 3}$	**e** $\frac{\sqrt{6}}{\sqrt{2} + \sqrt{3}}$	**f** $\frac{\sqrt{3} + 1}{\sqrt{2} - 1}$
g $\frac{5}{\sqrt{6} + 2}$		

<< RECALL AND CONNECT 3 <<

Determine the size of the angle marked x and explain your working.

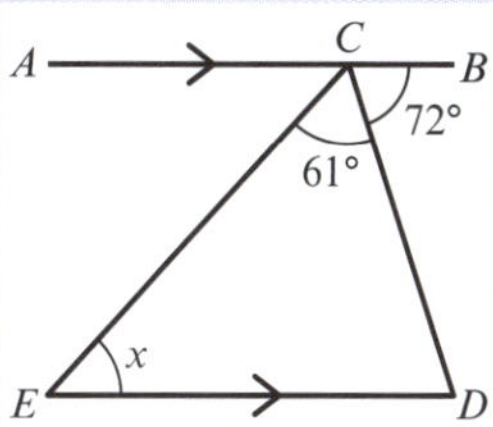

5 Show that $\frac{\sqrt{5}}{\sqrt{6}-\sqrt{2}}$ can be written in the form $\frac{\sqrt{10}+\sqrt{a}}{b}$,

where a and b are integers that you should find. [3]

[Total: 3]

6 The volume of a cone is given by the formula $V = \frac{1}{3}\pi r^2 h$.

The height of a cone is $3\sqrt{3}$ cm and the radius of its base is $\sqrt{7}$ cm.

Calculate the exact volume of the cone, leaving your answer in terms of π and any surds. [3]

[Total: 3]

REFLECTION

In which types of problems do you feel more confident using logic to 'determine' an answer? Are there types where you're still relying on trial and error? What can help you move from guessing to knowing?

9.4 Sets

UNDERSTAND THESE TERMS

- Set
- Element
- Venn diagram

1 List all the elements of each set.

a {prime numbers less than 10}

b {negative numbers greater than −7}

c {multiples of both 5 and 6 less than 100}

d {factors of 120}

e {multiples of 7 between 65 and 110}

2 a List two more members of the set {yellow, green, blue, …}.

b Describe, in words, the set {1, 3, 5, 7, 9}.

c Describe, in words, the set {2, 3, 5, 7, 11, 13, 17, 19}.

d True or false? If A = {multiples of 8 less than 100}, then $98 \in A$.

e True or false? If B = {prime numbers}, then $1 \in B'$.

3 Match each symbol to its definition.

Symbol	Definition
$n(A)$	Intersection of A and B
A'	Union of A and B
$\mathscr{E}$	Complement of set A
$A \cup B$	Universal set
$A \cap B$	Number of elements in set A

4 S = {multiples of 3 less than 50}

T = {multiples of 4 less than 50}

a List the members of

i $S \cup T$

ii $S \cap T$.

b Find

i $n(S \cap T')$

ii $n(S' \cap T)$.

5 Write each of the following using set notation.

a {1, 4, 9, 16, 25}

b Integers that are greater than −2 but are not greater than 14.

c Prime numbers greater than 70.

《 RECALL AND CONNECT 4 《

In a sale, all items are reduced by 15%.

Peter buys a pair of shoes for \$75.00 in the sale. Calculate the original price of the shoes. Give your answer correct to the nearest cent.

6 $A = \{1, 2, 4, 5, 6, 9\}$, $B = \{4, 5, 6, 7, 8, 10\}$ and $C = \{5, 6, 9, 10, 11\}$

a Copy and complete this Venn diagram. [3]

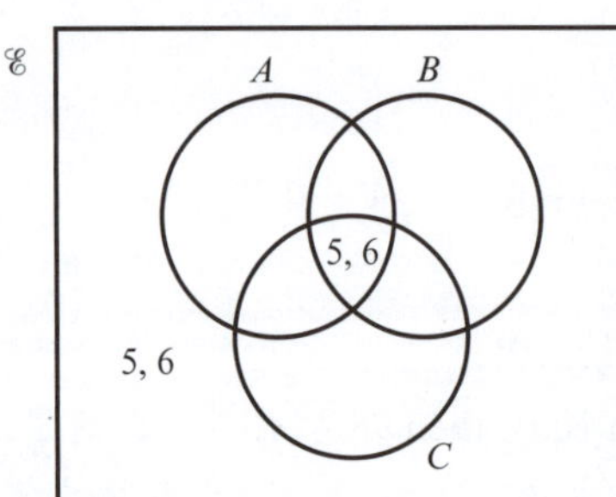

b List the elements of the set $A \cup B$. [2]

c Determine $n(A \cup B)$. [1]

d On your Venn diagram, shade $(B \cup C) \cap A$. [3]

[Total: 9]

7 160 students were asked whether they like playing football, basketball or tennis.

The results showed the following.

- 100 students like playing football.
- 80 students like playing basketball.
- 60 students like playing tennis.
- 40 students like playing both football and basketball.
- 30 students like playing both basketball and tennis.
- 25 students like playing both football and tennis.
- 10 students do not like playing any of the three sports.

a Letting x be the number of students who like playing all three sports, draw a Venn diagram to show this information. [3]

b Work out the number of students who like playing all three sports. [2]

c Determine the number of students who like playing basketball and tennis, but not football. [1]

[Total: 6]

REFLECTION

How did using the Venn diagram help you organise the information and make it easier to solve later parts of the question?

SELF-ASSESSMENT CHECKLIST

Let's revisit the Knowledge and Exam skills focus for this chapter.
Decide how confident you are with each statement.

	Now I can	Show it	Needs more work	Almost there	Confident to move on
1	describe the rule for continuing a sequence	State the term-to-term rule for the sequence −2, 1, 4, 7, ...			
2	find the nth term of some sequences	Find an expression for the nth term of the sequence above.			

CONTINUED

	Now I can	Show it	Needs more work	Almost there	Confident to move on
3	use the nth term to find terms from later on a sequence	Find the 35th term of the sequence −2, 1, 4, 7, ...			
4	generate and describe sequences from patterns of shapes	Write a rule for the number of matchsticks in pattern n of the triangle pattern in Section 9.1, Question 3.			
5	distinguish rational and irrational numbers	Which of the following are rational numbers? $0.\dot{6}$, $\sqrt{2}$, π			
6	express recurring decimals as fractions	Convert a recurring decimal like $0.\dot{7}\dot{4}$ into a fraction.			
7	simplify, calculate and solve problems with surds	Simplify $3\sqrt{12} - 2\sqrt{27}$			
8	use set language and notation to describe sets	Check you can answer all the questions that ask you to describe sets.			
9	find complements, unions and intersections of sets	Shade $A \cup B$ or $A \cap B$ on a Venn diagram.			
10	represent sets and solve problems using Venn diagrams	Solve a word problem like Section 9.4, Question 3 using a Venn diagram.			
11	show understanding of the command word 'determine' and answer a 'determine' question	Answer a question using clear reasoning to justify your final value. For example: 'Determine whether x is rational.').			
12	understand the difference between 'determine' and 'work out'.	Match examination questions to command words and explain how your working would differ.			

10 Straight lines and quadratic equations

KNOWLEDGE FOCUS

In this chapter, you will answer questions on:

- constructing a table of values and plot points to draw graphs
- finding the gradient of a straight-line graph
- recognising and determining the equation of a line
- determining the equation of a line parallel to a given line
- calculating the gradient of a line using coordinates of points on the line
- finding the gradient of parallel and perpendicular lines
- finding the length of a line segment and the coordinates of its midpoint
- expanding products of algebraic expressions
- factorising quadratic expressions
- solving quadratic equations by factorisation.

EXAM SKILLS FOCUS

In this chapter you will:

- show that you understand the command word 'plot' and can answer a 'plot' question
- understand the difference between plotting a graph and sketching a graph.

When answering questions involving graphs, you will often be asked to either 'plot' a graph or 'sketch' a graph.

Plot	mark point(s) on a graph.
Sketch	make a simple freehand drawing showing the key features.

When you are asked to plot a straight-line graph, you need to use a table of values to find three or more points that lie on the graph. You should then draw axes on graph paper and plot the points given in your table of values. You should then use a pencil and ruler to join the points.

'Sketch' is different to 'plot'. When you are asked to sketch a straight-line graph, you do not need to use graph paper. Instead, you should just find the points where the line crosses the coordinate axes and mark these on your sketch. Then, draw a line through these points. Later in the course, you will encounter curved graphs (such as parabolas), and in these cases, 'sketch' often means giving the correct shape and clearly indicating important points like turning points and axis intercepts – accuracy is less important than structure.

10.1 Straight-line graphs

UNDERSTAND THESE TERMS

- Parallel
- Perpendicular
- Perpendicular bisector

1 **a** For each of these equations, construct a table of values for $-3 \leqslant x \leqslant 3$.

On separate graphs, plot the points for each equation and draw the line.

i $y = 4x + 1$ **ii** $y = -2x + \frac{1}{2}$

iii $2y - x = 6$ **iv** $y + 3x - 4 = 0$

b Use each of your graphs to calculate the gradient of the line.
Did your calculated gradients match the coefficient of x in each equation?

2 Without constructing a table of values, draw the following lines on the same graph.

a $x = 3$ **b** $y = \frac{1}{2}$ **c** $x = -\frac{5}{2}$

3 For each pair of points, find the equation of the line that passes through both points.

a $A(4, 1)$ and $B(7, 7)$ **b** $A(-2, -1)$ and $B(2, 4)$

c $P(4, -1)$ and $Q(-7, 6)$ **d** $S(-3, 7)$ and $T(6, -2)$

e $V(-1, 2)$ and $W(3, 10)$ **f** $A(4, 0)$ and $B(-3, 6)$

g $C(-4, -6)$ and $D(2, 3)$ **h** $P(-5, -3)$ and $Q(1, 4)$

4 l is the line $y = 4x + 5$.

Find the equation of the line that is:

a parallel to l and passes through $(3, 1)$

b perpendicular to l and passes through $(-2, 4)$.

5 Find the distance between the points $(3, -1)$ and $(4, 6)$.
Give your answer in surd form.

6 Find the x- and y-intercepts for each of the following lines. Sketch the graph in each case.

a $y = -2x + 3$ **b** $3y - 4x = 5$

c $y = 2x + 5$ **d** $3x - 2y = 6$

e $y = -\frac{1}{3}x + 2$ **f** $4x + 5y - 20 = 0$

g $y + 2x + 3 = 0$ **h** $y - 4 = 2x - 2$

REFLECTION

Finding the equation of a perpendicular bisector requires you to work through several steps. How will you remember to do each of these steps in the correct order?

<< RECALL AND CONNECT 1 <<

a Make a the subject of the formula $s = ut + \frac{1}{2}at^2$.

b Make x the subject of the equation $a - \frac{b}{x} = c$.

7 Find the equation of the perpendicular bisector of $A(4, 5)$ and $B(8, 7)$. [5]

[Total: 5]

8 A company sells wooden crates for $12 each and charges a standard delivery fee of $5 for each order, irrespective of the number of crates ordered.

a Write an equation to represent the total cost C of buying x crates. [2]

b Plot the graph of x against C for $0 \leqslant x \leqslant 10$. [2]

c Determine the total cost of buying six crates in a single order. [2]

Emily paid $53, including the delivery fee, for her order.

d Work out the number of crates that Emily bought. [2]

[Total: 8]

9 A taxi company charges a flat booking fee and then a fixed price per kilometre.

The table shows the total cost, T, of a journey of d kilometres.

Distance, d (km)	0	1	2	3	4	5
Total cost, T ($)	4	6	8	10	12	14

a Plot a graph of T against d for $0 \leqslant x \leqslant 5$. [2]

b Use your graph to identify the cost of a 2.5 km journey. [1]

c i Calculate the gradient of your graph. [1]

ii Describe what the gradient tells you in the context of this question. [1]

d i Write the equation of the line in the form $y = mx + c$. [1]

ii State the meaning of the constant c in this context. [1]

[Total: 7]

10.2 Quadratic expressions and equations

UNDERSTAND THESE TERMS

- Expand
- Factorise

1 Expand and simplify each of the following products.

a $(x + 5)(x - 3)$ b $(x + 7)(x - 1)$ c $(5x - 2)(x + 6)$

d $(x - 4)(2x + 3)$ e $(2x - 4)(3x + 2)$ f $(3x + 1)(4x - 2)$

g $(5x + 2)(2x - 1)$ h $(3x + 4)^2$ i $(5x - 2)^2$

j $(x - 2)(2x + 4)(3x - 1)$ k $(4x + 1)(3x - 8)(x - 1)$

l $(2x + 3)(x - 4)(3x + 5)$ m $(x - 2)(3x + 1)(x + 4)$

2 Expand and simplify $(3 + 2x)^2 - (x + 4)(x - 1)$.

《 RECALL AND CONNECT 2 《

Factorise each expression as fully as possible.

a $14ab^2 - 63a^2$

b $15ab^4 + 25a^2b^2 - 40a^3b^2$

3 Factorise each quadratic expression completely.

a $x^2 + 5x + 6$ **b** $x^2 - 7x + 10$ **c** $x^2 + 4x - 21$

d $2x^2 + 7x + 3$ **e** $3x^2 + 5x - 2$ **f** $6x^2 + 5x - 6$

REFLECTION

It is important to find a method that you can use consistently to factorise a three-term quadratic expression into two linear brackets. Can you describe the method that you use? Can you break the method down into steps and write down each step in order?

4 Factorise each quadratic expression using the difference between two squares.

a $x^2 = 36$ **b** $16x^2 = 100y^2$ **c** $\frac{1}{4}p^4 - \frac{1}{25}q^4$

5 Solve each equation by factorising first.

a $x^2 + 6x + 9 = 0$ **b** $3x^2 = 11x + 4$ **c** $\frac{x^2}{16} - 81 = 0$

6 **a** Factorise the expression $a^2 - b^2$. [2]

b The number 225 can be written as a product of two factors: $225 = 5 \times 45$.

Use your answer to part **a** to write 225 as a difference of two square numbers. [2]

c Hence write 225 as a product of prime factors. [2]

[Total: 6]

7 Solve each equation.

a $\frac{x-8}{3} = -\frac{5}{x}$ [5]

b $2x = 7 - \frac{6}{x}$ [5]

[Total: 10]

8 A gardener is designing a rectangular garden.

The length of the garden is 3 metres more than its width.

If the area of the garden is 54 square metres, find the dimensions of the garden. [6]

[Total: 6]

REFLECTION

How does thinking about the purpose of a graph help you decide whether to plot it accurately or sketch it to show key features?

SELF-ASSESSMENT CHECKLIST

Let's revisit the Knowledge and Exam skills focus for this chapter. Decide how confident you are with each statement.

	Now I can	Show it	Needs more work	Almost there	Confident to move on
1	construct a table of values and plot points to draw graphs	Practise constructing tables of values and plotting graphs, for example $y = -3x - 4$.			
2	find the gradient of a straight-line graph	Find two points that lie on the graph of $y = -3x - 4$ and use them to find the gradient.			
3	recognise and determine the equation of a line	What is the gradient and what is the y-intercept of the line $y = -2x + \frac{3}{2}$?			
4	determine the equation of a line parallel to a given line	Find an equation of the line that is parallel to $y = -2x + \frac{3}{2}$ and passes through (1, 3).			
5	calculate the gradient of a line using coordinates of points on the line	Find the gradient of the straight line passing through (4, 6) and (7, −3).			
6	find the gradient of parallel and perpendicular lines	Use the fact that parallel lines have the same gradient and the product of perpendicular lines is −1.			
7	find the length of a line segment	Find the length of the line segment joining (4, 6) and (7, −3).			
8	find the coordinates of the midpoint of a line segment	Find the coordinates of the midpoint of the line segment joining (4, 6) and (7, −3).			

CONTINUED

	Now I can	Show it	Needs more work	Almost there	Confident to move on
9	expand products of algebraic expressions	Create a set of flashcards with an expression on one side and its expanded form on the back.			
10	factorise quadratic expressions	Factorise $2x^2 - x - 6$. Explain your reasoning out loud or to a friend.			
11	solve quadratic equations by factorisation	Solve $3x^2 - x - 6 = 0$. Then write your own question with two factors and include a mark scheme.			
12	show understanding of the command word 'plot' and answer a 'plot' question	Plot the graph of $y = 5x - 2$.			
13	understand the difference between plotting a graph and sketching a graph.	Write a short paragraph explaining when you would plot a graph versus when you would sketch one. Give examples from this chapter.			

11 Pythagoras' theorem and similar shapes

KNOWLEDGE FOCUS

In this chapter, you will answer questions on:

- using Pythagoras' theorem to find unknown sides of right-angled triangles
- using Pythagoras' theorem to solve problems
- deciding whether or not triangles are mathematically similar
- using properties of similar triangles to solve problems
- finding unknown lengths in similar figures
- recognising similar solids
- using the relationship between sides and areas of similar figures to find missing values
- calculating the volume and surface area of similar solids
- recognising whether shapes are congruent or not.

EXAM SKILLS FOCUS

In this chapter you will:

- understand how to answer questions that involve the use of a calculator, and those that do not
- recognise and make connections between different mathematical ideas.

In this chapter, you will use Pythagoras' theorem, explore similar and congruent shapes, and apply what you learn to solve real-world and exam-style problems. In an examination, some questions allow the use of a calculator, while others do not. Knowing the difference is key.

In calculator papers, you might see questions like Section 11.1, Question 1 (where you are asked to give side lengths to 3 significant figures). In non-calculator papers, you may be expected to leave answers as exact surds, like in Section 11.1, Question 4 (where the distance between two points must be given in surd form), or give your answer in terms of π.

A key part of succeeding when answering examination questions is being able to recognise connections between different mathematical concepts. For example, to find a missing length, you may need to decide whether to use Pythagoras' theorem, trigonometry, scale factors or even algebra. By making these connections confidently, you can choose the most efficient method and avoid unnecessary working.

11.1 Pythagoras' theorem

UNDERSTAND THESE TERMS

- Pythagoras' theorem
- Hypotenuse

1 Triangles **A–E** are right-angled triangles. Copy and complete the table with the missing side lengths.

Triangle	Side A (cm)	Side B (cm)	Hypotenuse (cm)
A	6		10
B	8	15	
C	5		13
D		24	25
E	9	12	

2 Find the unknown side length in each triangle.
Give your answers to 3 significant figures.

a

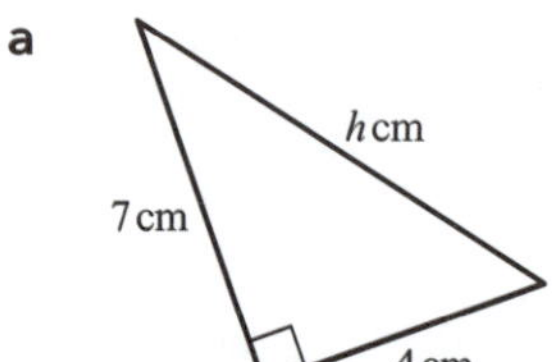

b

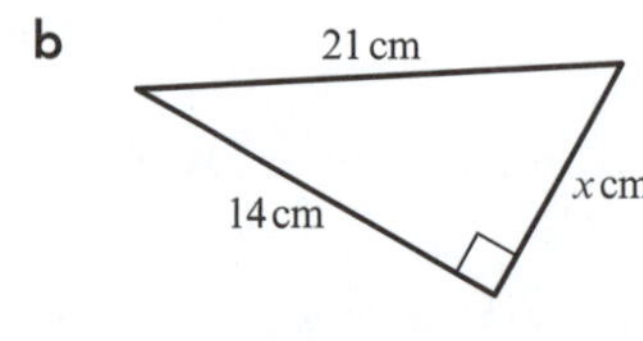

3 Find y.

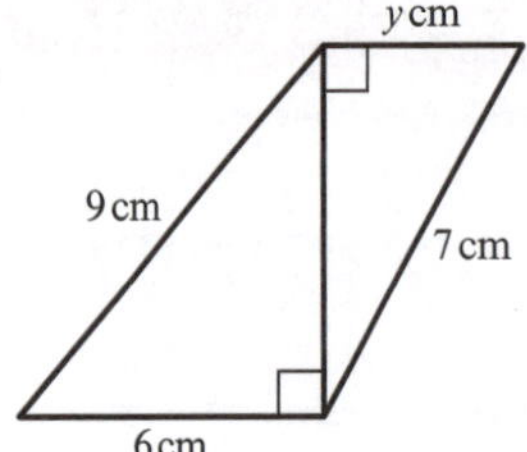

4 Use Pythagoras' theorem to determine whether each triangle, **A–E**, contains a right angle.

Triangle	Side A (cm)	Side B (cm)	Hypotenuse (cm)	Contains a right angle? (Yes/No)
A	3	4	5	
B	7	24	25	
C	8	15	17	
D	9	12	20	
E	5	6	10	

5 Use Pythagoras' theorem to determine whether or not each triangle contains a right angle.

a

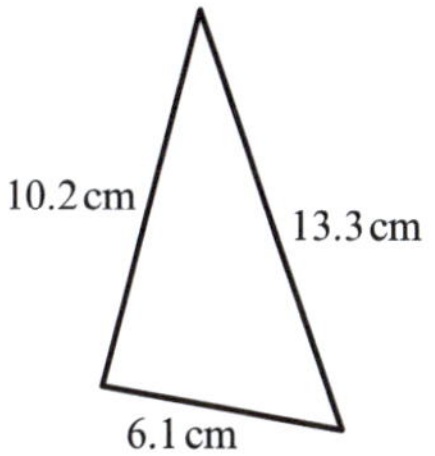

b

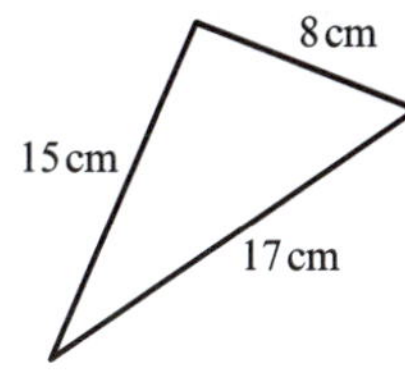

« RECALL AND CONNECT 1 «

A pentagon is made from an isosceles triangle connected to a rectangle, as shown.

Calculate the area and perimeter of the pentagon.

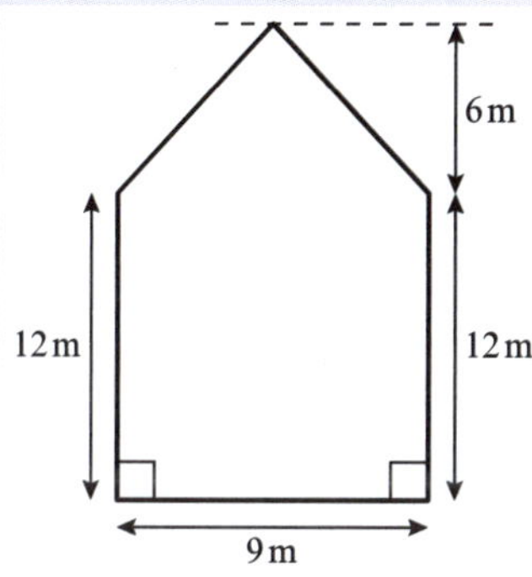

6 On a 1 cm squared grid, Steven draws a straight line segment between the points (3, 4) and (6, −2).

Find the exact length of Steven's line segment.

Give your answer in the form $a\sqrt{5}$, where a is a constant to be determined. [4]

[Total: 4]

7 *PQRS* is a quadrilateral with measurements as shown.

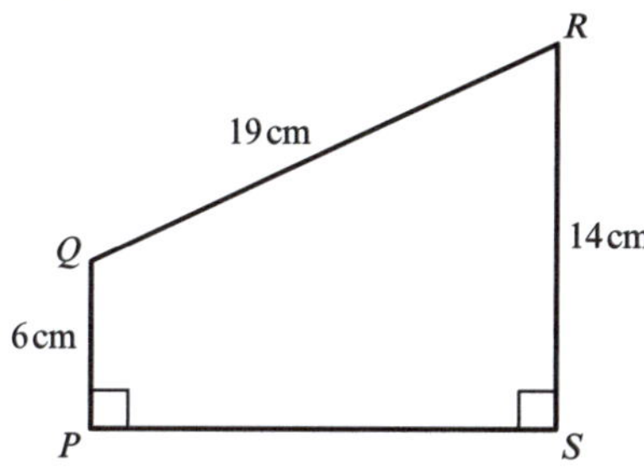

Calculate the length *QS*. [4]

[Total: 4]

REFLECTION

How can you recognise which method – such as Pythagoras' theorem, trigonometry or algebra – is needed to solve a problem? What patterns or clues help you decide, and how does this improve your confidence in tackling unfamiliar questions?

11.2 Understanding similar triangles

UNDERSTAND THESE TERMS

- Corresponding angles
- Corresponding lengths
- Similar

1 Complete the following sentences using the words from the list below.

Each word is used once.

corresponding angles	scale factor	
sides	similar	angles

a Two mathematically similar objects have the same shape and _______ but may be different in size.

b The ratio that compares the measurements of two similar shapes is called the _______.

c When two triangles are similar, all the _______ are equal.

d For similar triangles, the ratio of corresponding _______ is the same.

e If the corresponding sides of two triangles are proportional, the triangles are said to be _______.

2 For each pair of triangles, determine whether or not the triangles are similar. Give clear reasons to justify your answers.

a

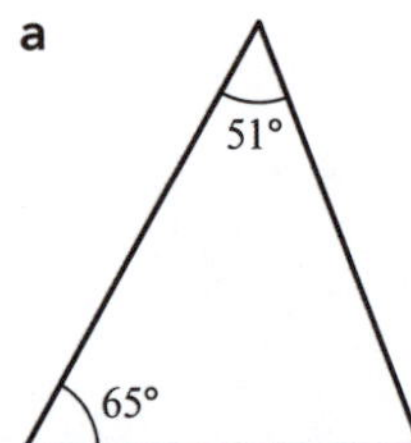

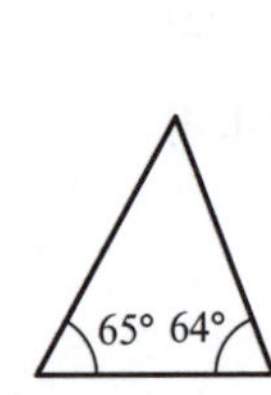

b

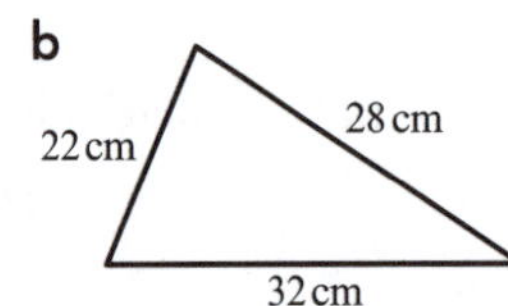

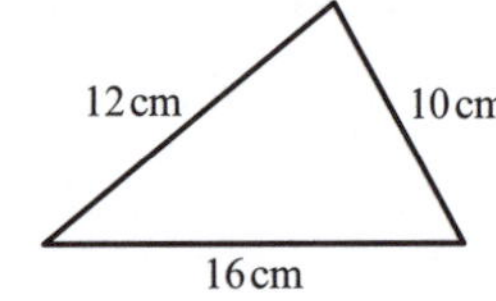

3 The two triangles in each pair are similar. Calculate the value of x in each case.

a

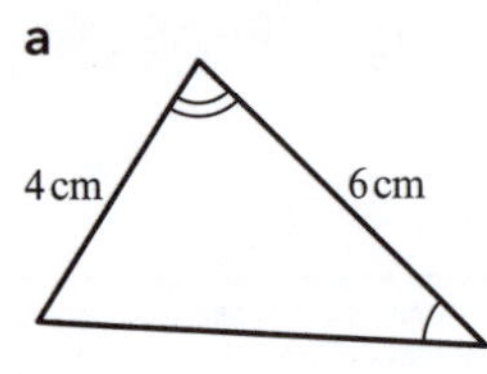

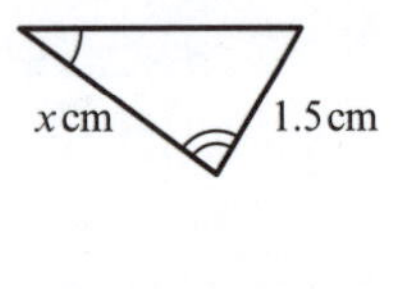

b

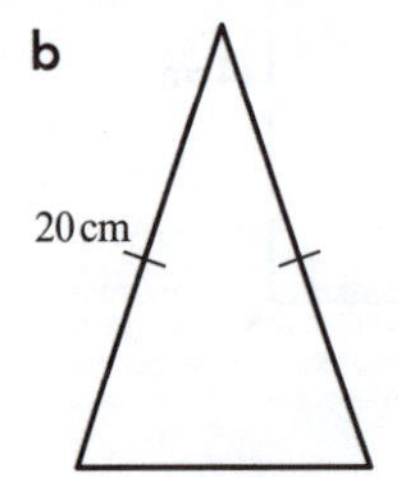

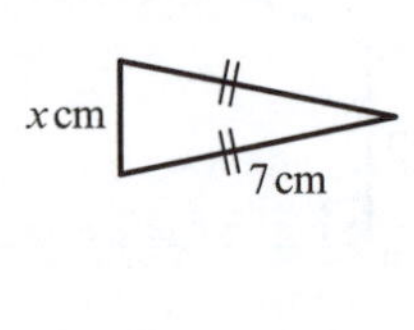

REFLECTION

In examination questions, similar triangles are usually not given in the same orientation.

When you recognise that triangles are not in the same orientation, what strategies do you use to decide how to rotate or reflect one triangle? How do you check that you have reoriented them correctly before starting your calculations?

Before attempting calculations, how does sketching the triangles in the same orientation help you plan your method more effectively? How can you use this strategy to reduce mistakes under exam conditions?

4 BD is parallel to AE.

Find the length BD.

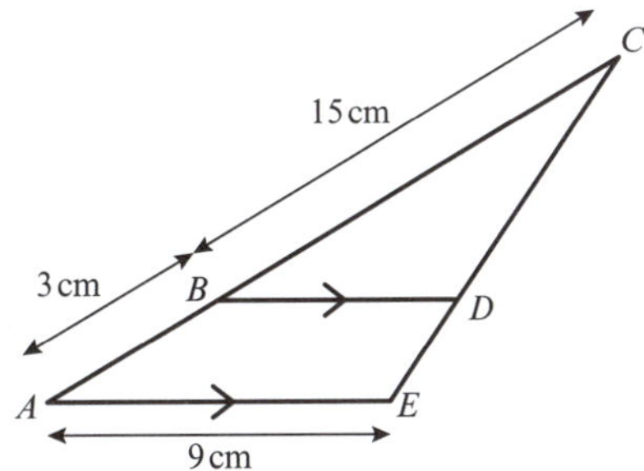

« RECALL AND CONNECT 2 «

Use a compass, a ruler and a pencil to construct triangle ABC, where $AB = 4.2$ cm, $BC = 6.7$ cm and $AC = 7.3$ cm.

5 Ioannis is on safari. He uses his camera to take a picture of a giraffe.

In the camera, the distance from the focal point to the image is 7 cm.
The image of the giraffe formed in the camera is 4 cm tall.

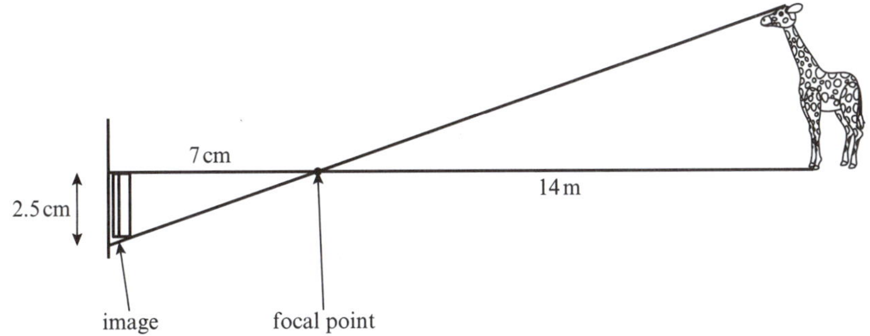

The safari guide tells Ioannis that the giraffe is 14 m away.

Calculate the height of the giraffe. [3]

[Total: 3]

11.3 Understanding similar shapes

1 What does it mean if two shapes are said to be similar?

- **A** The shapes are identical in both shape and size.
- **B** The ratio of corresponding sides is equal and the corresponding angles are equal.
- **C** The ratio of corresponding sides is different and the corresponding angles are equal.
- **D** The shapes have different proportions but the same angles.

2 Which of the following is true about similar shapes?

- **A** Similar shapes are identical in both shape and size.
- **B** Similar shapes have equal corresponding angles and the ratio of corresponding sides is different.
- **C** Similar shapes are identical in shape but may differ in size.
- **D** Similar shapes have different shapes but identical side lengths.

3 Determine whether or not each pair of shapes is similar.

Give reasons for your answer in each case.

a

4 cm

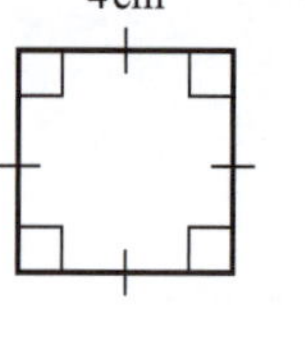

6 cm

b

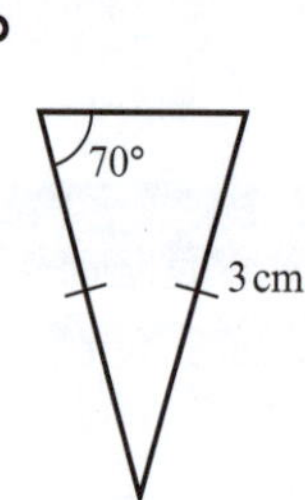

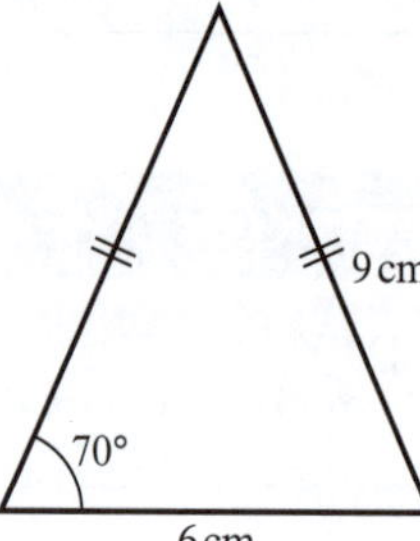

c

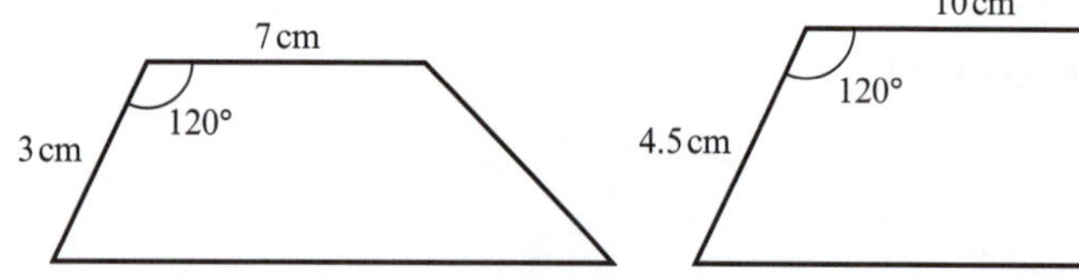

4 The two shapes shown are similar.

Calculate the lengths of x and y.

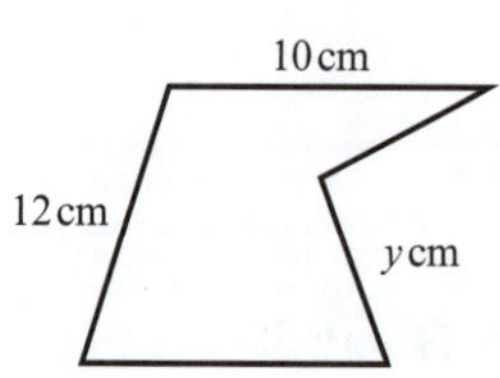

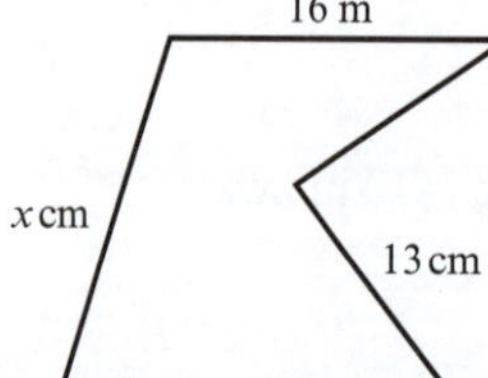

« RECALL AND CONNECT 3 «

A cylinder has a radius of 7 cm and height of 13 cm.

Calculate the following. In each case, give your answer to the nearest whole number.

a The volume of the cylinder.

b The surface area of the cylinder.

5 Evie draws two similar right-angled triangles.

The smaller triangle has hypotenuse length 8 cm and the larger triangle has hypotenuse length 14 cm.

The area of the smaller triangle is 44 cm^2.

Calculate the area of the larger triangle.

Give your answer correct to 3 significant figures. [3]

[Total: 3]

REFLECTION

When a question describes a situation, what steps do you take to decide whether drawing a diagram would help you? How can creating a diagram help you organise the information and plan your approach more effectively before you start answering?

6 The two cans of beans are similar.

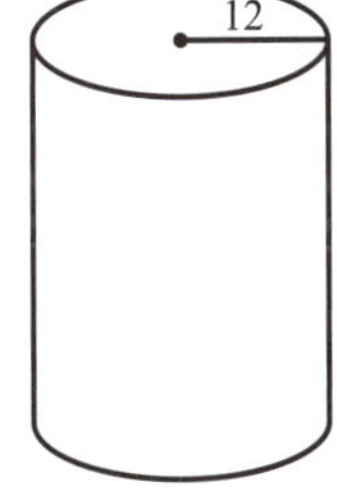

Volume = 480 cm^3

Find the volume of the larger can. [3]

[Total: 3]

7 Two solids are similar.

The larger solid has length 10 cm and surface area 140 cm^2.

The smaller solid has length l cm and surface area 60 cm^2.

Show that $l = \frac{\sqrt{2100}}{7}$ cm. [4]

[Total: 4]

8 Two pyramids are mathematically similar. They have surface areas and volumes as shown.

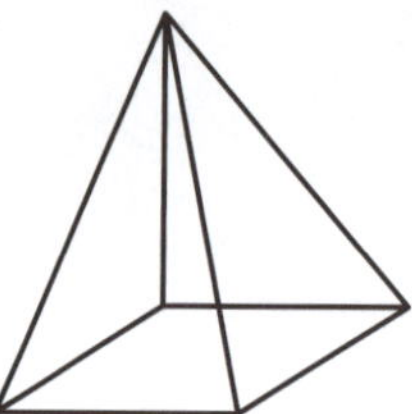

Calculate the volume of the smaller pyramid. [4]

[Total: 4]

11.4 Understanding congruence

UNDERSTAND THIS TERM

- Congruent

1 Which **three** statements are correct? If two shapes are congruent then ...

A corresponding sides are equal in length.

B the shapes have the same area.

C the shapes have the same perimeter but may have different areas.

D corresponding angles are equal.

E the shapes must have identical proportions but may differ in size.

F the shapes are the same size and may have different angles.

2 The two triangles shown are congruent.

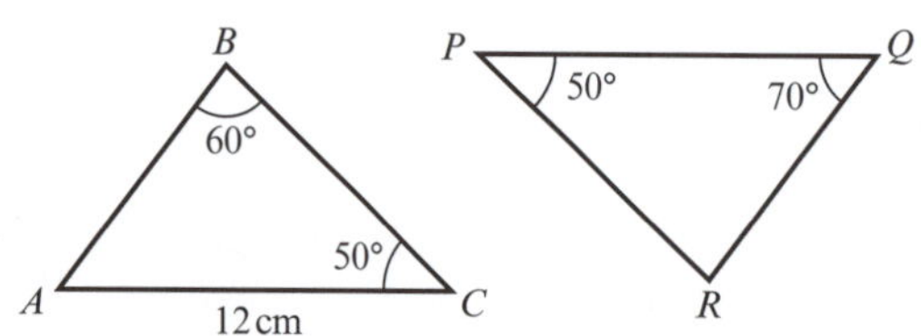

a Calculate the size of angle BAC.

b Calculate the size of angle PRQ.

c State which side in the first triangle has length 16 cm.

d State which side in the second triangle has length 12 cm.

《 RECALL AND CONNECT 4 《

Find the equation of the perpendicular bisector of the points (3, −1) and (−7, 4).

3 On the grid, the quadrilateral $ABCD$ has vertices at $A(2, 3)$, $B(4, 6)$, $C(7, 4)$ and $D(5, 1)$.

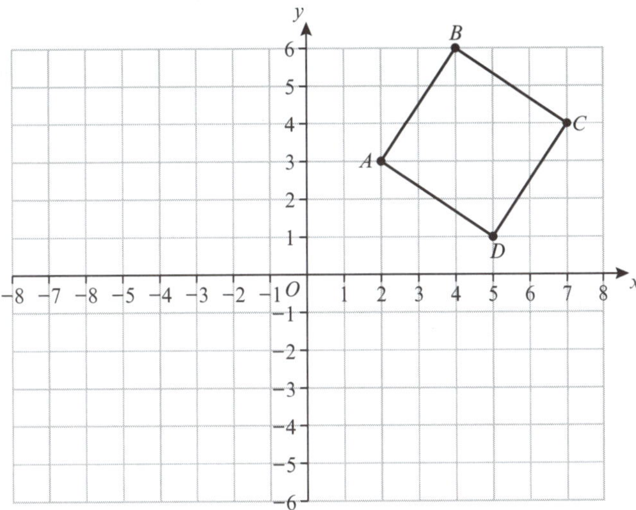

a On a copy of the grid, draw a quadrilateral that is congruent to $ABCD$ and is the reflection of $ABCD$ in the y-axis. Label the image as A', B', C' and D'. [4]

b Describe the transformation required to map quadrilateral $A'B'C'D'$ onto a new quadrilateral with vertices $W(-1, 2)$, $X(-3, 5)$, $Y(-6, 3)$ and $Z(-4, 0)$. [2]

[Total: 6]

SELF-ASSESSMENT CHECKLIST

Let's revisit the Knowledge and Exam skills focus for this chapter. Decide how confident you are with each statement.

	Now I can	Show it	Needs more work	Almost there	Confident to move on
1	use Pythagoras' theorem to find unknown sides of right-angled triangles	State Pythagoras' theorem for a right-angled triangle with shorter sides a and b and hypotenuse t.			
2	use Pythagoras' theorem to solve problems	Solve problems like the one given in Section 11.1, Question 5.			
3	decide whether triangles are mathematically similar	Write down the criteria that must be met for two shapes to be mathematically similar.			
4	use properties of similar triangles to solve problems	Solve problems like the one given in Section 11.2, Question 4.			

CONTINUED

	Now I can	Show it	Needs more work	Almost there	Confident to move on
5	find unknown lengths in similar figures	Find x in Section 11.2, Question 2.			
6	recognise similar solids	Determine whether two given cylinders are similar.			
7	use the relationship between sides and areas of similar figures to find missing values	Write down and memorise: $\left(\frac{\text{length } A}{\text{length } B}\right)^3 = \frac{\text{volume } A}{\text{volume } B}$			
8	calculate the volume and surface area of similar solids	Find past-paper questions that involve similar 3D shapes: one question on volume and one on surface area. Check the mark schemes to see how answers are structured.			
9	recognise whether or not shapes are congruent	Create a way of remembering: • corresponding sides are equal in length • corresponding angles are equal • the shapes have the same area. For example, 'SAA: Same Sides, Angles, Area'.			
10	understand how to answer questions that involve the use of a calculator, and those that do not.	Practise how to simplify surds. You often need to leave your answer in surd form if the final answer asks for an exact value.			

12 Averages and measures of spread

KNOWLEDGE FOCUS

In this chapter, you will answer questions on:

- calculating the mean, median and mode of sets of data
- calculating and interpreting the range as a measure of spread
- interpreting the meaning of average and range, and using them to compare sets of data
- calculating and working with quartiles
- constructing and using frequency distribution tables for grouped data
- dividing data into quartiles and calculating the interquartile range
- identifying the modal class from a grouped frequency distribution.

EXAM SKILLS FOCUS

In this chapter you will:

- show that you understand the command word 'state' and can answer a 'state' question
- understand the difference between 'state' and 'explain'.

In this chapter you will calculate measures of average and measures of range. You will work with both discrete and continuous data.

State	express in clear terms.
Explain	set out purposes or reasons/make the relationships between things clear/say why and/or how and support with relevant evidence.

You will practise answering questions that use the command word 'state'. Sometimes, 'state' is followed by 'explain', for example: *State and explain which café offers better average earnings.* When asked to 'state', you must give a specific name, value or other brief answer without explanation or calculation. When asked to 'explain', you must give reasons for the answer you stated. Generally, you will get two marks – one mark for stating the correct answer and the other mark for a correct reason.

12.1 Different types of average

1 For each of the following data sets, find the mode, mean and median.

a 3, 3, 4, 4, 5, 5, 5, 6, 6, 7, 8

b 12 000, 14 000, 15 000, 15 000, 15 000, 16 000, 17 000, 18 000, 19 000, 20 000

c 1, 100, 1000, 5000, 8000, 9000, 9500, 9700, 9900, 10 000

d 42, 45, 49, 50, 50, 50, 51, 52, 53, 60

e 2, 2, 2, 2, 3, 5, 7, 9, 11, 50

f 1.5, 2.1, 3.7, 2.1, 4.2, 5.6, 2.1, 6.0

g $\frac{1}{2}, \frac{3}{4}, \frac{3}{4}, \frac{1}{3}, \frac{2}{3}, 1, \frac{1}{4}, 1$

h 1.1, 2.2, 3.3, 4.4, 2.2, 1.1, 3.3, 2.2

i $3, \frac{7}{2}, \frac{2}{3}, 1.25, 2.5, 3.5, 1\frac{3}{4}, 2$

« RECALL AND CONNECT 1 «

Write $(0.3 \times 10^6) \div (2 \times 10^{-3})$ in standard form.

2 The heights (in cm) of ten plants are as follows.

32, 35, 30, 33, 35, 36, 34, 32, 33, 35

a State the mode. [1]

b Find the median. [2]

c Calculate the mean. [2]

[Total: 5]

3 The following are the times (in minutes) taken by 12 students to complete a quiz.

12.5, 14.0, 13.2, 15.3, 14.7, 13.2, 12.8, 14.0, 13.6, 15.3, 13.2, 14.5

a State the mode of the times. [1]

b Find the median time. [2]

c Calculate the mean time taken to complete the quiz. [2]

[Total: 5]

4 The mean mass of 15 apples in a crate is 180 grams.

A 16th apple with mass 195 grams is added to the crate.

Calculate the mean mass of all 16 apples in the crate.
Give your answer correct to the nearest gram. [4]

[Total: 4]

5 Amy has six items in her shopping basket.

The mean price per item for the six items is \$4.16.

Amy adds identical bottles of olive oil to her basket. The mean price per item for the eight items in her basket is \$6.02.

Calculate the cost of one bottle of olive oil. [4]

[Total: 4]

REFLECTION

How do you decide whether to use the mean, median or mode when comparing data sets? Can you think of a situation where one might give a misleading impression? How does recognising this help you feel more confident during exams?

12.2 Making comparisons using averages and ranges

1 Look at these data sets (**A**–**E**).

A	56	60	62	63	65	65	66	68	70	74
B	48	50	52	54	56	58	60	62	64	66
C	70	71	72	73	74	75	76	77	78	79
D	30	35	40	45	50	55	60	65	70	75
E	65	65	65	65	65	65	65	65	65	65

a For each data set, find the mean, median and range.

b Order the data sets from most to least consistent.

<< RECALL AND CONNECT 2 <<

Solve

$$\frac{3x - 2}{4} = \frac{x + 1}{2}$$

2 The scores out of 20 from two different classes in a maths quiz are as follows.

- Class A: 12, 15, 17, 14, 18, 16, 19, 13, 15, 17
- Class B: 13, 13, 15, 14, 16, 15, 17, 18, 12, 14

a Calculate the mean score for each class. [3]

b Find the range of scores for each class. [2]

c State which class performed better on average.
Give a reason for your answer. [2]

d State which class had more consistent scores.
Give a reason for your answer. [2]

[Total: 9]

3 The weekly earnings (in dollars) of part-time students working at two cafés are as follows.

- Café A: 85, 90, 90, 95, 100, 88, 92, 96, 91, 89
- Café B: 80, 85, 90, 105, 110, 87, 95, 93, 100, 84

a Calculate the mean, median and range of earnings for each café. [6]

b State and explain which café offers better average earnings. [2]

c State and explain which café offers more consistent earnings. [2]

[Total: 10]

4 The number of books read in a month by members of two reading clubs is recorded as follows.

- Club Alpha: 2, 4, 4, 4, 5, 6, 7, 5, 4, 6
- Club Beta: 3, 3, 3, 4, 5, 6, 8, 4, 4, 7

a Calculate the mean, mode and range for each club. [6]

b By referring to the mode, suggest which club shows more consistent reading patterns. [1]

c Explain whether the mean or the mode best represents each club's reading habits. [2]

[Total: 9]

5 Two teams, Team Storm and Team Thunder, played eight matches each. The number of goals they scored in each match is shown in the table.

Match	1	2	3	4	5	6	7	8
Team Storm	3	3	4	2	4	3	5	3
Team Thunder	2	2	1	3	3	2	4	1

a Calculate the mean, median, mode and range of goals scored for each team. [8]

b State which team performed better on average. Justify your answer by referring to the values you calculated in part **a**. [2]

[Total: 10]

12.3 Calculating averages and ranges for frequency data

1 For each of the following data sets, construct a frequency table and calculate

i the mean **ii** the median **iii** the mode **iv** the range.

a

7.0	6.5	5.5	6.0	5.0
7.0	6.5	5.0	6.0	5.5
6.5	7.0	6.0	5.5	7.0
6.0	6.5	5.0	7.0	7.0

b

11	12	11	13	15
12	12	13	11	14
12	11	14	15	13
13	12	14	14	15

c

16	17	18	19	15
15	18	18	17	19
19	15	18	17	16
17	18	19	15	16

d

13	15	14	18	19	11	12	13	11	17
16	16	19	15	14	18	12	17	11	13
19	16	12	11	13	17	13	11	19	14

≪ RECALL AND CONNECT 3 ≪

Solve for x

$4^{3x+1} = 8^{x+2}$

2 The number of hours per week spent on homework by students in a class is shown in the table.

Hours spent on homework	0	1	2	3	4	5	6	7	8	9	10
Number of students	3	2	4	5	6	7	5	4	3	2	1

a Find

i the mean [3]

ii the median [2]

iii the mode. [1]

The teacher says that, on average, students spend *less than* 5 hours per week on their homework.

The students disagree and say that, on average, they spend 5 hours per week on homework.

b **i** Suggest which measure of average the teacher is using. Justify your answer. [2]

ii Suggest which measure of average the students are using. Justify your answer. [2]

[Total: 10]

3 The heights (in metres) of 20 sunflowers are shown in the stem-and-leaf diagram.

0	9	8					
1	4	0	2	6	9	7	2
2	7	5	8	0	5	3	
3	6	0	1	9	4		

Key: 1 | 2 = 1.2 metres

a Redraw the stem-and-leaf diagram to make an ordered data set. [2]

b Calculate the mean height of the sunflowers. [2]

c Explain why the mode is not a helpful measure of the average height of sunflowers. [1]

d Calculate the median height of sunflowers. [2]

The garden centre will sell the sunflowers when their height is 2.5 m or more.

e Calculate what percentage of these sunflowers the garden centre can sell. [2]

[Total: 9]

12.4 Estimating the mean and finding the modal class for grouped data

1 For each data set, **a**–**e**, calculate

i an estimate of the mean

ii the median class

iii the modal class.

a

Data	Frequency
0–9	5
10–19	8
20–29	14
30–39	7
40–49	2

b

Data	Frequency
0–10	4
11–20	10
21–30	12
31–40	6
41–50	3

c

Data	Frequency
0–9	3
10–29	7
30–49	12
50–79	9
80–100	4

d

Data	Frequency
$0 < x \leqslant 15$	6
$15 < x \leqslant 40$	11
$40 < x \leqslant 70$	15
$70 < x \leqslant 100$	5

e

Data	Frequency
$0 < x \leqslant 30$	8
$30 < x \leqslant 60$	14
$60 < x \leqslant 80$	10
$80 < x \leqslant 100$	3

≪ RECALL AND CONNECT 4 ≪

Make a the subject of the equation $\sqrt{a+b} = c$.

2 A company surveyed its employees about their daily commute times to the office.

The table shows the results.

Commute time (minutes)	Frequency
$0 < t \leqslant 10$	4
$10 < t \leqslant 20$	7
$20 < t \leqslant 30$	12
$30 < t \leqslant 40$	9
$40 < t \leqslant 60$	3

a State the modal class for commute time, t. [1]

b Calculate an estimate for the mean commute time. [5]

[Total: 6]

3 A supermarket tracked how much money a group of 40 university students spent on groceries in one week. The spending amounts were grouped as shown in the table.

Weekly spending ($)	Frequency
$0 < S \leqslant 20$	5
$20 < S \leqslant 40$	8
$40 < S \leqslant 45$	14
$45 < S \leqslant 50$	9
$50 < S \leqslant 70$	4

Estimate the mean amount spent on groceries per week.

Write your answer to the nearest cent. [5]

[Total: 5]

4 The number of steps walked daily (in thousands) by employees from two different companies was grouped and recorded as shown in the tables.

Company A

Steps (000s)	Frequency
$0 < d \leqslant 4$	2
$4 < d \leqslant 8$	5
$8 < d \leqslant 10$	11
$10 < d \leqslant 12$	7
$12 < d \leqslant 15$	3

Company B

Steps (000s)	Frequency
$0 < d \leqslant 4$	1
$4 < d \leqslant 8$	7
$8 < d \leqslant 10$	15
$10 < d \leqslant 12$	12
$12 < d \leqslant 15$	1

a State the modal class

i for company A [1]

ii for company B. [1]

b Calculate an estimate for the mean number of steps walked per day by employees of

i company A [5]

ii company B. [5]

c Based on this data, state which company is likely to have the bigger office. Explain your answer using your calculations from part **b**. [2]

d Explain why the mean is a more helpful measure of average than the mode to help you answer part **c**. [1]

[Total: 15]

12.5 Quartiles

1 Find the median, quartiles and interquartile range for each set of data.

Make sure that you show your method clearly.

a 18, 22, 25, 20, 27, 30, 24, 21, 23, 26, 19, 22, 25, 20, 27, 28, 29, 24, 21, 23

b 45, 48, 50, 53, 49, 47, 52, 55, 51, 50, 48, 47, 49, 46, 51, 53, 54, 56, 52, 50

c 4.5, 6, 7.2, 6.8, 5, 7, 8, 6.5, 5.5, 9, 6, 5.8, 8.2, 4.9, 6.1, 7.5, 6.4, 7

d 12, 13.5, 14, 15, 14.5, 12.5, 13, 16, 15.5, 14.2, 13.8, 14.9, 15.3, 12.8, 13.2, 14.1

e 20, 19.5, 21, 22, 20.5, 18, 19, 21.5, 22.5, 23, 20.1, 19.8, 21.2, 18.5, 17.9, 21.1, 22.3, 20.8, 18.2, 23.1

f 30, 32, 33.5, 31, 30.5, 29, 28, 33, 31.5, 32.2, 34, 28.5, 29.5, 30.2, 31.8

g 45, 47, 44.5, 46, 48.5, 49, 47.5, 46.5, 45.5, 48, 44, 46.8, 47.3, 45.2, 44.8, 43.9, 49.2

《 RECALL AND CONNECT 5 《

Find the length of the line segment joining (2, 5) and (6, −3). Give your answer in simplified surd form.

2 A teacher recorded the times (in minutes) taken by 20 students to complete a maths test. The times (in minutes) are as follows.

32, 45, 39, 41, 47, 50, 36, 43, 42, 48, 40, 46, 38, 35, 44, 49, 33, 37, 41, 39

a i Write the data in ascending order. [1]

ii Find the median time. [1]

iii Find the lower quartile (Q1) and upper quartile (Q3). [1]

iv Find the interquartile range (IQR). [1]

b The teacher says, 'Most students took around 41 minutes to finish the test.'

Use your results from part **a** to comment on whether this is a reasonable statement. [2]

The times (in minutes) that 11 students took to complete a science test are as follows.

41, 42, 43, 40, 44, 39, 45, 38, 46, 90, 91

c Explain how the median and interquartile range give you a better measure of the time taken by the class in this situation. [3]

[Total: 9]

REFLECTION

In this chapter, you were sometimes asked to 'state' and at other times to 'explain'. How do you recognise the difference? What do you do to ensure you give only a brief answer when a question says 'state', but provide full reasoning when it says 'explain'?

SELF-ASSESSMENT CHECKLIST

Let's revisit the Knowledge and Exam skills focus for this chapter.
Decide how confident you are with each statement.

	Now I can	Show it	Needs more work	Almost there	Confident to move on
1	calculate the mean, median and mode of sets of data	Make flashcards: on one side, write the average type; on the other, write how to calculate it, with an example.			
2	calculate and interpret the range as a measure of spread	Collect a simple data set (for example shoe sizes or hours of screen time from friends/family) and calculate all three averages.			
3	interpret the meaning of average and range, and use them to compare sets of data	Explain to a classmate how two sets can have the same mean but different ranges, and what this means about the data.			
4	calculate and work with quartiles	Create your own small data set (10–20 values). Write it in order, then find Q1, Q2 (median), Q3 and the interquartile range. Highlight the middle 50%.			
5	construct and use frequency distribution tables for grouped data	Record some data (such as the number of steps you walk each day for a week), create a grouped table and estimate the mean and modal class using midpoints.			
6	divide data into quartiles and calculate the interquartile range	Use a large data set (more than 20 values) to find the lower quartile, upper quartile and IQR. Write down what the IQR tells you about the spread.			
7	identify the modal class from a grouped frequency distribution	Look at a grouped frequency table and state the modal class. Then explain how you know it is the most common group.			

CONTINUED

	Now I can	Show it	Needs more work	Almost there	Confident to move on
8	show understanding of the command word 'state' and answer a 'state' question	Write down a list of 'state' questions you might be asked (for example state the range, state the mode) and practise giving short, precise answers.			
9	understand the difference between 'state' and 'explain'.	Look through past-paper questions and mark schemes. Identify where 'state' is used alone and where it is followed by 'explain'. Make notes on how the required answers differ and how marks are awarded.			

Exam practice 3

This section contains past paper questions from previous Cambridge exams, which draw together your knowledge on a range of topics that you have covered up to this point. These questions give you the opportunity to test your knowledge and understanding.

The following question has an example student response and commentary provided. Work through the question first, then compare your answer to the sample response and commentary. Are your answers different to the sample responses?

1 **a** A sequence has nth term $3n^2 - 1$.

Find the second term in this sequence. [1]

b The table shows the first five terms of sequences **A** and **B**.

	1st term	2nd term	3rd term	4th term	5th term	nth term
Sequence A	−6	−2	2	6	10	
Sequence B	3	17	55	129	251	

Complete the table to show the nth term of each sequence. [4]

Cambridge IGCSE Mathematics (0580) Paper 21 Q13 November 2024 **[Total: 5]**

Example student response	Commentary
a $3 \times 2^2 - 1 = 11$	The student has correctly substituted $n = 2$ into the given formula for 1 mark. ***This answer scores 1 out of 1 mark.***
b Sequence A is linear: Common difference = +4 $4 \times 1 - 10 = -6$ So nth term is $4n - 10$ Sequence B is also linear: Common difference = +14 $14 \times 1 - 11 = 3$ So nth term is $14n - 11$	The student gains 1 mark for identifying that sequence A is a linear sequence, and 1 mark for finding the common difference and nth term. But they have incorrectly assumed that sequence B is linear. Although the difference between the first and second terms is 14, the difference between other consecutive terms is not 14. ***This answer scores 2 out of 4 marks.***

2

Sequence	1st term	2nd term	3rd term	4th term	5th term	nth term
A	13	9	5	1		
B	0	7	26	63		
C	$\frac{7}{8}$	$\frac{8}{16}$	$\frac{9}{32}$	$\frac{10}{64}$		

a Complete the table for the three sequences. [10]

b One term in Sequence C is $\frac{p}{q}$.

Write down the next term in Sequence C in terms of p and q. [2]

Cambridge IGCSE Mathematics (0580) Paper 42 Q11 November 2020 **[Total: 12]**

The following question has an example student response and commentary provided. Work through the question first, then compare your answer to the sample response and commentary. Are your answers different to the sample responses?

3 **a** The nth term of a sequence is $n^2 - 3$.

Find the first three terms of this sequence. [2]

b These are the first five terms of a different sequence.

1 3 9 27 81

Find the nth term of this sequence. [2]

Cambridge IGCSE Mathematics (0580) Paper 22 Q8 March 2024 **[Total: 4]**

Example student response	Commentary
a $0^2 - 3 = -3$ $1^2 - 3 = -2$ $2^2 - 3 = 1$	The student has incorrectly assumed that the first term is when $n = 0$. But they still achieve 1 mark for −3, −2 and 1; this is a 'special case' mark since those values *would* be correct if the $n = 0$ assumption was correct. ***This answer scores 1 out of 2 marks.***
b nth term is 3^{n-1}	The student has correctly identified that the terms are all powers of 3. ***This answer scores 2 out of 2 marks.***

4 Now that you have gone through the commentary, try to write an improved answer for your own solution and edit the sample student response to improve their answer to each part.

The following question has an example student response and commentary provided. Work through the question first, then compare your answer to the sample response and commentary. Are your answers different to the sample responses?

5 A is the point (6, 1) and B is the point (2, 7).

Find the equation of the perpendicular bisector of AB.

Give your answer in the form $y = mx + c$. [5]

Cambridge IGCSE Mathematics (0580) Paper 22 Q26 March 2024 **[Total: 5]**

Example student response	Commentary
Midpoint $= \left(\frac{6+2}{2}, \frac{1+7}{2}\right) = (4, 4)$ Gradient $AB = \frac{7-1}{2-6} = \frac{6}{-4} = -\frac{3}{2}$ Bisector is $y = -\frac{3}{2}x + c$ and passes through (4, 4) $4 = -\frac{3}{2}(4) + c \Rightarrow c = 10$ $y = -\frac{3}{2}x + 10$	The student has correctly found the midpoint for 1 mark, and the gradient of AB for 1 mark. However, the student lost a mark for not finding the gradient of the perpendicular bisector. The student gained a method mark for substituting (4, 4) into $y = -\frac{3}{2}x + c$ They lost another mark for the final equation being incorrect. ***This answer scores 3 out of 5 marks.***

6 Now that you have gone through the commentary, try to write an improved answer for your own solution and edit the sample student response to improve their answer to each part.

The following question has an example student response and commentary provided. Work through the question first, then compare your answer to the sample response and commentary. Are your answers different to the sample responses?

7 $\mathscr{E} = \{1, 2, 3, 4, 5, 6, 7, 8, 9, 10\}$

$P = \{\text{odd numbers}\}$

$Q = \{\text{multiples of } 3\}$

$R = \{\text{square numbers}\}$

a Find $P \cap Q \cap R$. [1]

b **i** Find $Q \cup R$. [1]

ii Find $n(P \cap (Q \cap R)')$. [1]

Cambridge IGCSE Mathematics (0580) Paper 21 Q19 November 2024 **[Total: 3]**

Example student response	Commentary
a $P \cap Q \cap R = 9$	The student correctly found that 9 was the only value in all three sets. ***This answer scores 1 out of 1 mark.***
b **i** $Q \cup R = \{1, 3, 4, 6, 9\}$	The student correctly understood that $Q \cup R$ are the values in either Q, or R, or both. ***This answer scores 1 out of 1 mark.***
b **ii** $(Q \cup R)' = \{2, 5, 7, 8, 10\}$ $P \cap (Q \cup R)' = \{5, 7\}$	The student correctly found that $(Q \cup R)'$ was the elements not contained in their answer to part **(b) (i)**. They also correctly worked out that $P \cap (Q \cup R)'$ was the odd numbers in $(Q \cup R)'$. However, the question asks for $n(P \cap (Q \cup R)')$, which is the size of the set, not the elements of the set. So they do not gain the mark. ***This answer scores 0 out of 1 mark.***

8 **a** $\mathscr{E}$ = {integers greater than 2}

A = {prime numbers}

B = {odd numbers}

C = {square numbers}

i Describe the type of numbers in the set $B' \cap C$. [1]

ii Complete the set labels on the Venn diagram.

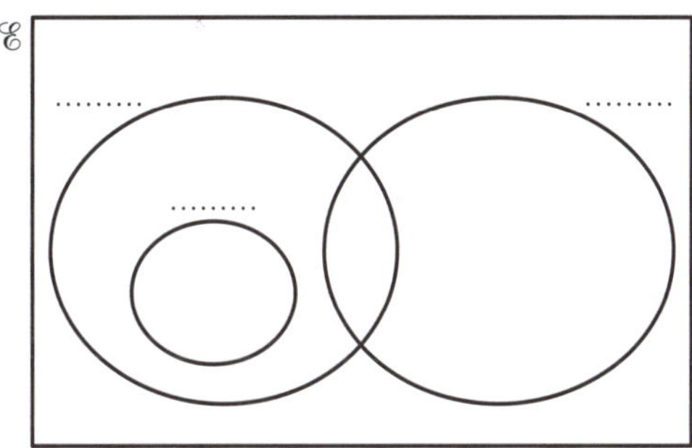

[1]

[Use Figure 1 in the Past Paper Practice Questions Resource Sheet.]

b

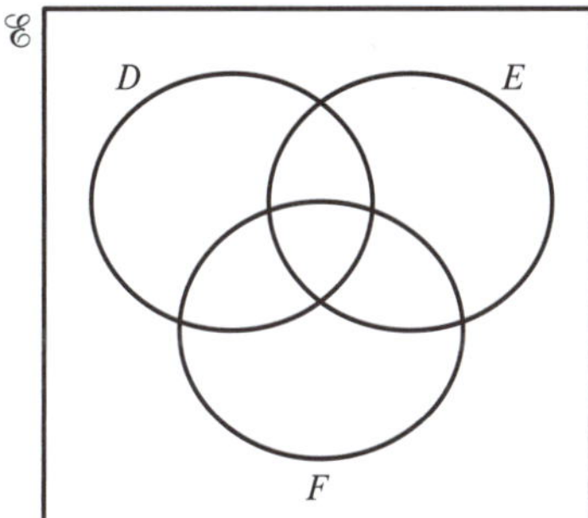

Shade the region $D' \cup (E \cap F)'$. [1]

[Use Figure 2 in the Past Paper Practice Questions Resource Sheet.]

Cambridge IGCSE Mathematics (0580) Paper 22 Q12 June 2021 **[Total: 3]**

The following question has an example student response and commentary provided. Work through the question first, then compare your answer to the sample response and commentary. Are your answers different to the sample responses?

9 Two solid steel statues are mathematically similar.

The smaller statue has height 12 cm and the larger statue has height 15 cm.

The larger statue has a mass 2.5 kg.

The density of steel is 8 g/cm^3.

Calculate the volume of the smaller statue. [4]

[Density = mass ÷ volume.]

Cambridge IGCSE Mathematics (0580) Paper 21 Q14 November 2024 **[Total: 4]**

Example student response	Commentary
Mass is proportional to volume, so $\frac{M_{small}}{M_{large}} = \frac{(h_{small})^3}{(h_{large})^3}$ $\frac{M_{small}}{2.5} = \frac{12^3}{15^3}$ $M_{small} = \frac{2.5 \times 12^3}{15^3} = 1.28\,\text{kg} = 1280\,\text{g}$ $V = \frac{M}{d} = \frac{1280}{8} = 160\,\text{cm}^3$	The student has correctly used the fact that mass is proportional to volume for 1 mark. They have found the mass of the small statue for another mark. Since the density is given in g/cm^3, the student has correctly converted mass to grams for the third mark. And their final answer is correct for the fourth mark. ***This answer scores 4 out of 4 marks.***

10 Now that you have gone through the commentary, try to write an improved answer for your own solution and edit the sample student response to improve their answer to each part.

The following question has an example student response and commentary provided. Work through the question first, then compare your answer to the sample response and commentary. Are your answers different to the sample responses?

11 a The table shows information about the marks gained by each of 10 students in a test.

Mark	15	16	17	18	19	20
Frequency	4	1	2	1	0	2

i Calculate the range. [1]

ii Calculate the mean. [3]

iii Find the median. [1]

iv Write down the mode. [1]

b Paulo's mean mark for 7 homework tasks is 17.

After completing the 8th task, his mean mark is 17.5.

Calculate Paulo's mark for the 8th task. [3]

Cambridge IGCSE Mathematics (0580) Paper 42 Q3a & b March 2024 **[Total: 9]**

Example student response	Commentary
a **i** Range = 4 − 0 = 4	The student has incorrectly found the range in the values for frequency. ***This answer scores 0 out of 1 mark.***
a **ii** Total marks = 15 × 4 + 16 ×1 + 17 × 2 + 18 ×1 + 19 × 0 + 20 × 2 = 168 Number of students = 10 Mean mark = $\frac{168}{10}$ = 16.8	The student has correctly found the total of all the marks (for 1 mark) and divided it by the number of students (for another mark). And they get the correct answer for the third mark. ***This answer scores 3 out of 3 marks.***
a **iii** Median = $\frac{17 + 18}{2}$ = 17.5	The student has incorrectly found the average of the two middle mark categories. Since there are 10 students, they should have found the category in which the $\frac{10 + 1}{2}$ = 5.5th student lies. ***This answer scores 0 out of 1 mark.***
a **iv** Mode = 19	The student has mistakenly found the category with the *lowest* frequency. ***This answer scores 0 out of 1 mark.***
b Total for 7 tasks = 7 × 17 = 119 Total for 8 tasks = 8 × 17.5 = 140 Mark for 8th task = 140 − 119 = 21	The student has correctly subtracted the total mark for the 7 tasks (for 1 mark) from the total mark from the 8 tasks (for another mark). And they've got the right answer for the third mark. ***This answer scores 3 out of 3 marks.***

12 Now that you have gone through the commentary, try to write an improved answer for your own solution and edit the sample student response to improve their answer to each part.

The following question has an example student response and commentary provided. Work through the question first, then compare your answer to the sample response and commentary. Are your answers different to the sample responses?

13 The height of each of 200 people is measured.

The table shows the results.

Height (h cm)	$100 < h \leqslant 120$	$120 < h \leqslant 130$	$130 < h \leqslant 150$	$150 < h \leqslant 190$
Frequency	32	55	64	49

Calculate an estimate of the mean height. [4]

Cambridge IGCSE Mathematics (0580) Paper 22 Q17 March 2024 **[Total: 4]**

Example student response	Commentary
Total marks = $32 \times 120 + 55 \times 130 + 64 \times 150 + 49 \times 190$ $= 29\,900$ Mean estimate $= \frac{29\,900}{200} = 149.5$	The student has not found the midpoints of each height category. Instead, they have incorrectly multiplied the frequency by the upper bound of the category. But they receive 2 marks because their method was correct in dividing their value for the total marks by the total frequency. ***This answer scores 2 out of 4 marks.***

14 The information about the 80 floor areas is shown in this frequency table.

Floor area (a m^2)	$40 < a \leqslant 60$	$60 < a \leqslant 80$	$80 < a \leqslant 100$	$100 < a \leqslant 130$	$130 < a \leqslant 160$	$160 < a \leqslant 200$
Frequency	14	17	18	15	9	7

Calculate an estimate of the mean floor area. [4]

Cambridge IGCSE Mathematics (0580) Paper 42 Q2b(i) November 2021 **[Total: 4]**

13 Understanding measurement

KNOWLEDGE FOCUS

In this chapter, you will answer questions on:

- converting between units in the metric system
- solving problems involving time calculations and timetables
- using a calculator to work out time calculations
- finding lower and upper bounds of numbers that are written to a given level of accuracy
- solving problems involving upper and lower bounds
- using conversion graphs to change units from one measuring system to another
- using exchange rates to convert currencies.

EXAM SKILLS FOCUS

In this chapter you will:

- show that you understand the idea of 'making connections' between different areas of mathematics
- recognise how to answer a measurement conversion question.

Often, a single examination question requires you to use knowledge from two or more topics within the IGCSE Mathematics course. In this chapter, you will encounter problems that combine ideas such as rounding and bounds, standard form, interpreting graphs or working with formulae – all within real-world measurement contexts.

To succeed in these questions, it helps to first identify the type of response needed. Are you expected to convert units, calculate upper and lower bounds, interpret a graph or solve a time-based problem? Recognising the type of task will guide you toward the correct method.

It can also be useful to underline or highlight key quantities and units in the question. Ask yourself: what skills from other chapters are relevant here? Many measurement problems rely on your wider understanding of number, algebra, and data handling – so keep making those connections as you go.

13.1 Understanding units

UNDERSTAND THIS TERM

- Standard form

1 Express each quantity in the units given in the brackets.

a 72 cm (mm, m, km)

b 34 g (mg, kg)

c 12 tonnes (kg, g)

d 140 ml (cl, l)

e 12 cm^2 (mm^2, m^2)

f 1.5 m^2 (cm^2, km^2)

g 10 ha (km^2, m^2)

2 Express each volume in the units given in the brackets. Give each answer in standard form.

a 150 cm^3 (mm^3, m^3)

b 0.43 km^3 (m^3, cm^3)

c 1600 ml (l, cm^3, m^3)

3 Convert 5.75 kilometres to centimetres.

REFLECTION

How can you remember what to multiply or divide by when you are converting units of area? What about when you are converting units of volume? Could drawing diagrams or writing powers help you understand unit conversions better?

4 The area of a rectangular field is 3.2 square kilometres.

Convert this area into square metres. Give your answer in standard form. [3]

[Total: 3]

5 A swimming pool has a volume of 120 000 litres.

Convert this volume to cubic metres. [2]

[Total: 2]

6 The length of a room is 8 metres and its width is 5.5 metres.

a Calculate the area of the room in square metres. [1]

b Hence find the area of the room in square centimetres.

Give your answer in standard form. [3]

[Total: 4]

« RECALL AND CONNECT 1 «

Calculate the following. Give your answer in standard form.

$(9.1 \times 10^{-3}) - (2.5 \times 10^{-4})$

13.2 Time

1 A movie starts at 7.20 p.m. and lasts for 2 hours and 15 minutes. What time does it end?

2 A flight departs at 14:30 and arrives at 21:05. How long is the flight?

3 A train journey takes 3 hours and 40 minutes. If the train arrives at 18:20, at what time did it depart?

4 A plane leaves London at 10:00 local time on Wednesday and takes 8 hours to reach Singapore. The local time in Singapore is 8 hours ahead of the local time in London. What time and day does the plane land in Singapore?

5 The bus timetable between Anytown and Ceeville is shown.

Anytown	06:30	07:45	12:00	16:30	17:15	18:00	20:30
Beecity	06:50	08:05	12:25	16:50	17:35	18:25	20:50
Ceeville	07:25	08:40	13:14	17:25	18:15	19:05	21:25

a Seb needs to catch a bus from Anytown and be at Ceeville by 18:00. Determine the time of the latest bus he can catch. [1]

b Calculate the time it takes for each of these buses to travel between Anytown and Ceevile.

Give your answers in hours and minutes.

i 07:45 bus [1]

ii 16:30 bus [1]

iii 18:00 bus [1]

iv 12:00 bus [1]

c Samantha arrives at the Beecity bus station at 11:37 and wants to travel to Ceevile.

Calculate how long it will be before:

i a bus arrives [1]

ii she arrives in Ceevile. [1]

d Bruce and Sheila live in Anytown and work in Ceevile.

Their office is a five-minute walk from Ceevile bus station.

Bruce catches the 06:30 bus to work.

Sheila sleeps through her alarm and misses the 06:30 bus, so she takes the next one.

Calculate the earliest time that they can schedule a meeting together at work. [2]

[Total: 9]

REFLECTION

What steps do you follow when calculating durations using a calculator? How do you check that your answer makes sense? Could drawing a timeline help you?

6 The tide times at Long beach are shown during a six-day period in May.

Date	High tide 1	Low tide 1	High tide 2	Low tide 2
2025-05-13	03:14	09:27	15:39	21:53
2025-05-14	03:55	10:12	16:22	22:37
2025-05-15	04:36	10:59	17:06	23:22
2025-05-16	05:17	11:45	17:50	--:--
2025-05-17	06:00	00:08	18:35	12:31
2025-05-18	06:42	00:54	19:20	13:18

a Calculate the time between the two high tides on 14 May. [2]

b Calculate the time between the High tide 2 on 16 May and the next low tide. [2]

c Emily likes to collect shells in the rockpools. She can only do this between an hour before low tide and an hour after low tide. Determine the times that Emily can collect shells on:

i 15 May at Low tide 1 [1]

ii 17 May at Low tide 2. [1]

[Total: 6]

« RECALL AND CONNECT 2 «

Solve $2(2x - 3) = 2x - 4$

13.3 Limits of accuracy – upper and lower bounds

UNDERSTAND THESE TERMS

- Lower bound
- Upper bound

1 Find the lower and upper bounds of the following values.

a 85 mm, to the nearest mm

b 37.6, to 1 decimal place

c 0.0465, to 3 significant figures

d 1400, to the nearest 50

2 Each value has been rounded to the level of accuracy given in brackets.

Find the upper and lower bounds of each.

a 72 (nearest ten)

b 15 000 (nearest thousand)

c 7.6 (1 d.p.)

d 9.42 (2 d.p.)

e 13.9 (1 d.p.)

f 0.05 (1 s.f.)

g 200 (nearest hundred)

h 0.072 (3 d.p.)

i 56.1 (1 d.p.)

j 0.876 (3 s.f.)

3 If $r = 12.75$ (to 2 d.p.), $s = 36$ (to the nearest whole number) and $t = 10.4$ (to 1 d.p.), find the upper and lower bounds for each of the following.

a $r + s$

b rs

c $\frac{r}{s}$

d $\frac{(r + s)}{r}$

e $r + t - s$

f $\frac{r}{s} - t$

g $\frac{st - r}{r^2}$

4 The length of a rectangle is 12.3 cm, rounded to the nearest tenth of a centimetre.

The width of the rectangle is 8 cm, rounded to the nearest centimetre.

Find the upper and lower bounds for the area of the rectangle. [4]

[Total: 4]

5 Hannah travels a distance of 78.4 km, rounded to the nearest tenth of a kilometre.

The time taken for the journey is 1.5 hours, rounded to the nearest tenth of an hour.

a Find the upper and lower bounds for the average speed of the car. [4]

The road that Hannah is travelling on has a speed limit of 50 km/h.

b Using your answer to part **a**, determine whether Hannah was speeding.

Give a reason for your answer. [2]

[Total: 6]

6 The mass of a block is measured as 12.75 kg (rounded to 2 decimal places).

The volume of the block is $8.6\,\text{m}^3$ (rounded to 1 decimal place).

a Find the possible range for the true value of the mass. [1]

b Given the formula: density $= \frac{\text{mass}}{\text{volume}}$,

calculate the upper and lower bounds for the density. [4]

c Hence determine the density of the block, giving your answer to an appropriate degree of accuracy. [2]

[Total: 7]

≪ RECALL AND CONNECT 3 ≪

Make b the subject of the equation $\sqrt{2b - 3c} = c^2$.

13.4 Conversion graphs

UNDERSTAND THIS TERM

- Conversion graph

1 The following graph shows the relationship between temperatures in degrees Celsius (on the x-axis) and degrees Fahrenheit (on the y-axis).

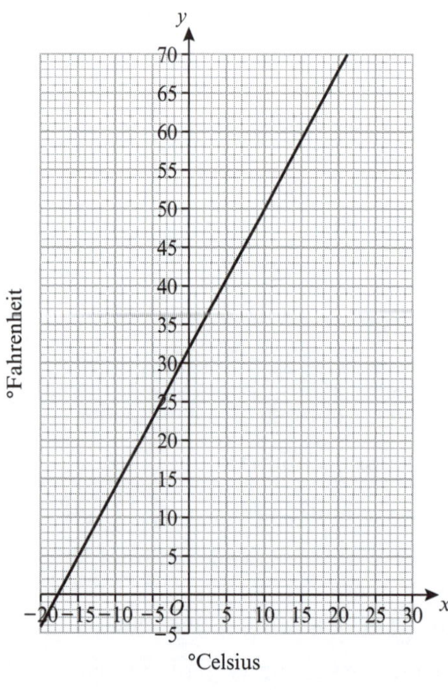

a Using the graph, convert the following temperatures from degrees Celsius to degrees Fahrenheit. Give your answers correct to the nearest whole number.

i	20 °C	**ii**	−10 °C	**iii**	17 °C
iv	0 °C	**v**	26 °C	**vi**	−4 °C

b Using the graph, convert the following temperatures from degrees Fahrenheit to degrees Celsius. Give your answers correct to 1 decimal place.

i	60 °F	**ii**	23 °F	**iii**	−1 °F
iv	36 °F	**v**	52 °F		

REFLECTION

When you are reading a conversion graph, how do you decide which axis to start from? What clues tell you whether to read across or read up? How does this help with graphs in other topics too?

2 The graph below shows the relationship between distance (in metres, y-axis) and time (in seconds, x-axis) for a car traveling at constant speed.

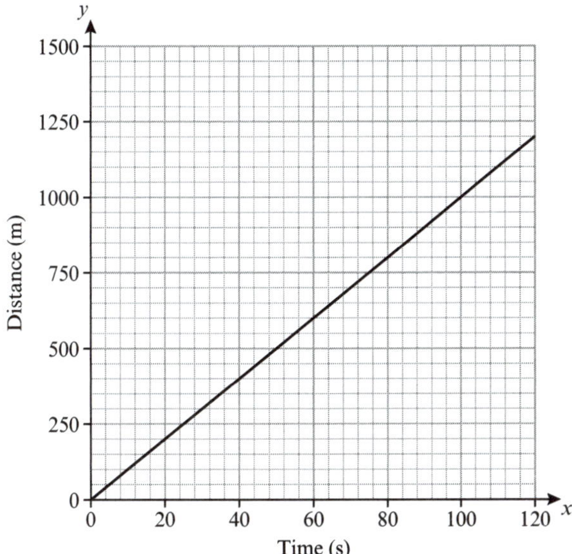

Using the graph, answer the following.

a How far does the car travel in 80 seconds?

b How far does the car travel in 1 minute 40 seconds?

c How far does the car travel between 10 s and 35 s?

d How long does it take for the car to travel 600 m?

e How long does it take for the car to travel 350 m?

f How long does it take for the car to travel 900 m?

g How long does it take for the car to travel 1.3 km? Give your answer in minutes and seconds.

h Find the speed of the car in metres per second.

3 The graph below shows the relationship between the length in inches (x-axis) and the length in centimetres (y-axis). The graph is linear, showing the conversion from inches to centimetres.

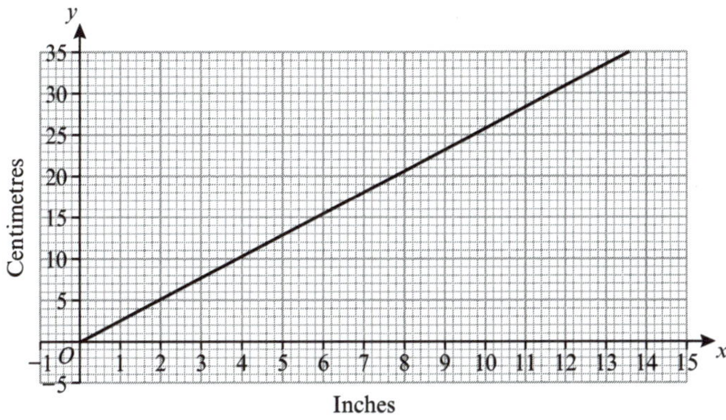

Using the graph, answer the following.

a A shoe box is 12 inches long. Determine its length in cm. [1]

b A piece of string is 15 cm long. Determine its length in inches. [1]

c A pizza has radius 7.5 inches. Determine the **area** of the pizza in cm^2. Give your answer correct to 3 s.f. [2]

d A cube has volume 1331 cm^3.

i Determine its side length in inches. [3]

ii Determine its surface area in cubic inches. Give your answer correct to 2 s.f. [2]

[Total: 9]

« RECALL AND CONNECT 4 «

Calculate $(3.2 \times 10^{-6}) \times (4.75 \times 10^{-11})$

13.5 Exchanging currencies

UNDERSTAND THIS TERM

- Exchange rate

1 Here is a currency conversion table for a new currency called the zyro.

Currency	1.00 zyro (Ʒ)
Japanese yen	Ʒ0.0059
Swiss franc	Ʒ0.84
Canadian dollar	Ʒ0.61
Australian dollar	Ʒ0.52
Indian rupee	Ʒ0.010
Euro	Ʒ0.86
UAE dirham	Ʒ0.22
South African rand	Ʒ0.045
Brazilian real	Ʒ0.16
Singapore dollar	Ʒ0.56

Use the table to work out the following conversions.

a Convert 10 000 yen to zyros.

b How many Swiss francs can you buy with 500 zyros?

c Convert 2000 Canadian dollars to zyros.

d How many Australian dollars can you buy with 400 zyros?

e Convert 50 000 rupees to zyros.

f How many euros can you buy with 750 zyros?

g Convert 3000 dirhams to zyros.

h How many rand can you buy with 200 zyros?

i Convert 1500 reals to zyros.

j How many Singapore dollars can you buy with 900 zyros?

2 The table shows the exchange rates between Thai Baht (THB) and some other currencies.

For example, 1 THB is worth 0.027 778 USD.

Thai Baht	1.00 THB
US dollar	0.027 778
Euro	0.025 583
British pound	0.018 560
Indian rupee	1.846 723
Australian dollar	0.038 600
Canadian dollar	0.038 324
Singapore dollar	0.039 245
Swiss franc	0.027 594
Malaysian ringgit	0.119 846
Japanese yen	3.403 587

a Ben exchanges 1000 THB into Euros.

Determine the number of Euros he will get. Give your answer to the nearest cent. [1]

b Samuel exchanges 40 Singapore dollars to THB.

Determine the number of THB he will get. Give your answer correct to the nearest whole Baht. [1]

c Lena has 5000 Japanese Yen.

She exchanges them to THB, and spends 150 THB.

She then exchanges what she has left over into Canadian dollars.

Work out the number of Canadian dollars Lena has, correct to the nearest dollar. [3]

[Total: 5]

REFLECTION

How can you convert between two currencies when you are not explicitly given the exchange rate between the two, but you do know the exchange rate between each one and a third currency?

3 The table shows the exchange rate between various currencies and the Euro (€).

Currency	Exchange Rate to EUR
US dollar (USD)	0.92
British pound (GBP)	1.16
Japanese yen (JPY)	0.0069
Swiss franc (CHF)	0.95
Canadian dollar (CAD)	0.68
Australian dollar (AUD)	0.60
Indian rupee (INR)	0.011
UAE dirham (AED)	0.25
South African rand (ZAR)	0.051
Brazilian real (BRL)	0.18
Singapore dollar (SGD)	0.64

a Determine how many US dollars can you buy with €800. [1]

b You have €600 and want to exchange it for British pounds. Work out how many British pounds will you receive. [1]

c Convert 500 Canadian dollars (CAD) to South African rand (ZAR). [2]

d Determine the number of Japanese yen (JPY) that 1200 Singapore dollars (SGD) can buy. [1]

[Total: 5]

REFLECTION

Which question(s) in this chapter made you use more than one topic at once? How did you work out which maths skills to use? What would you do differently if a similar problem came up in an exam?

‹‹ RECALL AND CONNECT 5 ‹‹

Calculate $8\frac{1}{3} \times \frac{9}{10}$.

SELF-ASSESSMENT CHECKLIST

Let's revisit the Knowledge and Exam skills focus for this chapter. Decide how confident you are with each statement.

	Now I can	Show it	Needs more work	Almost there	Confident to move on
1	convert between units in the metric system	Create a diagram showing area conversions in all metric units.			
2	solve problems involving time calculations and timetables	Write a timetable for your daily routine and calculate the time between events. Use colour to highlight overlaps or gaps.			
3	use a calculator to work out time calculations	Teach someone how to enter hours and minutes into a calculator and explain why it works.			
4	find lower and upper bounds of numbers that are written to a given level of accuracy	Find the upper and lower bounds of: $a = 2.46$ (rounded to 2 d.p.) $b = 7$ (rounded to the nearest whole number). Explain how you know the bounds are correct.			
5	solve problems involving upper and lower bounds	Write a word problem that includes a measurement with bounds, then solve it.			
6	use conversion graphs to change units from one measuring system to another	Create a sketch graph showing the difference between a linear and a curved conversion graph. Explain how to read the graph in both directions.			
7	use exchange rates to convert currencies	Design a short quiz with currency conversions, including an 'intermediate' exchange question.			

CONTINUED

	Now I can	Show it	Needs more work	Almost there	Confident to move on
8	show that you understand the idea of 'making connections' between different areas of mathematics	Choose a question from this chapter that uses more than one topic. Explain how you knew what skills to use and how you would describe your approach to someone else.			
9	recognise what type of response a measurement question requires.	Make flashcards for different types of measurement questions. On one side, write a typical exam-style question. On the other, write what topic it covers (e.g. 'upper bounds') and list the steps you'd take to solve it.			

14 Further solving of equations and inequalities

KNOWLEDGE FOCUS

In this chapter, you will answer questions on:

- deriving and solving simultaneous linear equations graphically and algebraically
- using number lines to represent and interpret inequalities
- solving linear inequalities algebraically
- deriving linear inequalities and finding regions in a plane
- solving quadratic equations by completing the square
- solving quadratic equations by using the quadratic formula
- factorising quadratics where the coefficient of x^2 is not 1
- simplifying algebraic fractions.

EXAM SKILLS FOCUS

In this chapter you will:

- learn to better reflect on your progress
- recognise how to choose the most appropriate method to solve an equation or inequality.

In this chapter, you will not only be learning new maths skills but also thinking about *how* you learn best. As you work through different problems, take time to notice which strategies help you understand and solve questions. You might find some methods work better for you than others.

In the 'Reflect' boxes throughout the chapter, you will reflect on your progress – what you have done well, and what you would like to improve. This kind of thinking helps you become a more confident learner. Remember, learning is not just about answers, it is about growing your thinking too.

This chapter introduces a variety of methods for solving equations and inequalities – such as elimination and substitution when solving simultaneous equations, to completing the square and using the quadratic formula when solving quadratic equations. Recognising which method suits which type of question helps you solve problems efficiently and confidently in examinations. Think about what the equation looks like before choosing your strategy.

14.1 Simultaneous linear equations

UNDERSTAND THESE TERMS

- Simultaneous equations
- Solve
- Graphical method
- Substitution method
- Elimination method

1 Use the graphs shown to find the solutions to the following pairs of simultaneous equations.

a $6x - 3y = 12$
$4x - 3y = 2$

b $2x - 4y = 10$
$2x + 3y = 24$

c $y = -5$
$y + x = -2$

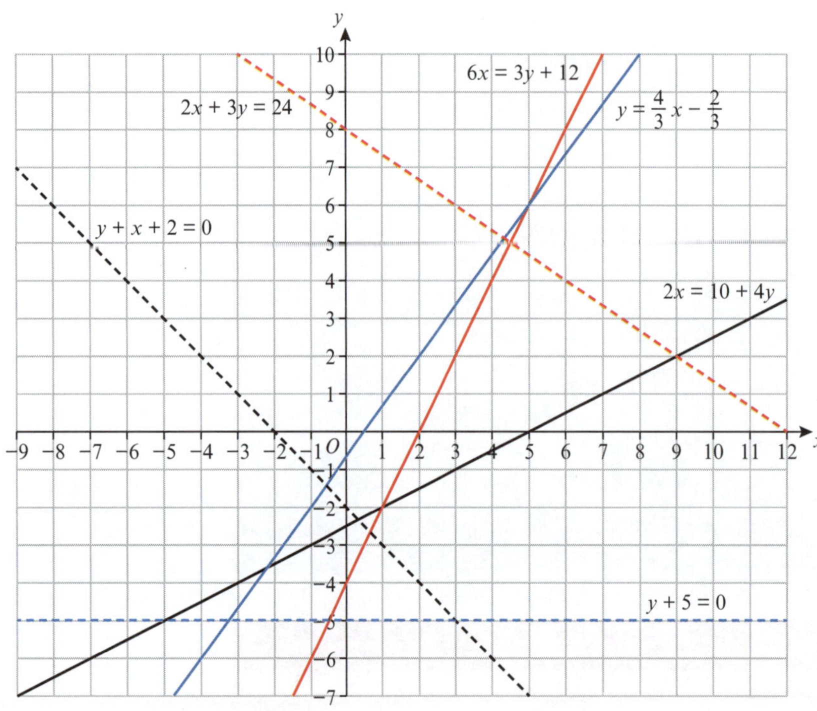

2 Solve for x and y by elimination.

a $3x + 2y = 16$
$x - y = 2$

b $5x + y = 19$
$2x + 3y = 16$

c $2x + y = 10$
$x + 3y = 16$

d $2x + 3y = 12$
$x - y = 1$

e $4x - y = 9$
$2x + 3y = 1$

f $7x + y = 20$
$3x - 2y = -6$

g $x + 4y = -8$
$3x - y = -11$

h $x - y = -4$
$3x + 2y = -2$

3 Solve for x and y by substitution.

a $4x - 12 = 2y$
$x + 3y = 19$

b $2x + 5y = 25$
$4x - y = 11$

c $6x - y = 17$
$3x + 2y = 16$

d $x + 2y = 7$
$3x - y = 7$

e $5x + 2y = 16$
$3x - y = 3$

f $3x + y = -1$
$x - 2y = -5$

g $4x + y = -7$
$x - 2y = 5$

4 Two chocolate bars and one packet of crisps cost \$5.50.

One chocolate bar and three packets of crisps cost \$9.00.

Find the price of one packet of crisps. [4]

[Total: 4]

5 Sam is 4 years older than his sister Emily.

The sum of their ages is 26.

Calculate their ages. [3]

[Total: 3]

6 Tom earns money by doing two part-time jobs.

In one week, he works 5 hours at Job A and 3 hours at Job B and earns \$74.

In another week, he works 2 hours at Job A and 6 hours at Job B and earns \$78.

Find his hourly rate for each job. Give your answers to the nearest number of cents. [4]

[Total: 4]

7 A train travels 240 km in total. It travels x km at 60 km/h and y km 80 km/h.

The total time taken is 3.5 hours.

Calculate x and y. [5]

[Total: 5]

8 A chemist has two solutions.

- Solution 1 is 30% salt.
- Solution 2 is 50% salt.

She wants to mix x ml of Solution 1 and y ml of Solution 2 to make 200 ml of a 40% salt solution.

Calculate x and y. [6]

[Total: 6]

« RECALL AND CONNECT 1 «

A shop advertises a computer for sale for \$448 during a 20% off sale.
What was the original price of the computer?

REFLECTION

How confident do you feel about drawing graphs to solve simultaneous equations? How can you work out what scale to use on each axis if you are not given a grid?

When solving simultaneous equations algebraically, can you explain the difference between the substitution and elimination methods? When is it easier to use substitution rather than elimination?

14.2 Linear inequalities

UNDERSTAND THESE TERMS

- Represent
- Solutions
- Inequality

1 Represent the solution to each inequality on a number line.

a $x > 3$ **b** $-4.5 \leqslant t < 5$ **c** $-3.7 < s \leqslant 0$

2 x is an integer that satisfies $\sqrt{2} \leqslant x < 2\pi$.

Write down all the possible values of x.

3 Find the set of values of x which satisfy each of these inequalities.

a $5x + 2 < 17$

b $3x - 4 \geqslant 8$

c $2x + 5 > 11$

d $-4x + 7 \geqslant 3$

e $2x - 5 < -3$

f $5(x - 2) + 3 \leqslant 2(x + 4)$

g $4(x + 1) - 2 \leqslant 3(x - 2) + 5$

h $2(x - 3) + 1 > 4(x + 2) - 5$

i $-8 \leqslant -2x + 5 < 4$

j $-5 \leqslant 2x - 3 \leqslant 7$

k $1 < 4x + 6 \leqslant 9$

l $-6 < 4(x - 2) - 2 \leqslant 10$

m $-10 < 2(x + 3) - x \leqslant 8$

n $-6 \leqslant 2(x - 5) - 4(x + 1) < 10$

4 A car rental company charges a flat rate of $24 per day plus an additional $0.08 per kilometre driven.

Adam would like to rent a car for two days and has $100 to spend.

Let x represent the number of kilometres driven.

a Write an inequality to show the condition on x if the maximum cost is $100. [2]

b Solve your inequality from part **a** to find the maximum number of kilometres Adam can drive over the days. [2]

[Total: 4]

5 You are selling concert tickets to raise money.

Each adult ticket sells for $11 and each child ticket for $7.

You need to raise at least $240.

You sell 10 adult tickets and x child tickets.

Write and solve an inequality to find the minimum number of child tickets you must sell. [3]

[Total: 3]

6 A bookshop sells children's books for $8 each.

If you purchase a membership card which costs $20 then the price of each book is reduced to $6.

Let x be the number of books you buy.

Write down and solve an inequality in x to find the smallest number of books you need to buy to make it worthwhile purchasing a membership card. [3]

[Total: 3]

≪ RECALL AND CONNECT 2 ≪

Insert brackets into the following calculations to make them true.

a $5 + 15 \div 4 - 3 = 20$

b $10 - 3 \times 4 - 2 = 4$

14.3 Regions in a plane

UNDERSTAND THIS TERM

- Region

1 By shading the desired region, show the region that represents the inequality $4x - 2y \leqslant 8$ on a set of coordinate axes.

2 Write down the three inequalities that define the unshaded region.

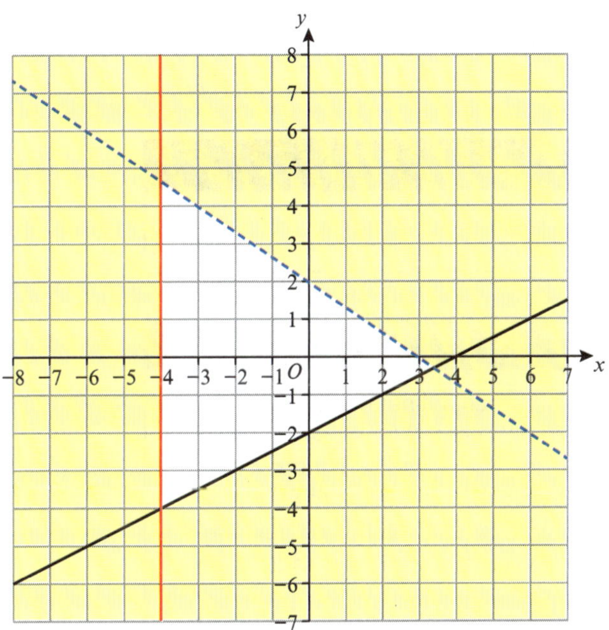

3 By shading the unwanted region, show the region defined by each set of inequalities on a set of coordinate axes.

a $x + y \geqslant 4$
$2x - y < 2$
$x - 2y \geqslant -8$

b $y > 3x - 4$
$y < 6$
$y + 2x \geqslant 0$

c $y < 3x + 6$
$x \leqslant 2$
$y \geqslant -x$

4 Aiman is training for a marathon, so he is using a food plan.

For each snack, he eats x plums and y bananas.

Each plum has 2 g of protein and 3 g of fat.

Each banana has 4 g of protein and 1 g of fat.

His nutritionist tells him that he must obey the following rules.

- Have at least one plum and one banana at each snack time.
- Eat a *maximum* of 15 g of protein.
- Eat *at least* 9 g of fat.

One of the inequalities that shows this information is $x \geqslant 1$.

a Write down three other inequalities in x and/or y that satisfy the conditions given by the nutritionist. [3]

b On a grid, draw four straight lines and shade the region that satisfies all the inequalities from part **a**. Label the region R. [3]

c Use the diagram to find the only possible number of plums and bananas that Aiman could eat. [1]

[Total: 7]

≪ RECALL AND CONNECT 3 ≪

Find the value of $\frac{10ac^2}{2(a-c)}$ when $a = 2$, $b = 6$ and $c = -3$.

REFLECTION

When shading regions, once you have drawn a particular line, how do you decide which side of the line represents the correct region? One useful strategy is to pick a test point – often (0, 0) if it's not on the line – and substitute its coordinates into the inequality. If the point satisfies the inequality, then it lies in the correct region. If it does not, the correct region must be on the other side. How confident are you in using this approach? Are there other methods you've found helpful?

14.4 Completing the square

1 Write each of the following expressions in the form $(x + p)^2 + q$.

a	$x^2 + 14x + 3$	**b**	$x^2 - 3x + 4$	**c**	$x^2 + 6x + 5$
d	$x^2 - 10x + 21$	**e**	$x^2 - 8x + 13$	**f**	$2x^2 + 8x + 7$
g	$5x^2 - 8x + 2$	**h**	$-3x^2 + 12x - 7$	**i**	$4x^2 + 4x - 15$
j	$-2x^2 - 16x - 27$				

UNDERSTAND THESE TERMS

- Quadratic expression
- Completing the square

2 Solve the following quadratic equations using the method of completing the square. Give your answer in surd form.

a $x^2 + 6x + 5 = 0$ b $x^2 - 4x - 3 = 0$ c $x^2 + 3x = -2$

d $2x^2 - 8x + 1 = 0$ e $3x^2 + 12x + 7 = 0$ f $-2x^2 + 4x + 6 = 0$

g $3x^2 + 9x + 4 = 0$ h $5x^2 = 12x - 3$ i $7x^2 = -28x - 25$

3 A farmer has 12 m of fencing.

He wants to use the fencing make a rectangular enclosure for ducks.

The width of the enclosure is x metres.

a Explain why the length of the enclosure is $(6 - x)$ m. [2]

b Express the area of the enclosure A as a quadratic expression. [2]

c Express A in the form $A = p - (x - q)^2$. [2]

d Find the maximum area of the enclosure and the value of the width that gives the maximum area. [2]

[Total: 8]

4 A factory finds that its monthly maintenance cost, C, in thousands of dollars is given by

$C(x) = x^2 - 12x + 50$

where x is the number of hours that each technician spends doing preventative maintenance each week.

Find the number of hours of preventative maintenance that minimises the cost, and what that minimum cost is. [3]

[Total: 3]

5 A theatre charges $20 per ticket and sells 100 tickets per show.

For every $1 increase in ticket price, 3 fewer tickets are sold.

Let x be the number of $1 increases above $20.

a Explain why the revenue for a show is $R = (20 + x)(100 - 3x)$. [2]

b Find the ticket price that maximises revenue. [4]

c Determine the maximum revenue. [1]

[Total: 7]

RECALL AND CONNECT 4

ABC is an isosceles triangle.

a Find the value of x.

b Find the value of y.

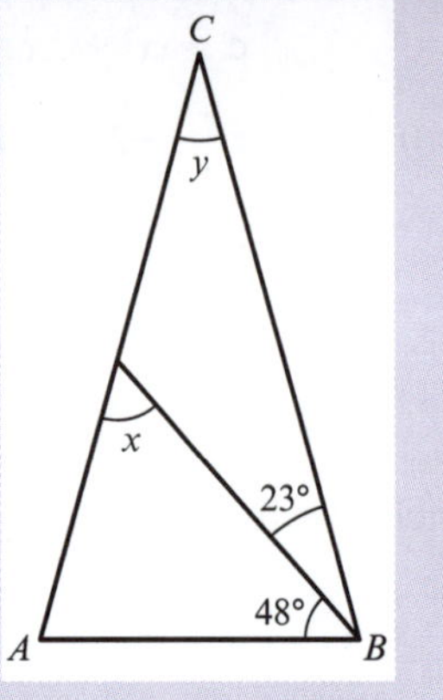

14.5 Quadratic formula

UNDERSTAND THIS TERM

- Factorise

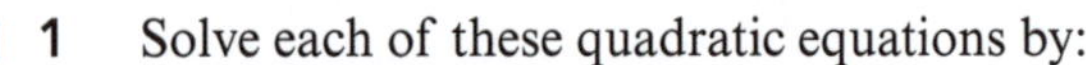

1 Solve each of these quadratic equations by:

i factorising

ii using the quadratic formula.

Check that you get the same answer from both methods.

a $x^2 - 7x + 12 = 0$ **b** $x^2 + 3x = 18$ **c** $x^2 = 2x + 35$

2 Solve each of these equations using the quadratic formula. Round your answers to 3 s.f.

a $3x^2 - 2x - 4 = 0$ **b** $5x^2 - 0.8x = 5$ **c** $\frac{1}{x} = x + 3$

d $0.5x^2 + x - 1 = 0$ **e** $\frac{2}{3}x^2 - x = \frac{1}{2}$ **f** $1.2x^2 = 3.6x - 2.4$

3 A rectangular garden has an area of $96\,\text{m}^2$. The length is 4 m more than the width.

Find the dimensions of the garden. [4]

[Total: 4]

4 An object is dropped from the top of a building. Its height, h metres, after t seconds is:

$h = -4.9t^2 + 19.6t + 1$

Find the time at which it hits the ground. [3]

[Total: 3]

5 Ben sits in a tree. He throws a ball directly upwards.

The height h (in metres) of the ball, t seconds after Ben throws it, is given by the equation

$h = -5t^2 + 20t + 15$

a Find the height that Ben threw the ball from. [1]

b By completing the square, find the maximum height of the ball. [3]

c Use the quadratic formula to find the time when the ball hits the ground. [3]

[Total: 7]

« RECALL AND CONNECT 5 «

Without using a calculator, evaluate $3\frac{1}{2} \div \left(2\frac{3}{8} - \frac{3}{4}\right)$

REFLECTION

Can you describe in your own words how completing the square allows you to find the maximum or minimum of a quadratic function?

14.6 Factorising quadratics where the coefficient of x^2 is not 1

1 Factorise each of these quadratic expressions.

a $2x^2 + 7x + 3$	b $3x^2 - 5x - 2$	c $4x^2 + 12x + 9$
d $6x^2 - 7x - 3$	e $5x^2 + 13x + 6$	f $3x^2 + 10x + 7$

2 Factorise each of these quadratic expressions.

a $-2x^2 + 5x + 3$	b $-3x^2 + 7x + 6$	c $-4x^2 + 11x - 7$
d $-6x^2 - 4x + 10$	e $-5x^2 + 3x + 2$	f $-8x^2 + 10x + 3$

3 A company's profit P (in thousands of dollars) is given by the equation:

$P = 4x^2 - 12x - 16$

when the company produces x thousand units.

a Find the profit when the company produces 10 000 units. [2]

b Factorise fully the quadratic expression for P. [2]

c Find the number of units the company must produce to break even (that is, when the profit is zero). [2]

[Total: 6]

« RECALL AND CONNECT 6 «

Write each of these as a single surd.

a $\sqrt{18} + \sqrt{8}$

b $\sqrt{45} - \sqrt{20} + \sqrt{5}$

14.7 Algebraic fractions

UNDERSTAND THIS TERM

- Simplify

1 Simplify each of these algebraic fractions.

a $\dfrac{24a^2bc}{8ab^2c}$ **b** $\dfrac{x^2 + 12x}{6x^2 + 15x}$

c $\dfrac{x^2 + 5x + 6}{x^2 - 4}$ **d** $\dfrac{2x^2 - x - 3}{2x^2 - 9x + 9}$

2 Simplify each expression by factorising. Then complete the calculation.

a $\dfrac{4y}{3x^2} \div \dfrac{8y^4}{9x}$ **b** $\dfrac{x^2 + 5x + 6}{x^2 - 4} \times \dfrac{x^2 - 9}{x^2 + 7x + 12}$

c $\dfrac{3x^2 + 2x - 1}{2x^2 + 6} \div \dfrac{6x^2 + x - 1}{7x^3 + 21x}$

3 Write each expression as a single fraction in its lowest terms.

a $\dfrac{1}{x + 2} + \dfrac{1}{2x + 1}$ **b** $\dfrac{3x - 1}{x} - \dfrac{1 - 2x}{x^2}$

c $\dfrac{9}{2a^2b} + \dfrac{4a}{3ab}$

4 A printing company prints posters using a cost model given by

$C = \dfrac{x^2 - 9}{x - 3}, x \neq 3$

where x is the number of hours spent printing and C is the cost in dollars.

a Simplify the expression. [2]

b Calculate the total cost when $x = 6$. [1]

[Total: 3]

5 Express $(2x + 4) - \dfrac{3x(x + 4)}{x(x - 4)}$ in the form $\dfrac{ax^2 + bx + c}{x - 4}$

where a, b and c are integers to be found. [4]

[Total: 4]

6 A painter uses the following expression for litres of paint needed to paint a fence

$$V = \frac{2x^2 + 4x}{x + 2}$$

where x is the number of fence panels and V is the volume of paint in litres.

a Simplify the expression. [2]

Simon wants to paint four panels. Paint is sold in tins of 330 ml, and each tin costs $3.26.

b Work out how many tins of paint Simon must buy, and calculate the change he will receive if he pays $100. [4]

[Total: 6]

7 Simplify the following expression fully:

$$\frac{6x^2 - 27x + 21}{x^2 - 4x + 3} \times \frac{x^2 - x - 6}{2x^2 - 10x + 12}$$ [4]

[Total: 4]

≪ RECALL AND CONNECT 7 ≪

Work out if this triangle contains a right angle.

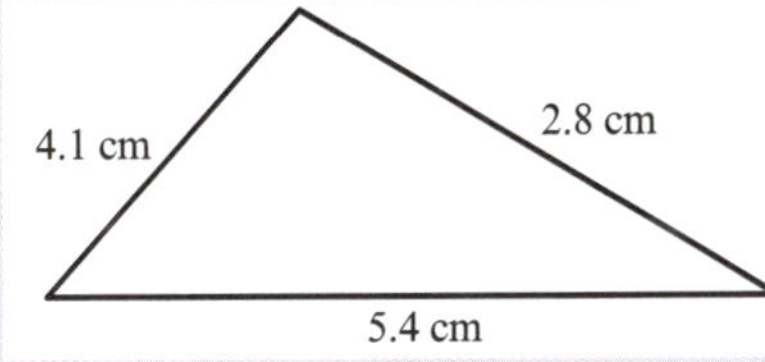

REFLECTION

Can you describe in your own words why factorisation allows you to simplify complicated quadratic expressions?

SELF-ASSESSMENT CHECKLIST

Let's revisit the Knowledge and Exam skills focus for this chapter.
Decide how confident you are with each statement.

	Now I can	Show it	Needs more work	Almost there	Confident to move on
1	derive and solve simultaneous linear equations graphically and algebraically	Solve $2x - 4y = 10$ $2x + 3y = 24$ graphically and by substitution. Check your answers agree.			

CONTINUED

	Now I can	Show it	Needs more work	Almost there	Confident to move on
2	solve linear inequalities algebraically	Solve $7 \leqslant 4x + 5 < 17$.			
3	use number lines to represent and interpret inequalities	On a number line, show the x-values that satisfy the inequality above.			
4	derive linear inequalities and find regions in a plane	Draw lines and find the region that satisfies a system of linear inequalities. See Section 14.3, Question 2.			
5	solve quadratic equations by completing the square	Express $5x^2 + 15x - 16$ in the form $a(x + b)^2 + c$			
6	solve quadratic equations by using the quadratic formula	Correctly substitute values into the formula $x = \dfrac{-b \pm \sqrt{b^2 - 4ac}}{2a}$.			
7	factorise quadratics where the coefficient of x^2 is not 1	Factorise $3x^2 - 2x - 8$.			
8	simplify algebraic fractions	Factorise expressions in the numerator and denominator and then divide through by common factors. See Section 14.7, Question 1.			
9	learn to better reflect on your progress	Write a note explaining what methods you found easiest and hardest in this chapter, and one goal for improving your confidence.			
10	recognise how to choose the most appropriate method to solve an equation or inequality.	Create a set of flashcards. On one side, write a type of equation or inequality. On the other side, write the method you would use to solve it.			

15 Scale drawings, bearings and trigonometry

KNOWLEDGE FOCUS

In this chapter, you will answer questions on:

- interpreting scale drawings
- calculating bearings
- calculating sine, cosine and tangent ratios for right-angled triangles
- using sine, cosine and tangent ratios to calculate the angles and lengths of sides of right-angled triangles
- solving trigonometric equations, finding all the solutions between 0° and 360°
- applying the sine and cosine rules to calculate unknown sides and angles in triangles that are not right-angled
- calculating the area of a triangle that is not right-angled using the sine ratio
- using the sine, cosine and tangent ratios, together with Pythagoras' theorem in three dimensions
- using exact sine, cosine and tangent ratios for certain angles.

EXAM SKILLS FOCUS

In this chapter you will:

- show that you understand the command word 'calculate' and can answer a 'calculate' question
- understand the difference between 'calculate' and 'solve'.

In this chapter you will practise answering questions that use the command word 'calculate' and other questions that use the term 'solve'.

Calculate	work out from given facts, figures or information.

Whenever you see the term 'solve', you must find the value of x (or whatever variable is used in the equation). In this chapter, you will solve trigonometric equations (equations involving sine, cosine or tangent).

'Solve' is different to 'calculate'. When you are asked to 'calculate', you need find a numerical answer to a question (such as calculating the size of a bearing). This will often involve a sequence of steps to get to the final answer. You should always show your working and give your final answer to the degree of accuracy that the question asks for (for example, 3 significant figures or 1 decimal place).

15.1 Scale drawings

UNDERSTAND THIS TERM

- Scale drawing

1 A map has a scale of 1 : 50 000. The distance between two towns on the map is measured to be 4.5 cm.

Calculate the actual distance between the two towns in kilometres.

2 A building is 120 m tall. A scale drawing of the building uses a scale of 1 : 200. What is the height of the building in the scale drawing, in centimetres?

3 A garden is 30 m long and 20 m wide. The scale of the plan is 1 : 100. Calculate

a the length of the garden on the plan, in cm

b the width of the garden on the plan, in cm

c the area of the garden on the plan, in cm^2

d the area of the garden on the plan, in mm^2.

4 In a scale drawing of a ship, 1 cm represents 20 m. The length of the ship in the drawing is 6 cm. What is the actual length of the ship, in m?

5 A blueprint is drawn where 1 cm represents 50 m. The length of a swimming pool on the drawing is 12 cm. What is the actual length of the swimming pool in metres?

6 Marie is drawing a scale model of a rectangular playground. She uses a scale of 1 cm to 2 m.

a State the scale of the model in the form $1 : n$, where n is a number that you must find. [1]

The actual width of the playground is 24 m.

b Calculate the width of the playground in Marie's model, in cm. [2]

In Marie's model, the length of the playground is 20 cm.

c Calculate the actual length of the playground. Give your answer in km. [2]

[Total: 5]

7 Telegraph poles are placed in the ground at A, B and C.

Wires are then used to connect A, B and C. The aerial view is shown in the scale diagram.

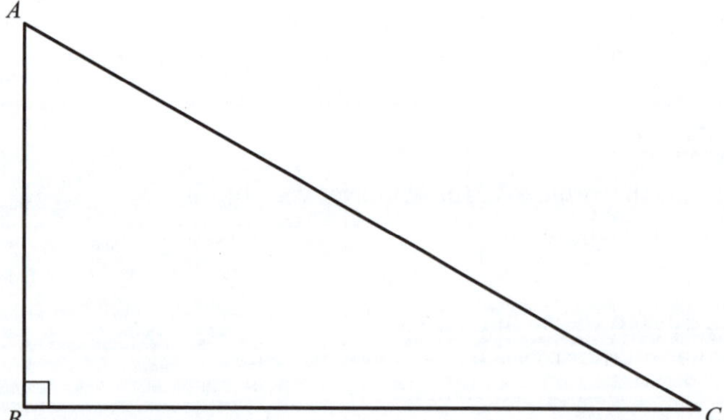

The scale of the diagram is 1 : 900.

a Calculate the distance, in metres

i between A and B [2]

ii between B and C. [2]

Hayley says that, in real life, the distance between A and C is 80 m.

b By referring to the scale diagram, explain why Hayley is wrong and calculate the true distance between A and C. [2]

[Total: 6]

« RECALL AND CONNECT 1 «

The distance from Earth to the Sun is approximately 1.5×10^8 km.

The distance from Earth to the nearest star, *Proxima Centauri*, is about 3.99×10^{13} km.

How many times further is it from the Earth to Proxima Centauri than from the Earth to the Sun?

Give your answer in standard form.

15.2 Bearings

UNDERSTAND THIS TERM

- Bearing

1 Here is a map of Cyprus.

Copy and complete the table with the three-figure bearings.

From	To	Bearing (°)
Limassol	Kyrenia	
Larnaca	Pafos	
Nicosia	Limassol	
Pafos	Larnaca	
Kyrenia	Famagusta	

REFLECTION

How can you measure a bearing greater than 180° if your protractor only measures angles between 0 and 180°? How can you use the fact that angles in a full turn add to 360°?

2 A scale diagram of a triangular-shaped field has vertices P, Q and R.

- The bearing of Q from P is 90°.
- The distance between P and Q on the map is 4 cm.
- The bearing of R from Q is 150°.
- The distance between Q and R on the map is 3 cm.
- The scale of the diagram is 1 cm = 150 m.

a Calculate the actual distances between P and Q, and between Q and R, in metres. [2]

b Draw a labelled, scale diagram of the field. [5]

[Total: 7]

3 Two points, A and B, are located on a scale map of a city. The scale is 1 : 50 000.

The bearing from A to B is 350° and the actual distance between A and B is 4 km.

a Calculate the distance between A and B on the map. Give your answer in cm. [3]

b On a scale drawing, plot the positions of A and B and indicate the bearing of 350° from A to B. [3]

[Total: 6]

« RECALL AND CONNECT 2 «

For the shape shown, calculate

a the area

b the perimeter, giving your answer to 3 s.f.

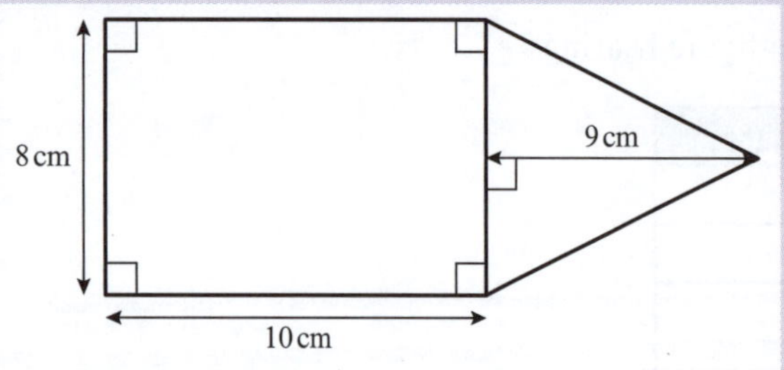

15.3 Understanding the tangent, cosine and sine ratios

1 Calculate the unknown length in each triangle. Give your answers correct to 3 significant figures.

a
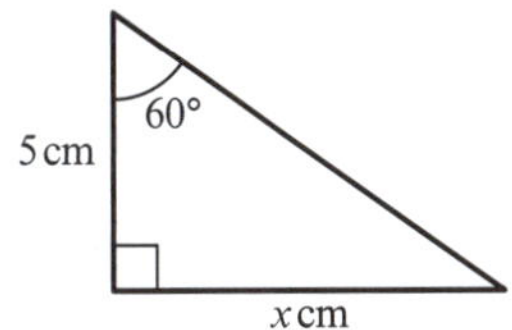

b
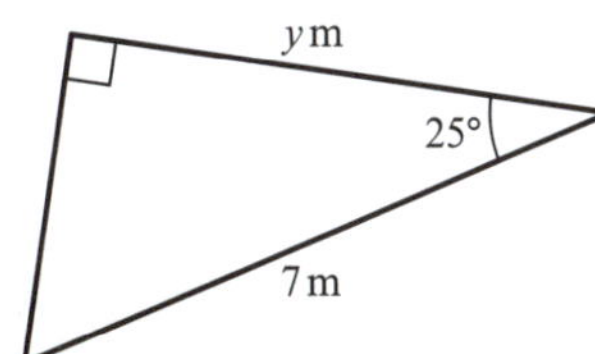

c
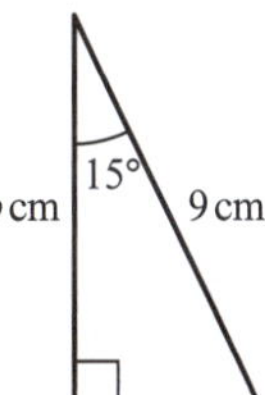

d
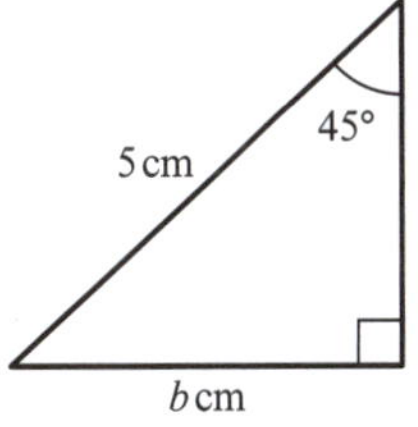

e
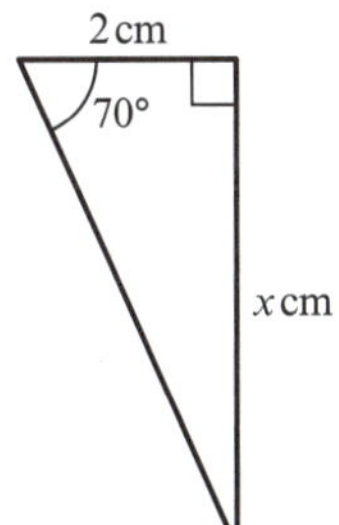

f
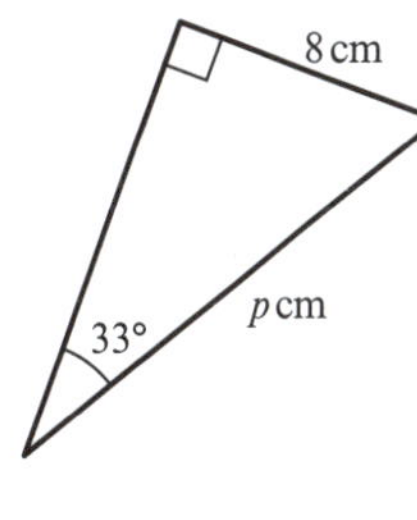

g
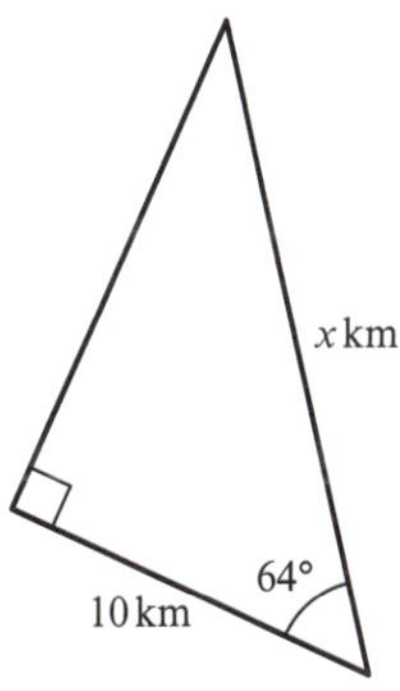

h
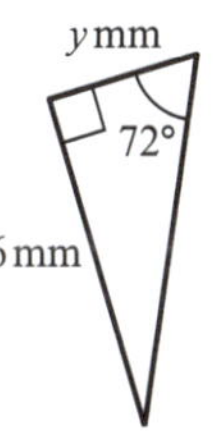

i
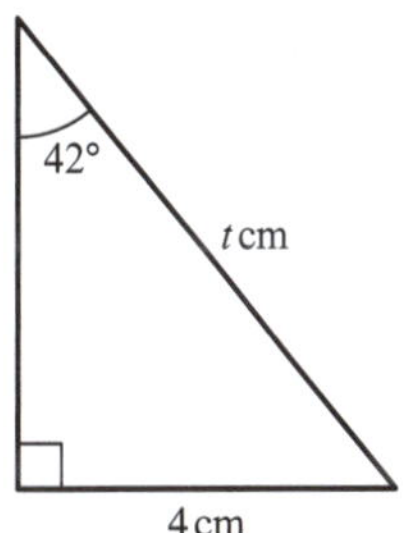

2 Calculate the unknown angle in each triangle. Give your answers correct to 1 decimal place.

a
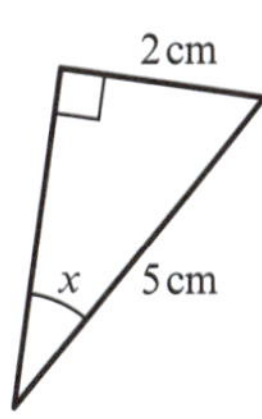

b
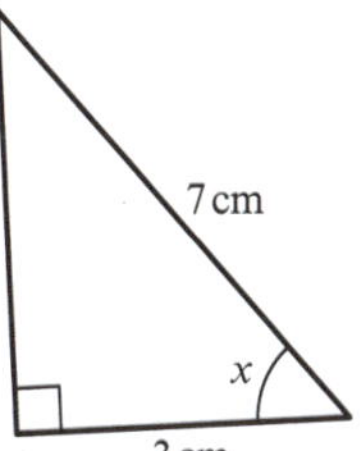

c
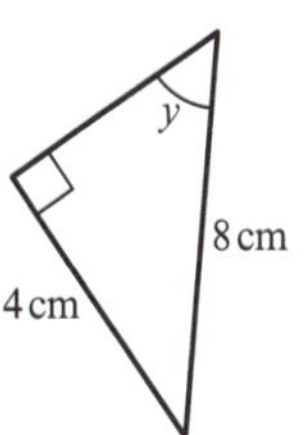

d
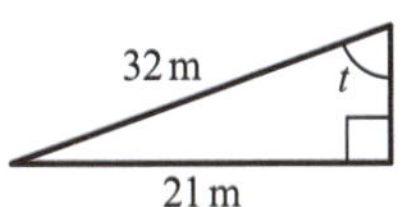

e
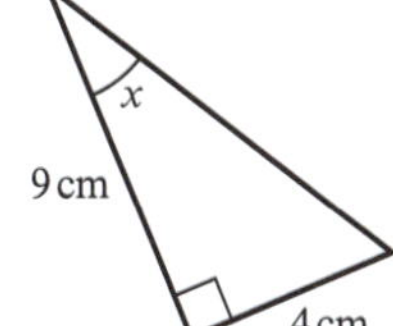

f
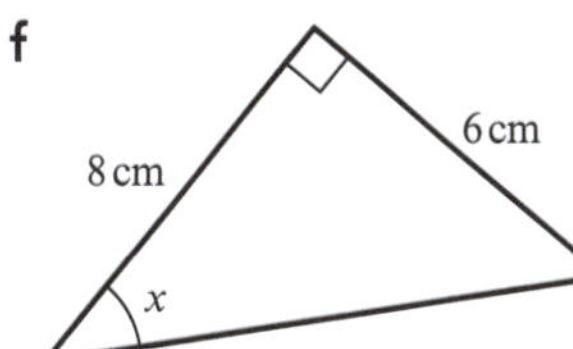

g

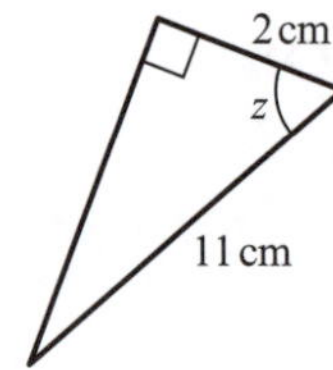

h

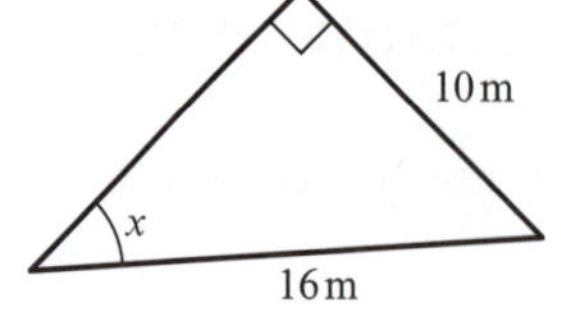

i

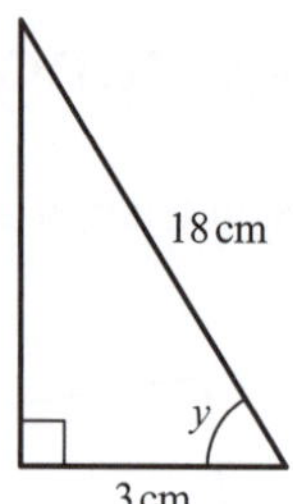

REFLECTION

Can you think of a mnemonic or rhyme to help you remember SohCahToa?

For example: Sense Of Humour Can Always Help To Overcome Awkwardness.

3 Sam and Pete both look at the top of a tower which is 42 m tall.

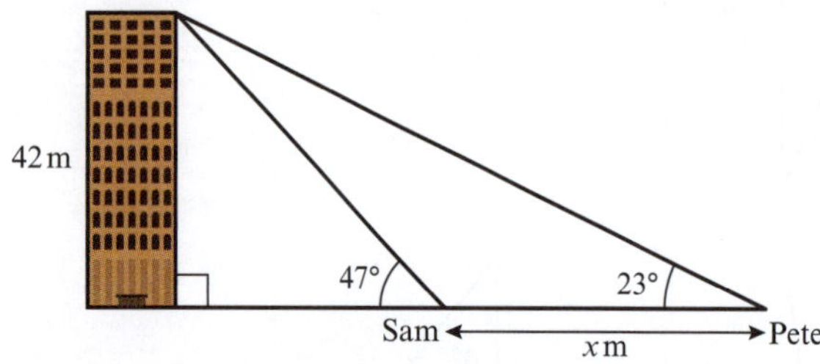

Sam is standing directly in front of Pete, x m away.

The angle of elevation from Pete to the top of the tower is 23°.

The angle of elevation from Sam to the top of the tower is 47°.

Calculate x. [4]

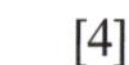

[Total: 4]

4 Calculate the value of y. [4]

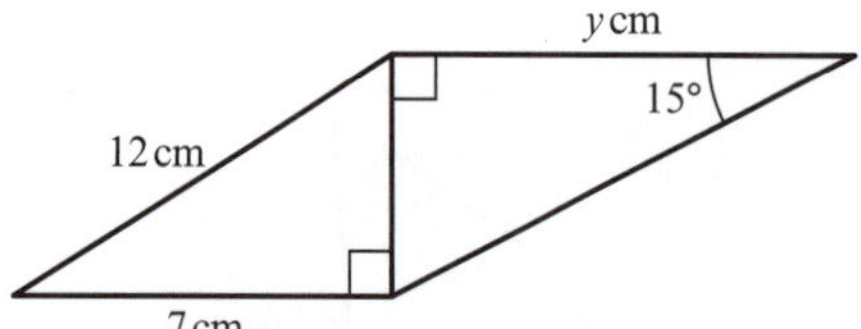

[Total: 4]

⟪ RECALL AND CONNECT 3 ⟪

Solve $5(x - 1) + 2 = 3(x + 3)$

15.4 Exact trigonometric ratios

UNDERSTAND THIS TERM

- Trigonometric ratio

1 Copy and complete this table. Give each value in exact form.

	$\sin x$	$\cos x$	$\tan x$
0°			
30°	$\frac{1}{2}$		
45°			
60°			$\sqrt{3}$
90°			

REFLECTION

How can you remember these trigonometric ratios without using a calculator? You may want to draw these two triangles.

a
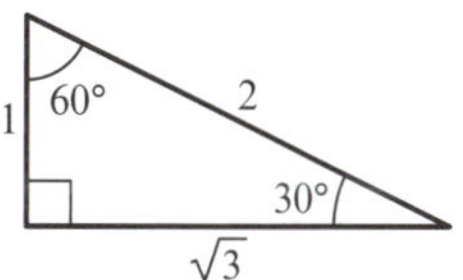

b
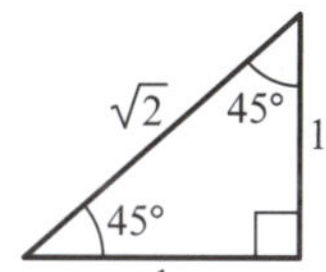

2 Find the exact value of the lettered side in each triangle.

a
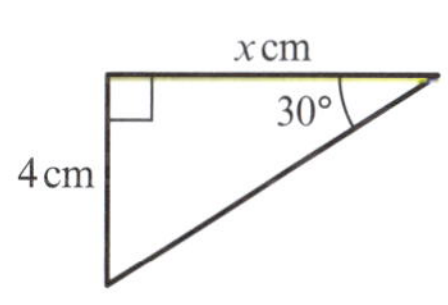

b
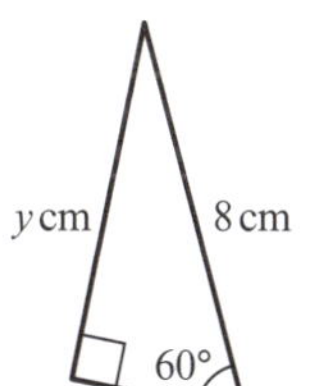

c
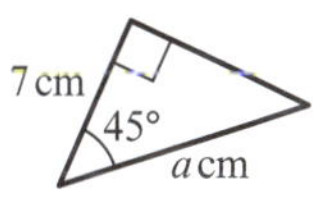

d
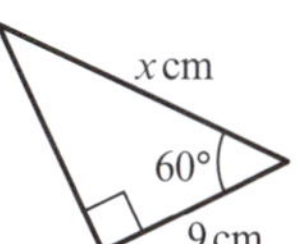

e
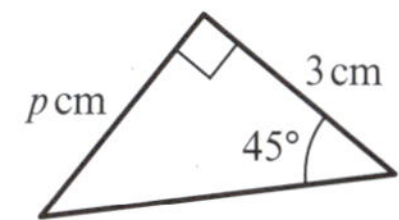

f
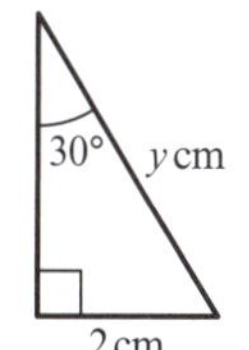

3 The diagram shows a triangle PQR.

The ratio of the lengths $PX : XR$ is $1 : 2$.

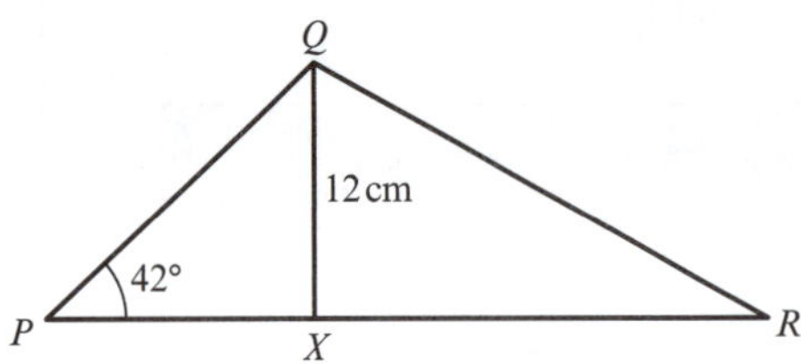

Calculate the size of angle PQR. Give your answer correct to 1 decimal place. [6]

[Total: 6]

4 The diagram shows a parallelogram.

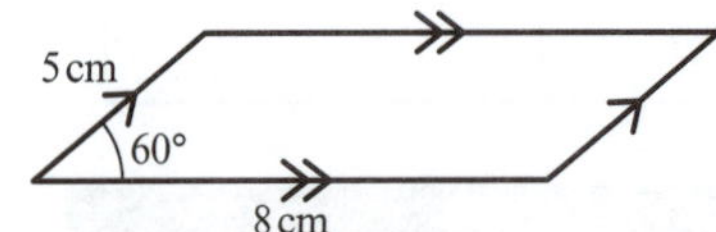

Calculate the exact value of the area of the parallelogram. Give your answer in the form $a\sqrt{b}$, where a and b are integers to be determined. [4]

[Total: 4]

« RECALL AND CONNECT 4 «

Rationalise the denominator

$\frac{5}{6+\sqrt{3}}$.

15.5 Solving problems using trigonometry

1 Harry wants to build a skateboard ramp so that he can jump over a small hedge.

The ramp will be safe if the angle it forms with the horizontal is at most 35°.

The hedge is 0.7 m high.

Calculate the shortest plank of wood that Harry can use for the ramp. [2]

[Total: 2]

2 The diagram shows a trapezium. AB is parallel to CD.

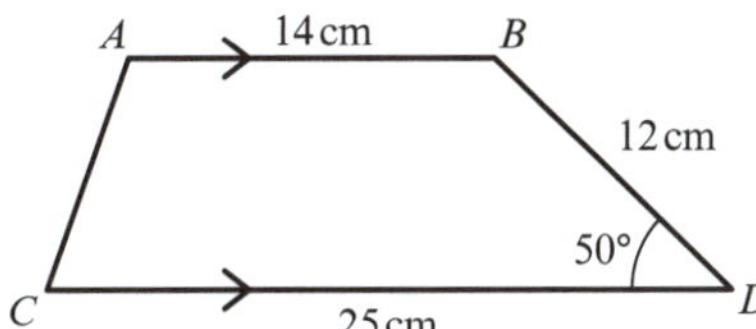

a Calculate the perpendicular height of the trapezium. [2]

b Calculate the area of the trapezium. [2]

[Total: 4]

3 A flagpole is held in place by two wires from points A and B, as shown.

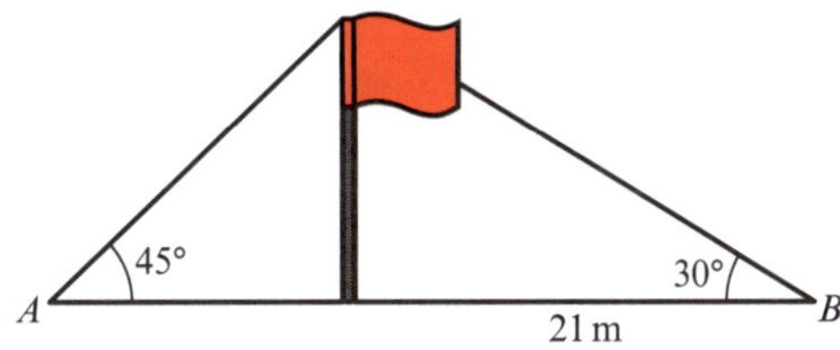

Calculate the exact distance between point A and the base of the flagpole. [4]

[Total: 4]

4 The diagram shows a regular hexagon $ABCDEF$ with sides of length 5 cm.

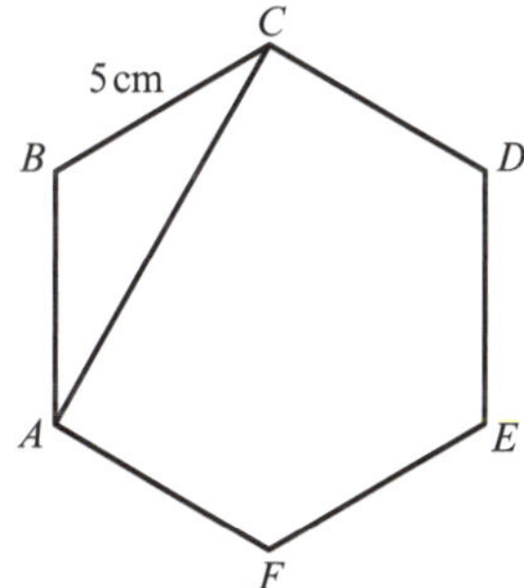

Calculate the exact length of AC. [6]

[Total: 6]

5 Calculate the area of triangle ABC. [5]

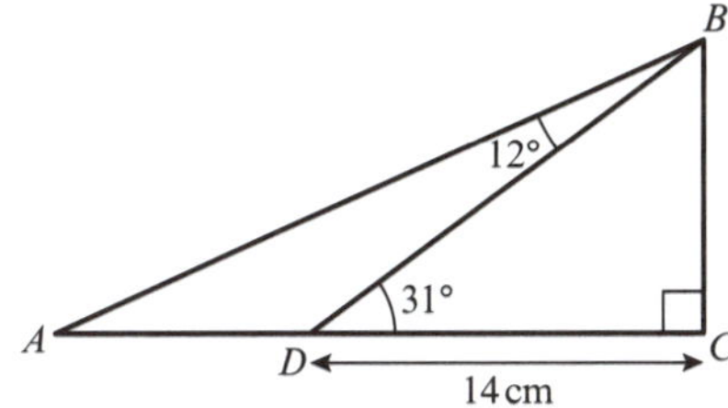

[Total: 5]

<< RECALL AND CONNECT 5 <<

Complete the square $4x^2 + 28x - 3$

15.6 Sines, cosines and tangents of angles greater than 90°

1 On the same set of axes, sketch the graphs of each of these functions for $-360° \leqslant x \leqslant 360°$.

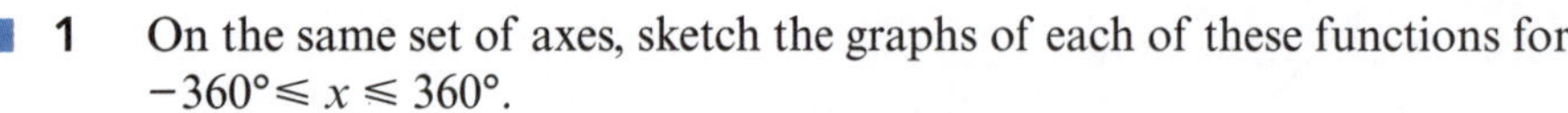

a $y = \sin(x°)$ **b** $y = \cos(x°)$ **c** $y = \tan(x°)$

REFLECTION

How can you remember the difference between the graphs of $y = \sin(x°)$ and $y = \cos(x°)$?

Remembering that $\sin 0 = 0$ and $\cos 0 = 1$ can help you remember where the graph of each intersects the y-axis.

2 Use the graphs that you drew in Question 1 to express each of the following in terms of the same trigonometric ratio of an acute angle ($0 \leqslant \theta \leqslant 90°$).

a $\sin 135°$ **b** $\tan 190°$ **c** $\cos 300°$

d $\sin 190°$ **e** $\tan 120°$ **f** $\cos 172°$

3 Solve each of the following equations, giving all solutions between 0° and 360°.

a $\cos x = \frac{1}{2}$ **b** $\tan x = \sqrt{3}$ **c** $\sin x = -0.6$

d $\tan x = -1$ **e** $\cos x = -0.4$ **f** $\sin x = -\frac{1}{\sqrt{2}}$

4 Solve $4\cos x - 3 = 0$, giving all solutions between 0° and 360°. [4]

[Total: 4]

5 Solve $(\tan x)^2 - 2 = 1$, giving all solutions between 0° and 360°. [5]

[Total: 5]

6 Solve $6(\sin x)^2 + \sin x - 2 = 0$, giving all solutions between 0° and 360°. [5]

[Total: 5]

≪ RECALL AND CONNECT 6 ≪

Solve the equation $2x^2 - 7x - 4 = 0$ by factorising.

15.7 The sine and cosine rules

UNDERSTAND THESE TERMS

- Sine rule
- Cosine rule

1 Use either the sine rule or the cosine rule to find the lettered side or angle.

Give each value correct to 1 decimal place.

a

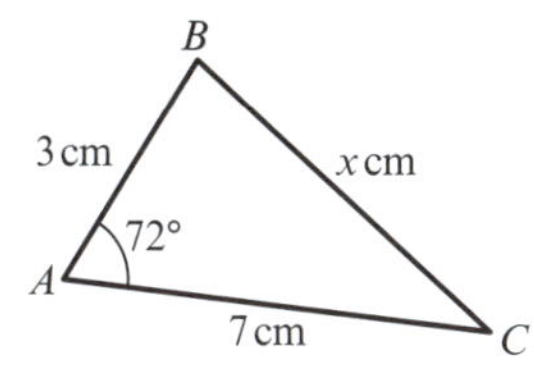

b

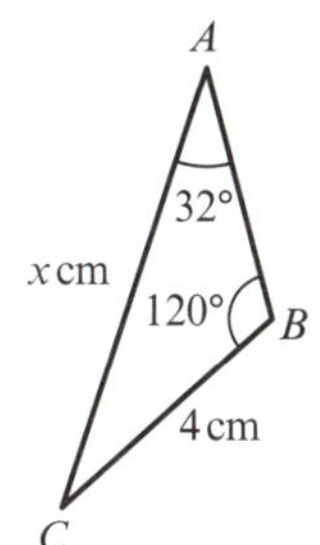

c

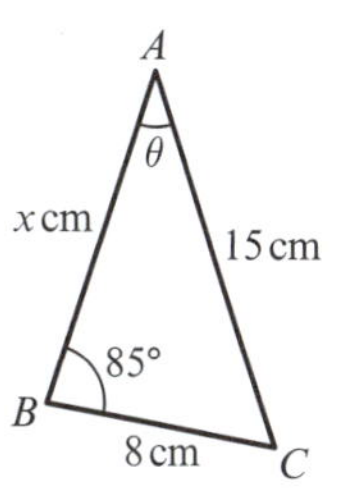

d

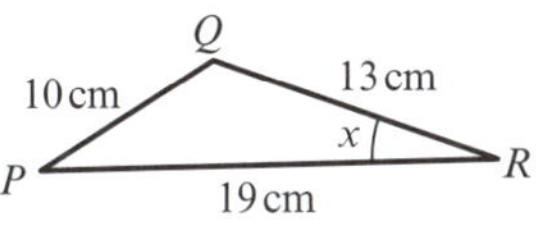

e

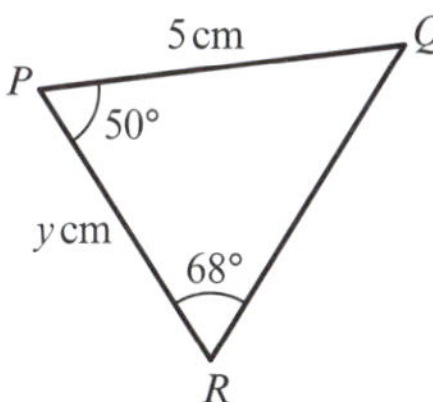

f

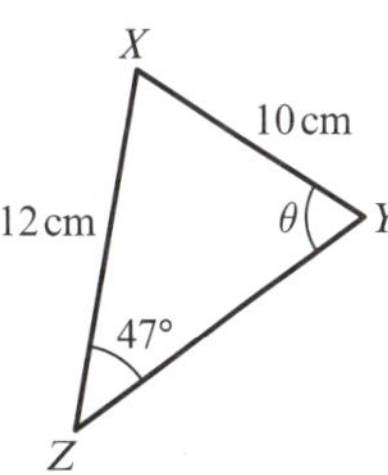

g

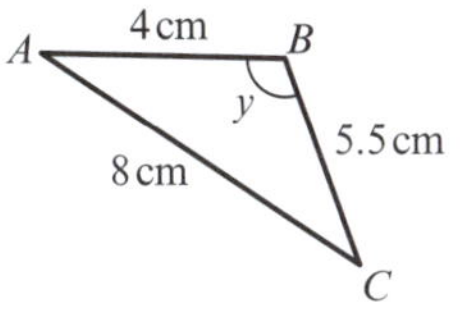

h

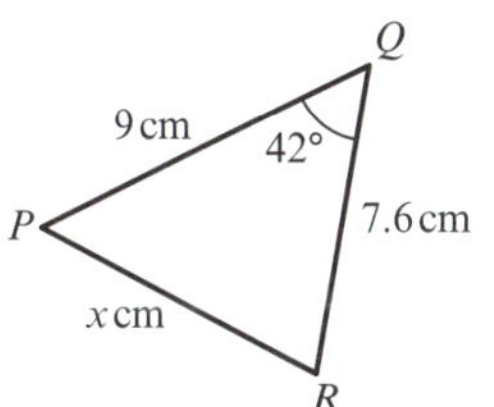

2 Find the size of angle x.

Give your answer correct to 1 decimal place. [4]

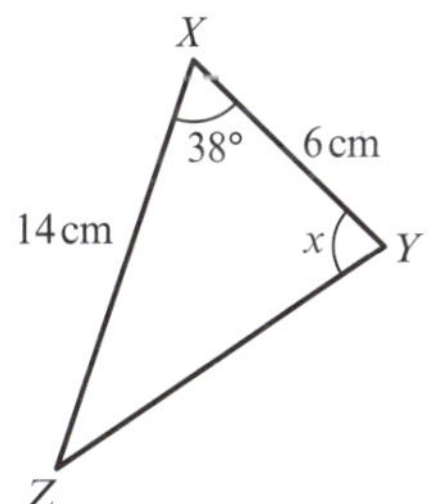

[Total: 4]

3 Ship A is 40 km from the port, P, on a bearing of 225°.

Ship B is 70 km from the port, P, on a bearing of 300°.

a Draw a diagram to show this information. [3]

b Find the distance between ships A and B. [2]

c Calculate the bearing of B from A. [7]

[Total: 12]

4 Two small boats are 50 m apart. They lie in a straight line with the cliff.

The angle of elevation from A to the top of the cliff is 23°.

The angle of elevation of B to the top of the cliff is 38°.

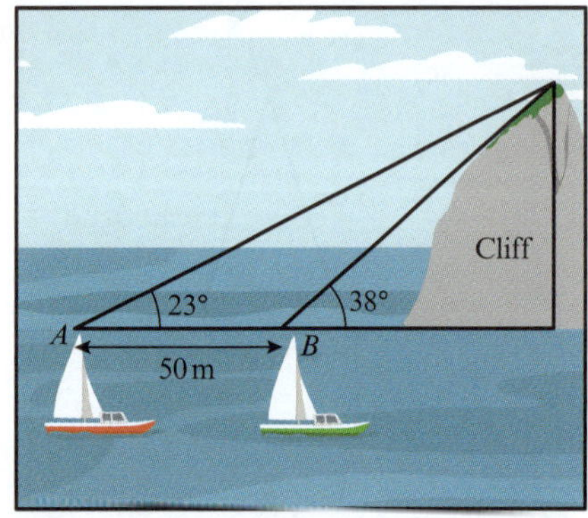

Calculate the height of the cliff. [6]

[Total: 6]

REFLECTION

Can you describe to a friend when you would use the sine rule and when you would use the cosine rule?

≪ RECALL AND CONNECT 7 ≪

Calculate the exact values of

a sin 60° **b** cos 45° **c** tan 30°

15.8 Area of a triangle

1 Calculate the area of each triangle. Give each answer correct to 3 significant figures.

a

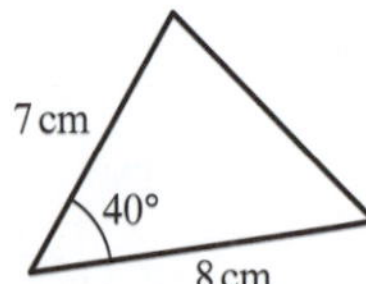

b

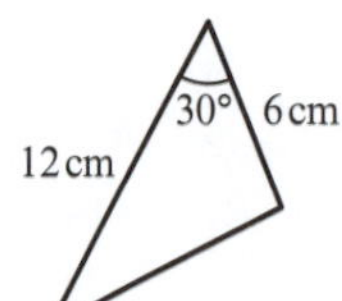

c

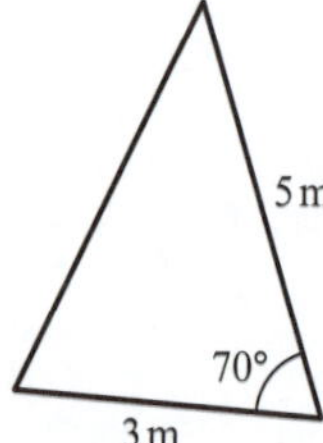

d

8 cm

8 cm

135°

2 The area of each triangle is given. Calculate the lettered side or angle. Give each answer correct to 1 decimal place.

a
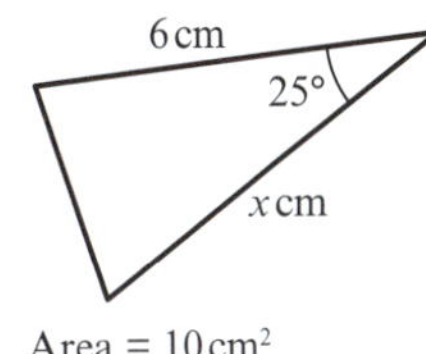

b
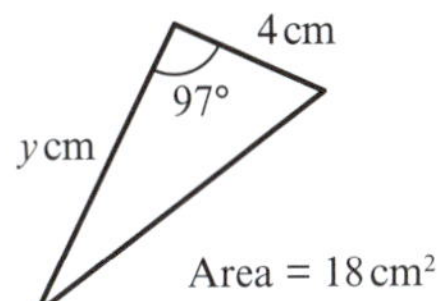

c
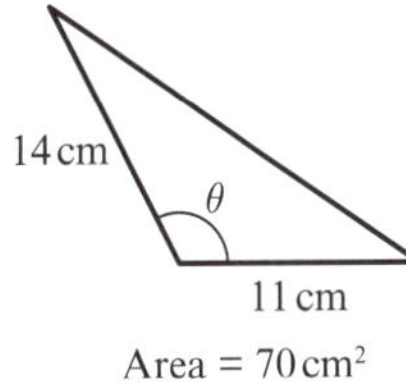

d
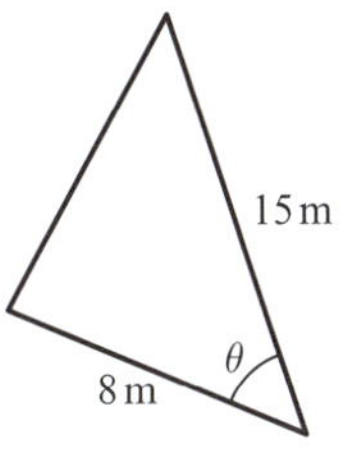

3 A regular hexagon has sides of length 8 cm.

Calculate the exact area of the hexagon. [2]

[Total: 2]

4 Calculate the area of this quadrilateral. [3]

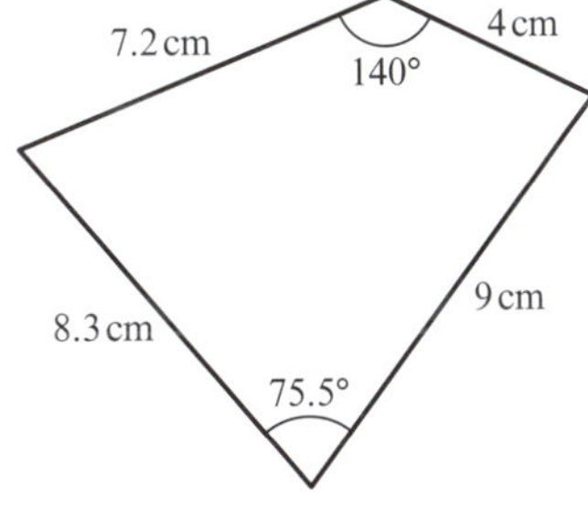

[Total: 3]

5 An architect is designing a triangular skylight. Two sides of the triangle measure 7 metres and 8 metres and the angle between these sides is **obtuse**. The area of the triangle must be 24 square metres. Calculate

a the angle between the sides of length 7 m and 8 m [3]

b the length of the third side. [2]

[Total: 5]

6 A surveyor is measuring a triangular plot.

Two sides of the plot are 100 metres and 150 metres long, and the angle between them is 45°.

The price of land is $850 per square metre.

Calculate the price of the plot. Give your answer to the nearest thousand dollars. [4]

[Total: 4]

« RECALL AND CONNECT 8 «

Simplify $\frac{3x^2 - 5x - 2}{x^2 + x - 6}$.

15.9 Trigonometry in three dimensions

1 A cuboid *ABCDEFGH* is shown.

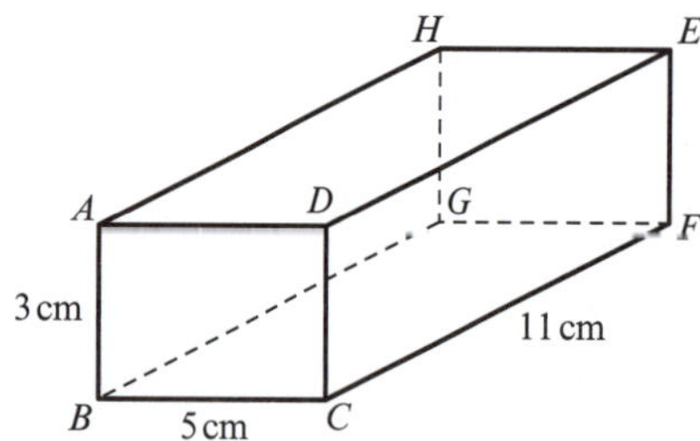

a Calculate the exact length of *BF*.

b Calculate the exact length of *BE*.

c Find the angle *EBF*.

2 *ABCDEF* is a right-angled triangular prism.

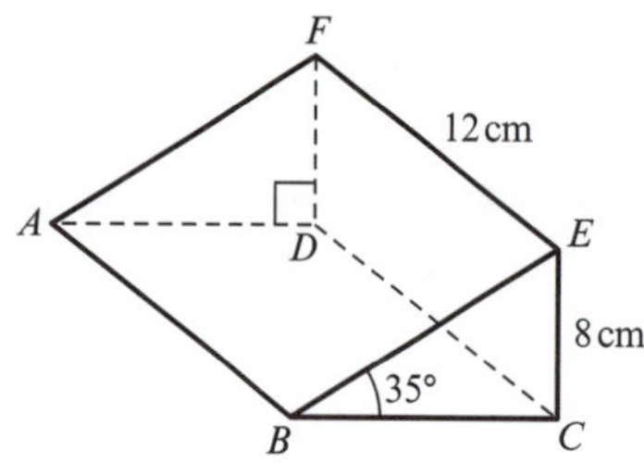

a Calculate the length of *BC*.

b Calculate the length of *AC*.

c Find the angle *BAC*.

d Calculate the area of the rectangle *BAEF*.

3 A cone has base radius 3 cm. The angle that the slanting edge makes with the base is 60°.

The volume of a cone is given by $V = \frac{1}{3}\pi r^2 h$.

The curved surface area of a cone is $A = \pi rl$.

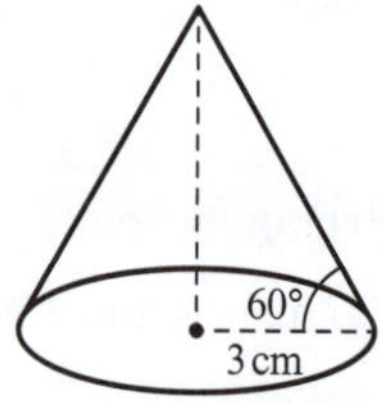

a Calculate the exact volume of the cone. [3]

b Calculate the total surface area of the cone. [3]

[Total: 6]

4 The diagram shows a square-based pyramid.

$AB = 7$ cm

The height of the point E is 15 cm vertically above the base.

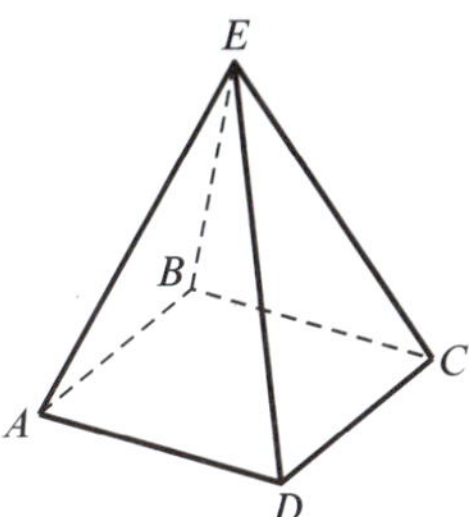

Show that $\tan ECA = \frac{15\sqrt{2}}{7}$. [4]

[Total: 4]

5 The diagram shows a right-angled triangular prism.

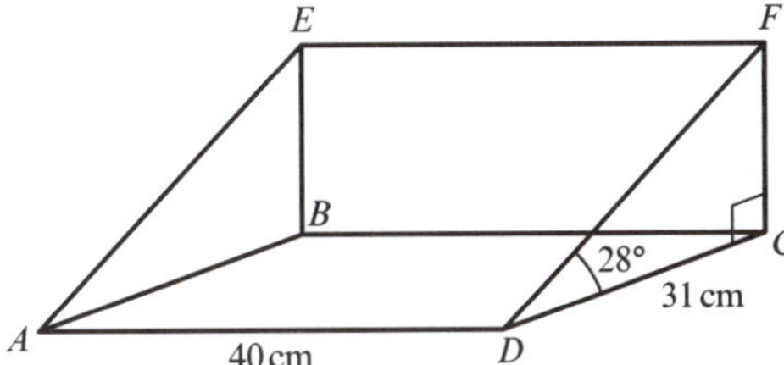

Calculate the angle that the line AF makes with the plane $ABCD$. [6]

[Total: 6]

≪ RECALL AND CONNECT 9 ≪

Calculate $(3 \times 10^{6}) \times (1.7 \times 10^{-3})$.

Give your answer in standard form.

SELF-ASSESSMENT CHECKLIST

Let's revisit the Knowledge and Exam skills focus for this chapter.
Decide how confident you are with each statement.

	Now I can	Show it	Needs more work	Almost there	Confident to move on
1	interpret scale drawings	Look back at Section 15.1, Question 7. Now create a new scale drawing for a real object (e.g. your room, school field, or bus stop route). Add a key and label one measurement clearly.			

CONTINUED

	Now I can	Show it	Needs more work	Almost there	Confident to move on
2	calculate bearings	Choose two cities on a map. Draw a line between them and label the bearing. Then, explain to a friend how you measured the bearing and why it is three figures.			
3	calculate sine, cosine and tangent ratios for right-angled triangles	Create a set of flashcards for sine, cosine and tangent. Add triangles with missing sides and angles on one side, and the correct ratio and calculation on the other.			
4	use sine, cosine and tangent ratios to calculate the angles and lengths of sides of right-angled triangles	Choose a triangle from your textbook or draw your own. Solve it, then write a step-by-step explanation of your method for a friend.			
5	solve trigonometric equations, finding all the solutions between 0° and 360°	Use one of the equations from Section 15.6. Write a mark scheme that includes correct rearrangement, correct values from calculator, all solutions within the interval. Swap and check with a peer.			
6	apply the sine and cosine rules to calculate unknown sides and angles in triangles that are not right-angled	Create flashcards. Front = diagram of a triangle. Back = state which rule to use (sine or cosine), explain why, and write the formula with substitutions.			
7	calculate the area of a triangle that is not right-angled using the sine ratio	Calculate the exact area of this triangle. 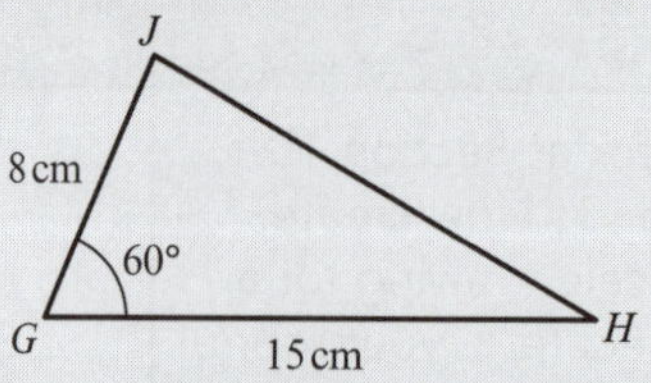 J 8 cm 60° G 15 cm H			

CONTINUED

	Now I can	Show it	Needs more work	Almost there	Confident to move on
8	use the sine, cosine and tangent ratios, together with Pythagoras' theorem in three-dimensions	Look back at Section 15.9, Questions 1 and 2.			
9	use exact sine, cosine and tangent ratios for certain angles	Show that $\tan 30° + \sin 60° = \frac{5\sqrt{3}}{6}$.			
10	show that you understand the command word 'calculate' and can answer a 'calculate' question	Look through past examination papers for multi-step 'calculate' questions. Solve them clearly, step by step, and check your method and answer against the mark scheme.			
11	understand the difference between 'calculate' and 'solve'.	Find and annotate two questions (one using 'solve', the other 'calculate') from the chapter. Explain the difference in required method and answer format.			

16 Scatter diagrams and correlation

KNOWLEDGE FOCUS

In this chapter, you will answer questions on:

- drawing scatter diagrams for bivariate data
- identifying whether or not there is a positive or negative correlation between two variables
- drawing a line of best fit
- using a line of best fit to make predictions
- deciding how reliable your predictions are
- recognising the common errors that are often made with scatter diagrams.

EXAM SKILLS FOCUS

In this chapter you will:

- practise how to give a good answer to a scatter graph examination question
- interpret data in context using mathematical language.

In this chapter you will practise answering questions that require you to draw a scatter diagram and interpret it in the context of the question.

Questions that require you to draw a scatter diagram will often use the command word 'plot'.

Plot	mark point(s) on a graph.

To answer one of these questions well, you should consider the following points.

- Always draw your graph using pencil and a ruler. Choose the scale on each axis carefully.
- Plot the points in the scatter table accurately.
- The line of best fit should generally have a similar number of points both above and below the line.
- When interpolating from the graph, draw your horizontal and vertical lines carefully. Make sure you know whether to start from the x-axis or the y-axis!

- Be mindful of the amount of marks available and adjust the time you spend accordingly.
- Know the different command terms – for example, here you will be plotting, *not* sketching.

But remember, it is not just about drawing graphs correctly – you also need to explain what those graphs show. You need to interpret patterns, trends and predictions using accurate mathematical language. This includes terms like positive correlation and line of best fit. Clear interpretation shows the examiner you understand what the data really means.

16.1 Introduction to bivariate data

UNDERSTAND THESE TERMS

- Correlation
- Line of best fit

1 For each of the following scatter diagrams:

  i State whether it shows positive, negative or no correlation.

  ii If the diagram shows correlation, comment on whether it shows strong, moderate or weak correlation.

a

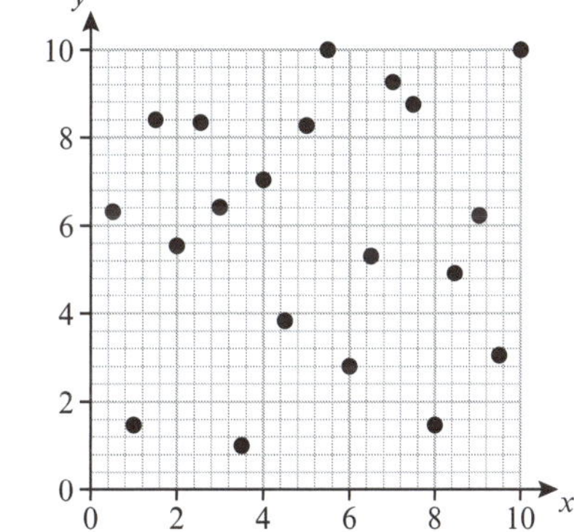

b

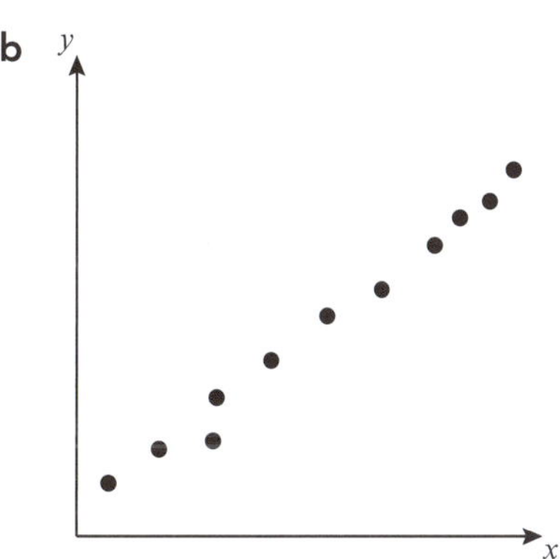

c

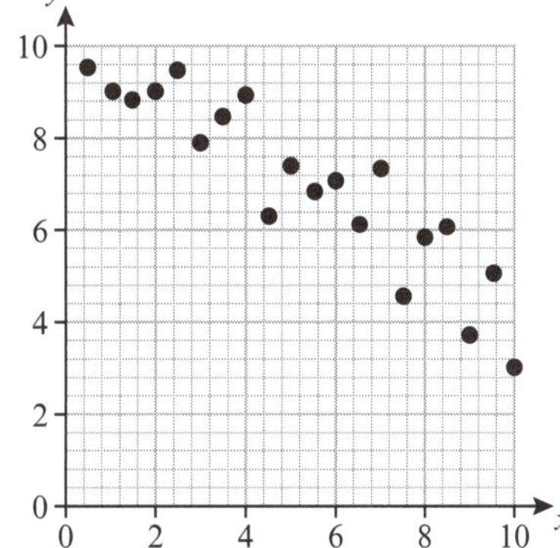

d

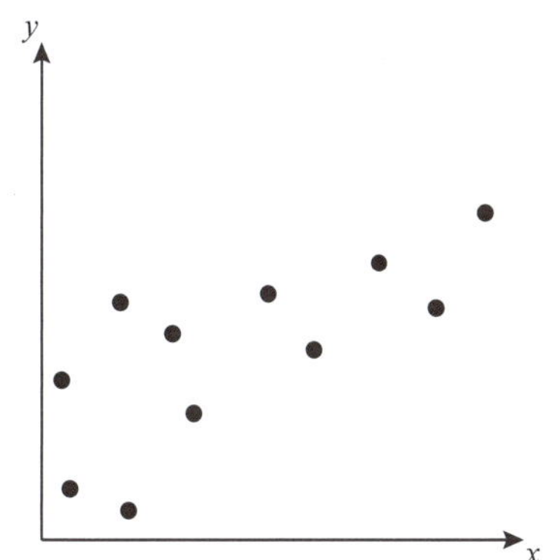

e

f

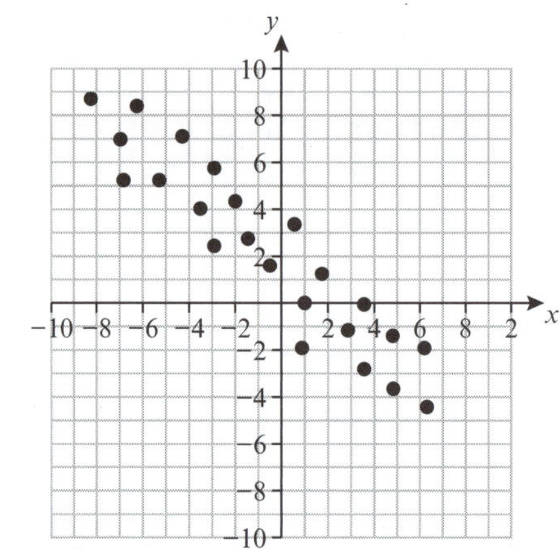

g

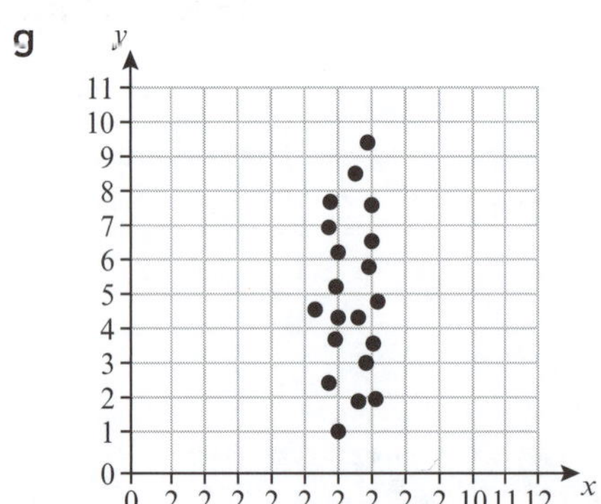

2 The heights and masses of 15 students are recorded below.

Height (cm)	150	160	155	165	170	152	158	162
Mass (kg)	45	50	47	55	60	46	48	53

Height (cm)	168	175	148	180	172	160	166
Mass (kg)	58	63	44	67	61	52	56

a Draw a scatter diagram with height on the horizontal axis. [2]

b Identify and explain the type of the correlation. [2]

c Draw a line of best fit. [1]

d Estimate the mass of a student who is 163 cm tall. [1]

[Total: 6]

3 Ben records the average outside temperature over the course of six months.

His heating bill for each month is also shown.

Month	Nov	Dec	Jan	Feb	Mar	Apr
Temperature (°C)	10	8	5	12	15	18
Heating bill ($)	120	130	150	100	80	60

a Draw a scatter diagram with temperature on the x-axis. [2]

b Describe the correlation and interpret what the correlation tells you about the connection between temperature and heating bills. [2]

c Draw a line of best fit. [1]

d Estimate the heating bill when the temperature is 11 °C. [1]

[Total: 6]

4 Beth thinks that her friends need to spend less time on social media.

She records the number of hours that six friends spend on social media on a Tuesday in the summer holidays, and the number of hours of sleep each one got.

Time on social media (hours)	1	3	3	4.5	5	4.5
Sleep (hours)	8.5	8.0	7.5	7.0	6.5	6.0

a Plot the data on a scatter diagram. [2]

b Describe the correlation and interpret what the correlation tells you about the connection between time on social media and hours of sleep. [2]

c Draw a line of best fit. [1]

d Estimate the number of hours of sleep for someone on social media for 2 hours. [1]

[Total: 6]

5 The examination scores of six piano students are shown, along with the number of hours they practise per day.

Hours of practice	2	2	3	3.5	4	4
Exam score (%)	45	55	60	70	75	80

a Plot a scatter diagram of the data. [2]

b Suggest what the correlation tells you about the link between hours of practice and exam score. [1]

c Draw a line of best fit. [1]

d John scores 65% in his exam.

Estimate the daily number of hours of practice that John does. [1]

[Total: 5]

6 Aiden records the shoe sizes and exam scores of seven students in his class.

Shoe size	4	5	6	7	8	9	10
Exam score (%)	72	65	80	75	68	74	69

a Draw a scatter diagram (shoe size on x-axis). [2]

b Describe the correlation. [1]

c What does this tell you about the relationship between shoe size and exam scores? [1]

[Total: 4]

7 Richard records the time that he spends on his cross-trainer and the number of calories he burns.

Time (min)	10	20	30	40	50
Calories burned	80	160	240	320	400

a Plot a scatter diagram. [2]

b Interpret what the correlation tells you. [1]

c Draw a line of best fit. [1]

d Estimate the calories Richard burned in 25 minutes. [1]

[Total: 5]

8 Samar records the reaction time of some friends and also looks at which brand of mobile phone they own.

Mobile brand code	1	2	1	3	4	3
Reaction time (ms)	320	290	310	300	295	315

a Draw a scatter diagram. [2]

b Describe the correlation. [1]

c Suggest what can you conclude about mobile brand and reaction time from this data. [1]

[Total: 4]

9 Paula recorded the ages and resting heart rates of ten people. The table shows some of Paula's results, but it is incomplete.

Age (years)	16		20	22	24		28	30	32	
Resting heart rate (bpm)	70	72	74		75	76	77		80	81

Paula drew a scatter diagram to show her results.

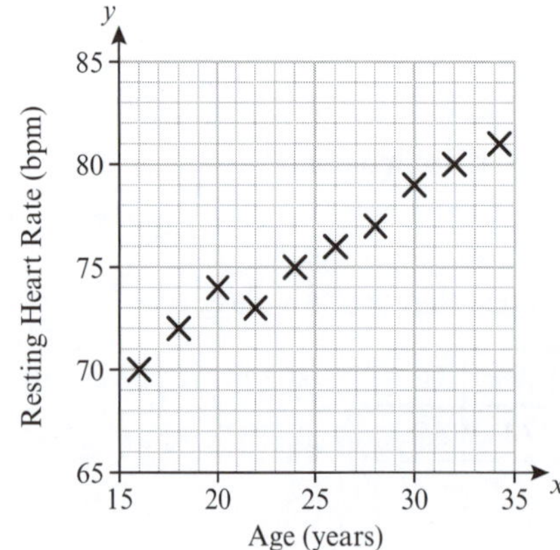

a Use the scatter diagram to complete the table. [2]

b Comment on the correlation between age and resting heart rate. [2]

c Draw a line of best fit. [1]

d Predict the heart rate for a 25-year-old. [1]

e Suggest whether the scatter diagram could be used to predict accurately the resting heart rate of an 85-year-old. Give a reason for your answer. [2]

[Total: 8]

REFLECTION

How does understanding the correlation help you to work out how the two variables are connected?

When you were asked to describe a graph or trend, what made your explanation effective or less effective? Did you use words like 'positive correlation' or 'inversely proportional'? How might you improve your explanations next time?

≪ RECALL AND CONNECT 1 ≪

$a = 2.75$ to 3 s.f.

$b = 7.3$ to 1 d.p.

Calculate the upper and lower bounds for $\frac{2ab}{b - a}$.

Give your answers to 2 d.p.

SELF-ASSESSMENT CHECKLIST

Let's revisit the Knowledge and Exam skills focus for this chapter.
Decide how confident you are with each statement.

	Now I can	Show it	Needs more work	Almost there	Confident to move on
1	draw scatter diagrams for bivariate data	Collect data from friends and family and create your own scatter diagram (e.g. shoe size vs height)			
2	identify whether there is a positive or negative correlation between the two variables	Write a statement describing correlation for three diagrams in past exam papers.			
3	draw a line of best fit	Look for scatter diagrams in past papers, or by using an internet search, and add lines of best fit to them.			

CONTINUED

	Now I can	Show it	Needs more work	Almost there	Confident to move on
4	use a line of best fit to make predictions	Predict a value using one of the graphs in this chapter			
5	decide how reliable your predictions are	After completing the above, write a short note to explain how reliable each prediction is.			
6	recognise the common errors that are often made with scatter diagrams	Create a list of 'Mistakes to avoid' when creating scatter diagrams.			
7	give a good answer to a scatter graph exam question	Write your own exam-style question based on scatter diagrams. Write a sample answer and create a mark scheme showing how each part would be awarded marks.			
8	interpret data in context using mathematical language.	Pick a scatter diagram and write three different ways of explaining what it shows. Then ask a friend which is the clearest explanation.			

Exam practice 4

This section contains past paper questions from previous Cambridge exams, which draw together your knowledge on a range of topics that you have covered up to this point. These questions give you the opportunity to test your knowledge and understanding.

The following question has an example student response and commentary provided. Work through the question first, then compare your answer to the sample response and commentary. Are your answers different to the sample responses?

1 Solve the simultaneous equations.

You must show all your working.

$3x - 2y = 19$

$x + y = 3$

[3]

Cambridge IGCSE Mathematics (0580) Paper 22 Q9 March 2023 **[Total: 3]**

Example student response	Commentary
$x = 3 - y$ $3(3 - y) - 2y = 19$ $9 - 3y - 2y = 19$ $9 - 5y = 19$	The question does not say that students must use either substitution or elimination, so this student has chosen to use substitution.
Solve for y: $-5y = 10$ $y = -2$ Find x: $x = 3 - y$ $x = 3 - 2$ $x = 1$	The student correctly substitutes $x = 3 - y$ into the first equation and finds the correct value for y. The student made a calculation error when finding the value of x, so loses a mark for this. ***This answer scores 2 out of 3 marks.***

2 Now that you have gone through the commentary, try to write an improved answer for your own solution and edit the sample student response to improve their answer to each part.

The following question has an example student response and commentary provided. Work through the question first, then compare your answer to the sample response and commentary. Are your answers different to the sample responses?

3 The diagram shows a triangular prism $ABCDQP$ of length 7 cm.

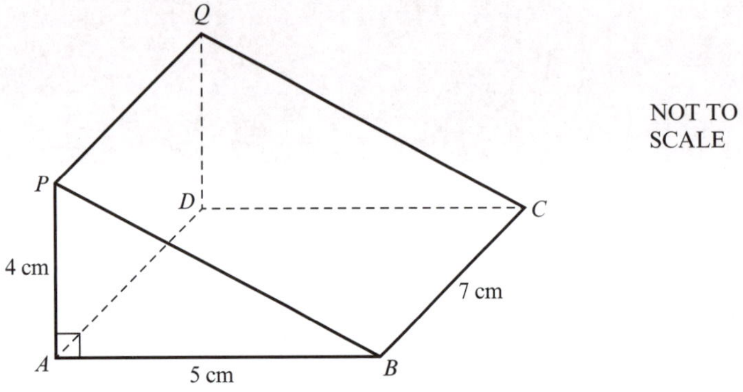

The cross-section is triangle PAB with $PA = 4$ cm, $AB = 5$ cm and angle $PAB = 90°$.

Calculate the angle between the line PC and the base $ABCD$. [4]

Cambridge IGCSE Mathematics (0580) Paper 22 Q22 March 2023 **[Total: 4]**

Example student response	Commentary
$AC = \sqrt{5^2 + 7^2} = \sqrt{74}$ $\tan PCA = \frac{4}{\sqrt{74}}$	The student has correctly used Pythagoras' theorem to find the length of AC.
$PCA = \tan^{-1}\left(\frac{4}{\sqrt{74}}\right) = 3.1°$	The student then uses trigonometric ratios in triangle PCA to find the angle between PC and the base $ABCD$. However, they make an error with the final calculation (it looks like they forgot to calculate the square root of 74), so the answer is incorrect. ***This answer scores 3 out of 4 marks.***

4 Now that you have gone through the commentary, try to write an improved answer for your own solution and edit the sample student response to improve their answer to each part.

The following question has an example student response and commentary provided. Work through the question first, then compare your answer to the sample response and commentary. Are your answers different to the sample responses?

5 Simplify.

$$\frac{5x^2 - 19x + 12}{x^2 - 9}$$ [4]

Cambridge IGCSE Mathematics (0580) Paper 22 Q23 March 2023 **[Total: 4]**

Example student response	Commentary
$\frac{5x^2 - 19x + 12}{x^2 - 9} = \frac{(5x + 4)(x + 3)}{(x - 3)(x + 3)}$ $= \frac{(5x + 4)(x + 3)}{(x - 3)(x + 3)}$	The student correctly identifies that they must factorise both the top and the bottom to simplify. This attempt, with the $5x$ and x terms correct and $4 \times 3 = 12$, scores 1 mark. But both the top and bottom are incorrectly factorised. ***This answer scores 1 out of 4 marks.***

6 Simplify.

$$\frac{2x^2 - 5x - 12}{3x^2 - 12x}$$ [4]

Cambridge IGCSE Mathematics (0580) Paper 22 Q22 June 2021 **[Total: 4]**

The following question has an example student response and commentary provided. Work through the question first, then compare your answer to the sample response and commentary. Are your answers different to the sample responses?

7

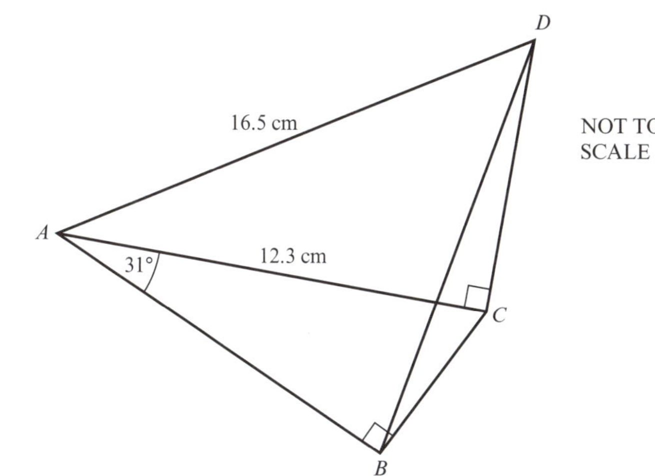

The diagram shows a quadrilateral $ABCD$.

$AC = 12.3$ cm and $AD = 16.5$ cm.

Angle $BAC = 31°$, angle $ABC = 90°$ and angle $ACD = 90°$.

a Show that $AB = 10.54$ cm, correct to 2 decimal places. [2]

b Show that angle $DAC = 41.80°$, correct to 2 decimal places. [2]

c Calculate BD. [3]

d Calculate angle CBD. [4]

Cambridge IGCSE Mathematics (0580) Paper 42 Q10a–d March 2023 **[Total: 11]**

Example student response	Commentary
a $\sin 31° = \frac{AB}{12.3}$ $AB = 12 \sin 31 = 10.54$	The student has incorrectly used sine. If they had calculated 12 sin 31°, they would find it is not equal to the value they are asked to show. ***This answer scores 0 out of 2 marks.***
b $\cos DAC = \frac{12.3}{16.5}$ $DAC = \cos^{-1}\left(\frac{12.3}{16.5}\right) = 41.80°$	The student has correctly used cosine and the answer is correct. ***This answer scores 2 out of 2 marks.***

c $DAB = 41.80 + 31 = 72.80$ $(BD)^2 = 16.5^2 + 10.54^2 - 2(16.5)(10.54)\cos 72.8$ $BD = 280.488 = 280.49$ to 1 d.p.	The student has spotted they need to use the cosine rule and has correctly applied the formula. The student has forgotten to take the square root of 280.49. ***This answer scores 2 out of 3 marks.***
d $\frac{\sin ABD}{16.5} = \frac{\sin 72.8°}{280.49}$ $ABD = 3.2$ $CBD = 90 - 3.2 = 86.8°$	The student has used the fact that $CBD = 90 - ABD$ They have correctly applied the sine rule to calculate ABD. Their incorrect answer in part **c** was correctly carried through. They only lose one mark for the final answer being wrong. ***This answer scores 3 out of 4 marks.***

8

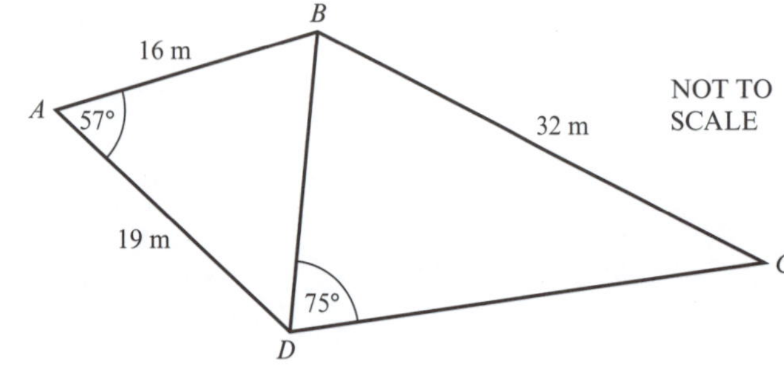

The diagram shows a quadrilateral $ABCD$ made from two triangles, ABD and BCD.

a Show that $BD = 16.9$ m, correct to 1 decimal place. [3]

b Calculate angle CBD. [4]

c Find the area of the quadrilateral $ABCD$. [3]

Cambridge IGCSE Mathematics (0580) Paper 42 Q6 June 2021 **[Total: 10]**

The following question has an example student response and commentary provided. Work through the question first, then compare your answer to the sample response and commentary. Are your answers different to the sample responses?

9 **a** Sketch the graph of $y = \tan x$ for $0° \leqslant x \leqslant 360°$.

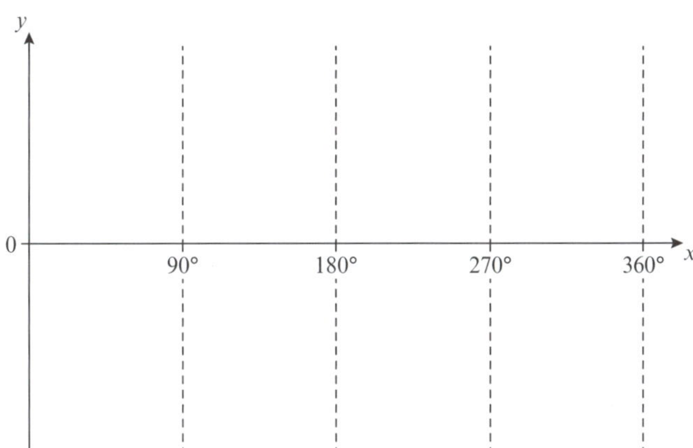

[2]

[Use Figure 3 in the Past Paper Practice Questions Resource Sheet.]

b Find x when $\tan x = \frac{1}{\sqrt{3}}$ and $0° \leqslant x \leqslant 360°$. [2]

Cambridge IGCSE Mathematics (0580) Paper 42 Q12 March 2023 **[Total: 4]**

Example student response	Commentary
a	The student has correctly sketched the graph. They are awarded full marks. If the student had only sketched one part of the graph correctly, they would have scored one mark. ***This answer scores 2 out of 2 marks.***
b $x = \tan^{-1}\left(\frac{1}{\sqrt{3}}\right) = 30°$	The student has correctly found the first solution of $x = 30°$. However, they have forgotten to find the second solution using the graph. ***This answer scores 1 out of 2 marks.***

10 Find all the solutions of $4 \sin x = 3$ for $0° \leqslant x \leqslant 360°$. [2]

Cambridge IGCSE Mathematics (0580) Paper 22 Q23 June 2021 **[Total: 2]**

The following question has an example student response and commentary provided. Work through the question first, then compare your answer to the sample response and commentary. Are your answers different to the sample responses?

11 Anil changes \$830 into euros when the exchange rate is 1 euro = \$1.16.

He spends 500 euros.

He then changes the remaining money back into dollars at the same exchange rate.

Work out how much, in dollars, Anil receives. [3]

Cambridge IGCSE Mathematics (0580) Paper 42 Q2a June 2023 **[Total: 3]**

Example student response	Commentary
Anil gets 830 × 1.16 = €962.80 He spends €500 so has €962.80 – €500 = €462.80 left After exchanging back, he gets 462.80 ÷ 1.16 = \$398.97	Unfortunately, the student has misunderstood the exchange rate. After this initial mistake, the whole answer is incorrect. ***This answer scores 0 out of 3 marks.***

12 Now that you have gone through the commentary, try to write an improved answer for your own solution and edit the sample student response to improve their answer to each part.

The following question has an example student response and commentary provided. Work through the question first, then compare your answer to the sample response and commentary. Are your answers different to the sample responses?

13 a Find all the positive integers which satisfy the inequality.

$3n - 8 > 5n - 15$ [2]

b

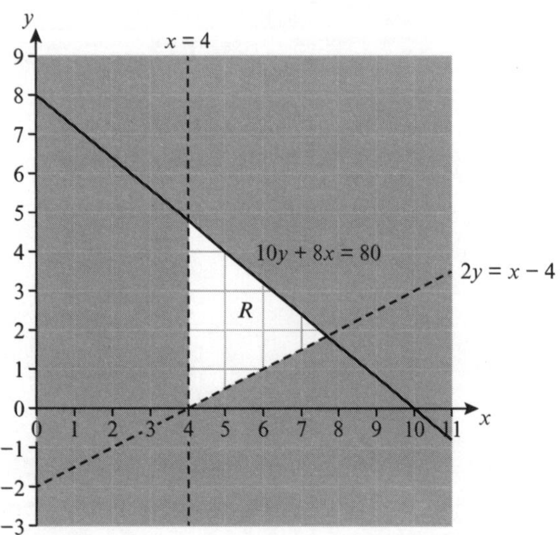

The region marked R is defined by three inequalities.

Find these three inequalities. [3]

Cambridge IGCSE Mathematics (0580) Paper 42 Q10a, b(i) June 2022 **[Total: 5]**

Example student response	Commentary
a $15 - 8 > 5n - 3n$ $7 > 2n$ $3.5 > n$ $n = 1, 2, 3$	The student has correctly solved the inequality, being careful to keep the inequality symbol the correct way around. They have then correctly identified that the only positive integers smaller than 3.5 are 1, 2 and 3. ***This answer scores 2 out of 2 marks.***
b $x > 4$ $2y > x - 4$ $10y + 8x \geqslant 80$	The student has correctly identified the inequalities $x > 4$ and $2y > x - 4$, along with the fact that these are dashed lines so the inequalities must be strict. The third inequality should be the other way around. To see this, you can pick a test point in R, say (5, 1), and substitute $x = 5$, $y = 1$ into $10y + 8x$ to see whether it is less than or greater than 80. ***This answer scores 2 out of 3 marks.***

14 Now that you have gone through the commentary, try to write an improved answer for your own solution and edit the sample student response to improve their answer to each part.

The following question has an example student response and commentary provided. Work through the question first, then compare your answer to the sample response and commentary. Are your answers different to the sample responses?

15 A picture in a small frame has length 15 cm and width 10.5 cm, both correct to the nearest 5 mm.

Calculate the upper bound for the area of this picture. [2]

Adapted from Cambridge IGCSE Mathematics (0580) Paper 42 Q7b March 2022 **[Total: 2]**

Example student response	Commentary
5 mm = 0.5 cm $0.5 \div 2 = 0.25$ UB for length = $15 + 0.25 = 15.25$ UB for width = $10.5 + 0.25 = 10.25$ UB for area = $10.25 \times 15.25 = 156.3\ \text{cm}^2$	The student employs the correct method to calculate the upper bounds of both the length and the width. They achieve a mark for $15 + 0.25 = 15.25$. However, they have incorrectly calculated $10.5 + 0.25$. They then correctly multiply the upper bounds for length and width together to find the upper bound for the area. ***This answer scores 1 out of 2 marks.***

16 Now that you have gone through the commentary, try to write an improved answer for your own solution and edit the sample student response to improve their answer to each part.

The following question has an example student response and commentary provided. Work through the question first, then compare your answer to the sample response and commentary. Are your answers different to the sample responses?

17 Darpan runs a distance of 12 km and then cycles a distance of 26 km.

His running speed is x km/h and his cycling speed is 10 km/h faster than his running speed.

He takes a total time of 2 hours 48 minutes.

a An expression for the time, in hours, Darpan takes to run the 12 km is $\frac{12}{x}$.

Write an equation, in terms of x, for the total time he takes in hours. [3]

b Show that this equation simplifies to $7x^2 - 25x - 300 = 0$. [3]

c Use the quadratic formula to solve $7x^2 - 25x - 300 = 0$.

You must show all your working [4]

Cambridge IGCSE Mathematics (0580) Paper 42 Q8a–c March 2022 **[Total: 10]**

Example student response	Commentary
a 2 hours 48 min = 2.8 hours $\frac{12}{x} + \frac{26}{x+10} = 2.8$	The student correctly applies the formula time = distance ÷ speed for both parts of the journey. ***This answer scores 3 out of 3 marks.***
b $\frac{12(x+10)+26x}{x(x+10)} = \frac{2.8x(x+10)}{x(x+10)}$ $12(x+10) + 26x = 2.8x(x+10)$ $12x + 120 + 26x = 2.8x^2 + 28x$ $0 = 2.8x^2 - 10x - 120$ $0 = 7x^2 - 25x - 300$	The student correctly puts all terms over a common denominator and then manipulates the algebra to get the required quadratic equation. ***This answer scores 4 out of 4 marks.***
c $x = \frac{-25 \pm \sqrt{25^2 - 4(7)(-300)}}{2(7)}$ $x = 5, x = -8.57$	The student has incorrectly substituted into the quadratic formula. ***This answer scores 1 out of 4 marks.***

18 Now that you have gone through the commentary, try to write an improved answer for your own solution and edit the sample student response to improve their answer to each part.

The following question has an example student response and commentary provided. Work through the question first, then compare your answer to the sample response and commentary. Are your answers different to the sample responses?

19 a Henrik draws this scatter diagram.

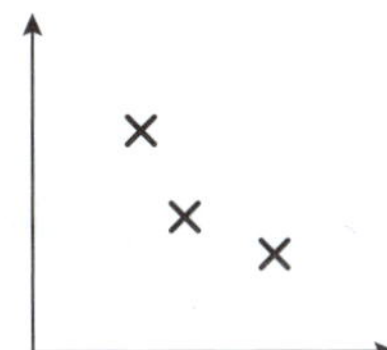

Identify the **one** correct statement about this scatter diagram.

It shows no correlation.	It is not possible to tell if there is correlation as there are not enough points.	It shows negative correlation.	It shows positive correlation.

[1]

b Each of the four scatter diagrams shows the same set of data.

A line has been drawn on each diagram.

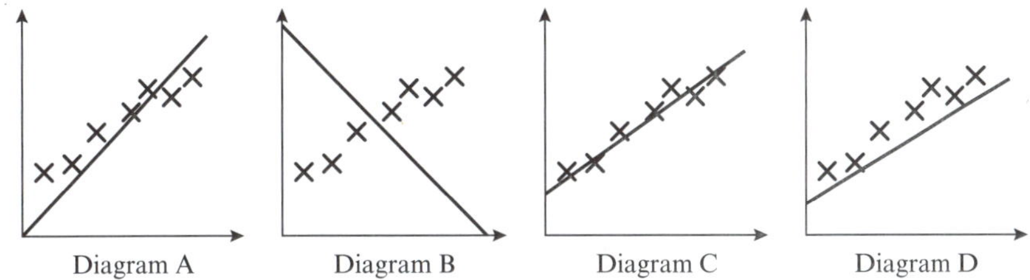

Complete the statement.

The line in Diagram _______ is the most appropriate line of best fit. [1]

Adapted from Cambridge IGCSE Mathematics (0580) Paper 22 Q5 June 2021 **[Total: 2]**

Example student response	Commentary
a It shows negative correlation	Although the three plotted points may appear to be negatively correlated, there are not enough points plotted to make a judgement about correlation. ***This answer scores 0 out of 1 mark.***
b Diagram C	The student has correctly identified that the line of best fit should follow the trend of the points, where roughly half the points should be above the line and half the points should be below the line. ***This answer scores 1 out of 1 mark.***

20 Now that you have gone through the commentary, try to write an improved answer for your own solution and edit the sample student response to improve their answer to each part.

17 Managing money

KNOWLEDGE FOCUS

In this chapter, you will answer questions on:

- calculating earnings (wages and salaries) in different situations
- using and manipulating formulae to calculate simple and compound interest
- solving problems related to simple and compound interest
- applying what you already know about percentages to work out discounts, profit and loss in everyday contexts
- using a calculator effectively to perform financial calculations
- reading and interpreting financial data provided in tables and charts
- using exponential growth and decay in relation to finance.

EXAM SKILLS FOCUS

In this chapter you will:

- demonstrate that you understand the command word 'show' and can successfully answer 'show' questions
- practise using your calculator effectively and show clear working.

In this chapter, the questions involve working with money, percentages, and interest. Accurate calculation and clear communication are both essential. You will often be given a final result and asked to 'show that' it is correct.

Show (that)	provide structured evidence that leads to a given result.

When you see the command word 'show (that)', you are being asked to prove a result, usually by starting with known information and taking logical steps to arrive at the target answer. These questions test your ability to build an argument using maths, not just get the answer. Even if you are confident in your calculator work, you will still need to show your reasoning line by line.

This chapter is also a great opportunity to practise using your calculator effectively. On calculator papers, it is not enough to just type in the numbers – you must lay out your method and give answers to the required level of accuracy (such as 2 decimal places or the nearest dollar).

17.1 Earning money

UNDERSTAND THESE TERMS

- Compound interest
- Cost price
- Discount
- Interest
- Interest rate
- Loss
- Profit
- Selling price
- Simple interest

1 A bricklayer earns $7.56 per hour.

How much would she earn for a 7-hour shift?

2 Calculate the hourly rate for each of the following payments.

a $85.98 for six hours.

b $554 for a 40-hour week.

c $508.55 for five 7-hour shifts.

d $9.54 for half an hour.

e $70.25 for 6 hours and 15 minutes.

f $12.33 for 20 minutes.

g 87 cents for 1.5 minutes.

3 Jamin is paid $13.86 for each kilogram of salt he scrapes from a salt pan. If Jamin delivers 58 kilograms, how much will he earn?

4 A group of 5 friends is raising money for a trip by washing cars. They are paid $22 for each car. If the group washes eight cars and then divides the money equally, how much will each member of the group be paid?

5 Justine sells pizzas and is paid a retainer of $220 per week plus a commission on sales. The rate of commission is 3.2% on all sales. How would Justine earn in three weeks if she sold 152 pizzas at $5 each?

6 An executive transport company pays drivers $9.24 per hour. Drivers earn time and a half for hours worked between 10.00 p.m. and 2.00 a.m. and double time for hours worked between 2.00 a.m. and 6.00 a.m.

The table shows a full-week timesheet for four drivers.

Driver	Normal hours	Hours between 10 p.m. and 2 a.m.	Hours between 2 a.m. and 6 a.m.
Michael	27	8	4.5
Anna	18	6.5	3
Brigita	35	7	1.5
Nigel	39	7	2

a Calculate the total amount paid to all four drivers for the week. [2]

b The company wants to reduce costs and considers removing double pay for the hours between 2.00 a.m. and 6.00 a.m., instead paying these hours at time and a half after 10.00 p.m.

Work out how much money the company would save on the total weekly wages for the four drivers under the new pay structure. [2]

[Total: 4]

7 Jacqueline is paid $875.60 per week before any tax or other deductions are taken off. The tax rate on Jacqueline's earnings is 34% and she also pays other deductions of $123 per week.

a Work out how much money Jacqueline has left each week after tax and other deductions have been taken off. [2]

b Calculate this amount as a percentage of the amount she earns before deductions. Give your answer to the nearest whole percent. [2]

[Total: 4]

8 Consider the following tax table and answer the questions that follow.

Taxable income	Income tax payable
$0–$9384	12% of the amount over $0
$9385–$32 400	15% of the amount over $9384
$32 401–$85 000	25% of the amount over $32 400
$85 001– $125 000	55% of the amount over $85 000

a Janin earns $5400, working as a member of staff on a summer camp.

Show that Janin pays $648 tax. [2]

b Bertrand earns $102 000 by selling cars at a used car dealership.

Show that Bertrand will pay a total of 26.5% of his earnings in tax. [2]

[Total: 4]

REFLECTION

How do you know that your solution has shown the given answer to be correct? How can you check that you have not left out important steps?

17.2 Borrowing and investing money

1 Mr Ritornello took out a loan to pay for a violin.

The amount he borrowed was $11 240, and he pays simple interest of 3.2% each year.

Work out how much interest Mr Ritornello will have paid after four years.

« RECALL AND CONNECT 1 «

When reporting pay or prices, explain why it is usually sensible to give answer to *at most* 2 decimal places.

2 Chu bought a car for $12 340. If the value of the car depreciates by 4.3% per year, what will the value of the car be after:

a 1 year? b 2 years? c 5 years? d 8 years?

Give your answers to the nearest dollar.

3 A painting is bought for \$350. If the value of the painting increases in value by 12% each year, after how many whole years will the value of the painting be more than \$1000?

4 The number of fish in a lake increases by 15% each year. After how many years will the fish population in the lake be doubled?

5 Oscar takes out a loan for \$15 000 and pays compound interest of 6.4% each year. What is the total amount that Oscar will have paid after three years?

6 A games enthusiast bought a computer for \$1240 on installment. The deposit was 10% and interest on the remaining balance is paid at a simple rate of 15% per year. The enthusiast is going to pay the remaining balance in 36 equal instalments. Calculate each instalment.

7 Sumon invests \$360 at 5.6% per year simple interest.

a Work out the amount of interest Sumon will earn after 5 years. [2]

b Calculate the total value of Sumon's investment after 5 years. [1]

c Determine the minimum number of whole years it will take for the value of Sumon's investment to be more than \$1000. [3]

[Total: 6]

8 Andrea invests a sum of money at a simple interest rate of 5% per year.

a Write down a formula for the total value of Andrea's investment after t years. [1]

b Calculate the number of years that it will take for the value of her investment to double. [2]

c Andrea is offered a compound interest rate of 3.6% instead. She invests \$1000.

Determine which investment will give her more money after 20 years. Show all your working. [3]

[Total: 6]

9 A driver buys a car for \$32 000 on a finance deal.

She pays a 12.5% deposit and agrees to pay simple interest of 12% per year on the remaining balance.

She will repay the rest in 24 equal monthly instalments.

a Calculate the deposit she pays. [1]

b Calculate the loan amount (the amount still to pay after the deposit). [1]

c Work out the total interest charged. [1]

d Calculate the value of each of the 24 monthly instalments. Give your answer to 2 decimal places. [3]

[Total: 6]

« RECALL AND CONNECT 2 «

If Jessica and Anwar both earn \$40 000 per annum to the nearest \$10 000, what is the maximum possible difference in the actual salaries? Remember, you studied upper and lower bounds in Chapter 13. Use this information to help you.

10 Bashir pays simple interest on a \$7000 loan for 6 years.

The total interest paid is £1155.

Show that the rate of simple interest is 2.75%. [2]

[Total: 2]

11 Jansit takes out a loan that is repaid using compound interest.

The compound interest rate is 5% per year and the amount owed after 6 years is \$16 751.20.

a Show that the amount Jansit borrowed was \$12 500. [3]

b Explain why compound interest results in a larger repayment than simple interest over the same time period and interest rate. [2]

[Total: 5]

REFLECTION

When completing a 'show that' question, how can you use the final answer to help you work out a good solution?

17.3 Buying and selling

1 Nicholas buys a house for \$430 000 and then sells it for \$520 000.

a Calculate Nicholas's profit.

b Calculate Nicholas's *percentage* profit.

2 Jason buys bottles of cola and sells the bottles with a 15% markup. If the bottles cost \$3.00 each and Jason sells all 60 that he buys, calculate Jason's profit.

3 Sara sells a textbook to a second-hand bookshop at a 15% loss. She is paid \$13.60 for the book. What was the original price of the book?

4 Alpinee provides fitness classes, usually priced at \$25 per class. If Alpinee decides to offer a 25% discount for new class members, how much does each new member save?

5 Brock is providing dance lessons at a 60% discount. If the discount price is \$7.40, what was the original price of a dance lesson?

6 Sangrika buys 500 shares in a motor repair company for $4.30 per share.

She sells half of them at a 20% loss and the other half at a 20% profit.

a Calculate the amount Sangrika received from selling

i the first 250 shares at a 20% loss [1]

ii the remaining 250 shares at a 20% profit. [1]

b Determine whether Sangrika makes an overall profit or loss, or breaks even. [3]

[Total: 5]

7 Frank buys 60 bottles of cola for $3.00 each.

He sells three-quarters of the bottles at a price 6% higher than what he paid and returns the remaining bottles to the wholesaler at a price 9% lower price than what he paid.

a Calculate how much profit Frank makes on the bottles he sells. [2]

b Calculate how much money Frank loses on the returned bottles. [2]

c Determine whether Frank makes an overall profit or loss, or breaks even. [1]

[Total: 5]

8 On Monday, tennis rackets in a sports store are being sold at a 15% discount.

On Tuesday, a further 20% discount is applied.

a Explain why the total discount is not 35% of the original price. [2]

b Show that the actual final discount on the original price is 32%. [2]

[Total: 4]

« RECALL AND CONNECT 3 «

When carrying our percentage changes, we always calculate the change of a particular value. What is that value?

REFLECTION

When you use a calculator, how do you make sure your input is correct? How do you show your method even when you used the calculator to find the answer?

SELF-ASSESSMENT CHECKLIST

Let's revisit the Knowledge and Exam skills focus for this chapter.
Decide how confident you are with each statement.

	Now I can	Show it	Needs more work	Almost there	Confident to move on
1	calculate earnings (wages and salaries) in different situations	Look up examples of pay slips online and check to see if you understand the calculations.			
2	use and manipulate formulae to calculate simple and compound interest	Complete Section 17.2 and write some more questions of your own. Do your answers agree with those of your friends?			
3	solve problems related to simple and compound interest	Find an online savings calculator and compare results with your manual calculations.			
4	apply what you already know about percentages to work out discounts, profit and loss in everyday contexts	Find some sale advertisements online and check the calculations of new prices. Do your new prices match those in the advertisements?			
5	use a calculator effectively to perform financial calculations	Work through questions from past papers, using the mark scheme. Make sure your answers match those given.			
6	read and interpret financial data provided in tables and charts	Find examples of financial data online and read the explanations. Can you repeat the calculations for yourself?			
7	use exponential growth and decay in relation to finance	Find examples of exponential growth online and try to repeat the calculations for yourself.			

CONTINUED

	Now I can	Show it	Needs more work	Almost there	Confident to move on
8	answer questions that use the 'show that' command	Complete the Exam practice questions for this chapter successfully, giving full explanations. Compare your solutions to those provided and check that you have no details missing.			
9	use a calculator effectively and show clear working.	Find a compound interest question on a past examination paper. Solve it using your calculator, then write down each step clearly. Annotate your answer to show what each line in your working means.			

18 Curved graphs

KNOWLEDGE FOCUS

In this chapter, you will answer questions on:

- constructing a table of values to draw graphs called parabolas
- sketching and interpreting parabolas
- constructing a table of values to draw graphs called hyperbolas
- interpreting curved graphs
- using graphs to find the approximate solutions to quadratic equations
- constructing tables of values to draw graphs of the form ax^n, $\frac{a}{x}$, $\frac{a}{x^2}$ and $ab^x + c$
- recognising, sketching and interpreting graphs of functions
- estimating the gradients of curves by drawing tangents
- using graphs to find the approximate solutions to associated equations
- differentiating functions to find gradients and stationary (turning) points.

EXAM SKILLS FOCUS

In this chapter you will:

- demonstrate that you understand the command word 'sketch' and can answer a 'sketch' question
- develop your understanding of the command word 'show (that)'.

This chapter focuses on curved graphs, including parabolas and hyperbolas. You will frequently be asked to 'sketch' in this chapter.

Sketch	make a simple freehand drawing showing the key features.
Show (that)	provide structured evidence that leads to a given result.

To sketch a graph means to draw a freehand diagram showing the key features: shape, intercepts and turning points. You will practise this throughout Section 18.1, where you are asked to sketch quadratic graphs and label important points.

You will also answer more 'show (that)' questions, especially in Section 18.7, where you are expected to provide clear algebraic or graphical reasoning that leads to a stated result. For example, you may need to show a given derivative or demonstrate where a curve has turning points.

18.1 Review of quadratic graphs (the parabola)

UNDERSTAND THESE TERMS

- Minimum
- Maximum
- Asymptote
- Derivative of function
- Differentiation
- Exponential
- Stationary point
- Turning point

≪ RECALL AND CONNECT 1 ≪

The order in which you work out each calculation can be remember by using either BODMAS or BIDMAS. Write down what this means and explain how you use it.

1 Complete the following tables of values, then sketch each graph.

a

x	−3	−2	−1	0	1	2	3
$y = x^2 + 2$							

b

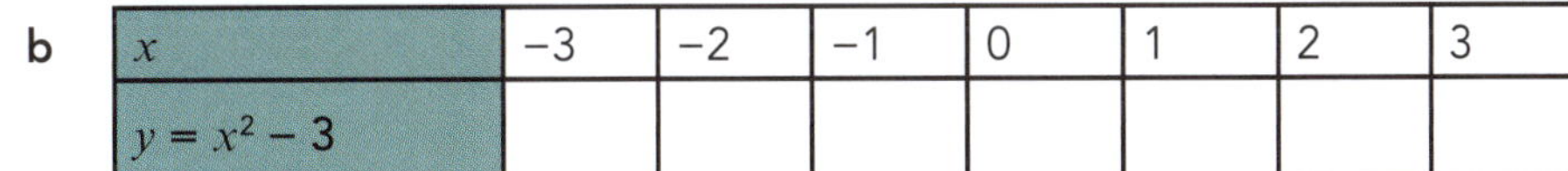

x	−3	−2	−1	0	1	2	3
$y = x^2 - 3$							

c

x	−3	−2	−1	0	1	2	3
$y = x^2 + 2x + 2$							

d

x	−3	−2	−1	0	1	2	3
$y = x^2 - 2x + 1$							

e

x	−3	−2	−1	0	1	2	3
$y = -x^2 + 2x + 1$							

f

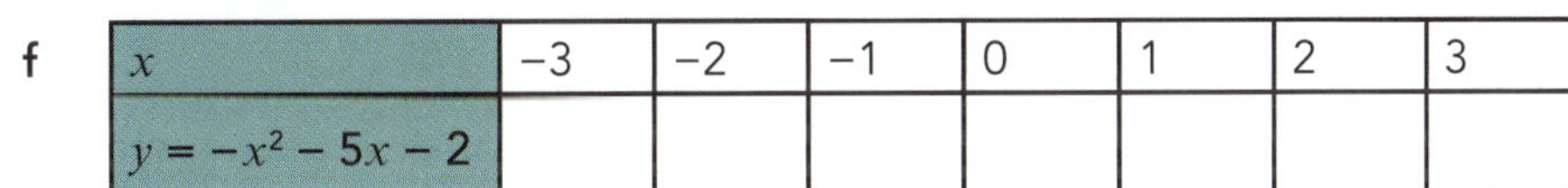

x	−3	−2	−1	0	1	2	3
$y = -x^2 - 5x - 2$							

2 A quadratic graph has minimum point at $(3, -16)$ and x-intercepts at -1 and 7. Find the equation of the graph.

3 Sketch the graph of $y = x^2 - 16$. [3]

[Total: 3]

4 Sketch the graph of $y = -x^2 + 4$. [3]

[Total: 3]

5 Sketch the graph of $y = 2x^2 - 18$. [3]

[Total: 3]

6 Sketch the graph of $y = x^2 + 2$. [3]

[Total: 3]

7 The graph of a curve is given by

$y = x^2 - 4x - 5$

a Complete the square to find the coordinates of the turning point. [2]

b Hence solve the equation $x^2 - 4x - 5 = 0$ to find the x-intercepts of the curve. [2]

c Find the y-intercept of the curve. [1]

d Hence sketch the graph of the curve. [2]

[Total: 7]

REFLECTION

Some questions require you to plot the graphs as accurately as possible. Others expect you to provide the general shape and main features. How do you know which approach you need to take for each question?

18.2 Drawing reciprocal graphs (the hyperbola)

1 Complete the following tables of values, then sketch each graph.

a

x	−6	−4	−3	−2	−1		1	2	3	4	6
$y = \frac{3}{x}$											

b

x	−6	−4	−3	−2	−1		1	2	3	4	6
$y = -\frac{2}{x}$											

c

x	−6	−4	−3	−2	−1		1	2	3	4	6
$y = -\frac{4}{x}$											

d

x	−6	−4	−3	−2	−1		1	2	3	4	6
$y = \frac{6}{x}$											

2 Sketch the graph of $y = \frac{5}{x} - 2$. Label the asymptotes and the coordinates of one point. [3]

[Total: 3]

18.3 Using graphs to solve quadratic equations

1 Explain how drawing the graph of $y = x^3 - 3x - 7$ helps you find approximate solutions to the equation $x^3 - 3x - 7 = 0$.

Why is drawing a graph sometimes better than using trial and improvement to solve an equation?

2 Explain why solutions from graphs are, usually, only approximations.

3 a Construct a table of values for $y = x^2 - 3x - 7$, for $-4 \leqslant x \leqslant 6$. [1]

b Plot the points on a grid and join them with a smooth curve. [2]

c Use your graph to solve the equation $x^2 - 3x - 7 = 0$.
Give your answers correct to 1 decimal place. [1]

d Use your graph to solve the equation $x^2 - 3x - 7 = 1$.
Give your answers correct to 1 decimal place. [2]

[Total: 6]

4 a Construct a table of values for $y = x^2 - 2x - 1$, for $-2 \leqslant x \leqslant 4$. [1]

b Plot the points on a grid and join them with a smooth curve. [2]

c Use your graph to solve the equation $x^2 - 2x - 1 = 0$.
Give your answers correct to 1 decimal place. [1]

d Use your graph to solve the equation $x^2 = 2x + 2$.
Give your answers correct to 1 decimal place. [2]

[Total: 6]

5 a Construct a table of values for $y = -x^2 + 3x + 2$, for $-2 \leqslant x \leqslant 5$. [1]

b Plot the points on a grid and join them with a smooth curve. [2]

c Use your graph to solve the equation $-x^2 + 3x + 2 = 0$.
Give your answers correct to 1 decimal place. [1]

d Use your graph to solve the equation $-x^2 + 2x + 7 = -x$.
Give your answers correct to 1 decimal place. [2]

[Total: 6]

18.4 Simultaneous linear and non-linear equations

≪ RECALL AND CONNECT 2 ≪

Can you remember how to solve quadratic equations in the form $ax^2 + bx + c = 0$, using the quadratic formula? Write out the equation and make sure you understand how to substitute the coefficients into it.

1 Use a graphical method to solve each pair of simultaneous equations, giving your answers to 1 decimal place.

a $y = x^2$ and $y = 2x$

b $y = \frac{3}{x}$ and $y = 3x$

c $y = x^2 - 4x - 5$ and $y = x - 1$

2 Solve each pair of simultaneous equations algebraically. Give your answers to 2 decimal places where necessary.

a $x^2 + y^2 = 13$
$y = x + 5$

b $y^2 = 27 - x^2$
$2x - y - 3 = 0$

c $y = \frac{3}{x}$
$x + y = 7$

3 These equations represent a curve and a straight line.

$y = x^2 + 4$

$y = x - 3$

a Draw the graph of $y = x^2 + 4$ for $-3 \leqslant x \leqslant 3$. [2]

b On the same grid, draw the line $y = x - 3$. [1]

c Use your graph to determine whether the equations have any solutions in common. Explain your reasoning. [1]

[Total: 4]

REFLECTION

How can you check that you have the correct solutions for these equations? Do you check every time?

18.5 Other non-linear graphs

1 a Draw the graph of $y = x^3 + 2$ for $-3 \leqslant x \leqslant 3$ by completing the table.

x	−3	−2	−1	0	1	2	3
x^3							
2							
y							

b Use the graph to solve the following equations.

i $x^3 + 2 = 0$

ii $x^3 + 2 = 2x + 1$

《 RECALL AND CONNECT 3 《

Write down what m and c mean in the context of sketching a line with the equation $y = mx + c$.

2 a Draw the graph of $y = x^3 + 3x$ for $-3 \leqslant x \leqslant 3$ by completing the table.

x	−3	−2	−1	0	1	2	3
y							

b Use the graph to solve the following equations.

i $x^3 + 3x = 0$

ii $x^3 + 2x - 1 = 0$

3 Complete the table, then draw the graph of $y = x^3 + 2x^2 - 11x - 12$ for $-4 \leqslant x \leqslant 4$.

x	−4	−3	−2	−1	0	1	2	3	4
x^3									
$2x^2$									
$-11x$									
−12									
y									

4 a Sketch the graphs of $y = \frac{12}{x}$ and $y = x^3 - 1$ for $-3 \leqslant x \leqslant 3$ on the same set of axes. [3]

b Use the graphs to find the approximate solutions to the equation $x^3 + 3 = 4 + \frac{12}{x}$. [1]

[Total: 4]

5 a Sketch the graph of $y = 1.5^x$ for $-6 \leqslant x \leqslant 4$. [2]

b Use your graph to estimate the value of $1.5^{2.5}$. [2]

[Total: 4]

18.6 Finding the gradient of a curve

1 As part of an experiment, Jack poured liquid into a container of unusual shape at a steady rate. Jack recorded the depth of the liquid at 10-second intervals.

Time, t (s)	0	10	20	30	40	50	60	70	80
Depth, d (cm)	0	2.8	5.8	9.0	12.2	15.7	20.8	26.5	33.9

a Plot the graph of d against t.

Draw the tangent to the curve at $t = 50$ seconds.

Find the gradient of the tangent.

b Explain what this gradient means in this context.

c Draw the shape of a possible container.

2 **a** Copy and complete the table of values for $y = x^2 - 2x - 3$.

x	−2.5	−2.0	−1.5	−1.0	−0.5	0	0.5	1.0
y	8.25	5						

x	1.5	2.0	2.5	3.0	3.5	4.0	4.5
y							

b Plot these points and join them to form a smooth curve.

c Find the gradient of the graph at the point where $x = 3$.

d Give the coordinates of the point where y stops decreasing and begins increasing.

e Find the gradient of the curve at this point and comment on the significance of the result.

REFLECTION

What steps have you taken to make sure your diagrams and calculations are as accurate as possible?

3 A goldfish bowl is being filled with water. The graph shows how the diameter of the surface of the water changes as the depth of the water increases.

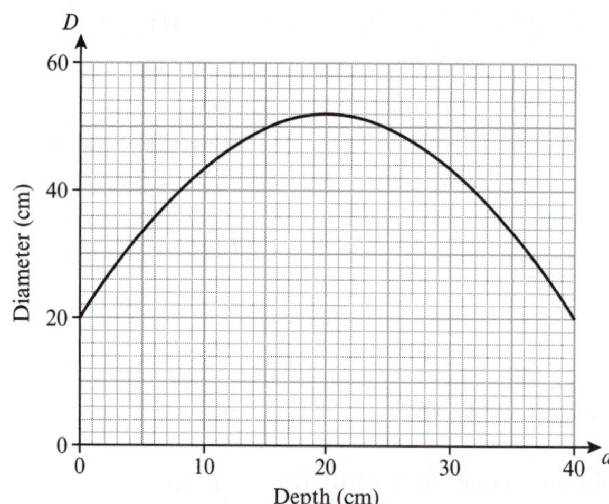

a On a copy of the graph, draw the tangent at the point where $d = 10$ cm and find its gradient. [3]

b Explain what this gradient tells you. [1]

c Without drawing another tangent, state the gradient of the curve where $d = 30$ cm. [1]

[Total: 5]

18.7 Derivatives of functions

1 Find $\frac{dy}{dx}$ for each of the following.

a $y = x^3$

b $y = x^7$

c $y = 5x^6$

d $y = -2x^8$

e $y = 12x^2$

f $y = x^3 + x^4$

g $y = 3x^4 + 4x^3$

h $y = 6x^7 - 4x^2$

i $y = -7x^3 - 3x$

j $y = 6x^3 - \frac{1}{2}x^{12}$

k $y = 3x^3 + 4x^2 - 3x + 2$

l $y = \frac{2}{3}x^9 + \frac{1}{4}x^{52} + 1$

m $y = \frac{2}{5}x^3 - \frac{3}{4}x^7 - \frac{1}{8}$

2 Find the gradient of each curve at the point with the given x-coordinate.

	Graph	x-coordinate
a	$y = 4x^3$	$x = 3$
b	$y = 14x^2$	$x = 1$
c	$y = 4x^3 + 3x^2 - 6x + 1$	$x = 3$
d	$y = \frac{1}{3}x^4 - \frac{4}{5}x^3 + x^2$	$x = \frac{1}{2}$

3 Find the coordinates of the point where the curve with equation $y = 3x^3 - 2x + 1$ has gradient 2.

4 Find the x-coordinates of the points where the curve with equation $y = 4x^3 - 3x - 1$ has gradient zero.

5 Differentiate each of the following.

a $y = 5(x + 4)$

b $y = 3(x^2 + 4x)$

c $y = x(x^2 - 4x)$

d $y = 5x^4(2x^3 - 4x^2)$

e $y = (x + 3)(x + 4)$

f $y = (x + 3)(x + 4) + (x + 5)(x + 6)$

g $y = (3x - 1)^2$

h $y = \frac{1}{4}(x^2 + 4x)$

i $y = 3(x + 4)(x - 4)$

j $y = \frac{2}{5}x^3\left(x + \frac{1}{3}\right)$

6 Find the turning point or points on the following curves and explain whether each point is a maximum or a minimum.

a $y = x^2 - 4x + 1$

b $y = -3x^2 + 2x - 2$

c $y = 2x(x - 3)$

d $y = 3x(x^2 + 2x + 2)$

e $y = x^4 + 5$

7 The curve with equation $y = ax^2 + ax$ is parallel to the line with equation $y = 2x + 1$ at the point where $x = 2$.

Show that $a = \frac{2}{5}$. [4]

[Total: 4]

8 Show that the equation of the tangent to the curve $y = 2x^2 - 3$ at the point where $x = -1$ is $y = -4x - 5$. [4]

[Total: 4]

9 A curve has equation $y = x^3 - 21x + 37$.

a Using differentiation, find the equation of the tangent to the curve at the point where $x = 3$. [3]

b This tangent meets the coordinate axes at points A and B.

Show that the area of the triangle OAB is $\frac{289}{12}$. [2]

[Total: 5]

REFLECTION

There are often several ways of completing questions like this. Review your solutions and think carefully about whether you could have found the same answers, but more quickly.

10 a Show that the curve $y = x^3 - 3x + 1$ has two turning points at $(1, -1)$ and $(-1, 3)$. [3]

b Determine which is the maximum point and which is the minimum point. [2]

c Hence sketch the curve. [2]

[Total: 7]

11 A rectangle has a perimeter of 24 cm.

a If the length of the rectangle is x cm, write down an expression for the width and hence show that the area, A cm^2, is given by $A = 12 - x^2$. [2]

b Differentiate your expression for A and find the value of x for which A is a maximum. [3]

c Calculate the maximum area of the rectangle. [2]

[Total: 7]

12 A rectangular tin box without a lid has a square base of side x cm and a height of h cm.

a If the surface area is A cm^2, express A in terms of h and x. [2]

b If $A = 48$, express h in terms of x. [2]

c Hence show that the volume V cm^3 is given by

$V = 12 - \frac{1}{4}x^3$ [2]

d Calculate the value of x for which the volume is a maximum and find its maximum volume. [3]

[Total: 9]

SELF-ASSESSMENT CHECKLIST

Let's revisit the Knowledge and Exam skills focus for this chapter.
Decide how confident you are with each statement.

	Now I can	Show it	Needs more work	Almost there	Confident to move on
1	construct a table of values to draw graphs called parabolas	Plot the curve with the equation $y = x^3 - 4x^2 + 3x + 1$. Use an online graph plotter to check your answer.			
2	sketch and interpret parabolas	Draw sketches of all the possible shapes for quadratic and cubic graphs.			
3	construct a table of values to draw graphs called hyperbolas	Create a table of values and plot the graph of $y = 3 - \frac{1}{x}$. Label any asymptotes.			
4	interpret curved graphs	Pick a graph from this chapter. Write a sentence explaining its key features (e.g. where it increases or turns).			
5	use graphs to find the approximate solutions to quadratic equations	Plot the curve with the equation $y = x^3 - 3x - 4$ and use your graph to solve the equation $x^3 - 3x - 4 = 0$.			

CONTINUED

	Now I can	Show it	Needs more work	Almost there	Confident to move on
6	recognise, sketch and interpret graphs of functions	Sketch the curve with equation $y = x^2 - 4x + 3$ and label your diagram with the most significant features. Check your answer using an online graph plotter.			
7	estimate the gradients of curves by drawing tangents	Plot the graph of $y = x^3$ and estimate the gradient at several points. Then use differentiation to check your answers. How close were your estimates? Can you make them any better? How?			
8	use graphs to find the approximate solutions to associated equations	Use the graph with the equation $y = x^3 - 4x + 1$ to solve the equation $x^3 - 3x + 2 = 0$.			
9	differentiate functions to find gradients and stationary (turning) points	Find the stationary points on the curve with the equation $y = x^3 - 4x + 1$. Work out which is a maximum and which is a minimum.			
10	demonstrate understanding of the command word 'sketch' and answer a 'sketch' question	Sketch the curve with the equation $y = x^3 - 4x^2 + 3$ and label your diagram with the most significant features. Check your answer using an online graph plotter.			
11	demonstrate understanding of the command word 'show (that)'.	Show that the turning point on the curve with the equation $y = x^2 - 8x + 1$ is $(4, -15)$ and explain why you know it is a minimum.			

19 Symmetry

KNOWLEDGE FOCUS

In this chapter, you will answer questions on:

- identifying line symmetry in two-dimensional shapes
- finding the order of rotational symmetry of two-dimensional shapes
- recognising and using symmetrical properties of triangles, quadrilaterals and circles
- recognising symmetry properties of prisms and pyramids
- applying symmetry properties of circles to solve problems.

EXAM SKILLS FOCUS

In this chapter you will:

- identify when a question requires explanation or justification, rather than simple calculation or recall.

In this chapter, you will explore symmetry in both two-dimensional and three-dimensional shapes, as well as how symmetrical properties help you solve problems involving angles, circles and solids.

Describe	state the points of a topic/give characteristics and main features.
Explain	set out purposes or reasons/make the relationships between things clear/say why and/or how and support with relevant evidence.

Some examination questions ask you to 'describe' or 'explain' your reasoning, not just give a numerical answer. It is important to identify when an explanation is required and to use correct mathematical vocabulary (for example, in this chapter, that might be cyclic quadrilateral, perpendicular bisector or angle in a semicircle). These are the kinds of answers that mark schemes reward with method marks, so practice is essential.

19.1 Symmetry in two dimensions

1 Copy each of the following shapes and draw dotted lines to show as many lines of symmetry as you can. If there are none, write 'none'.

a

b 

c 

d 

e 

f 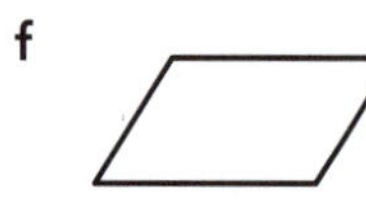

g 

h 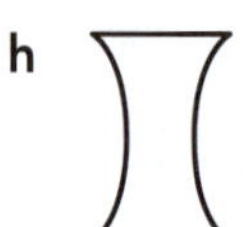

i 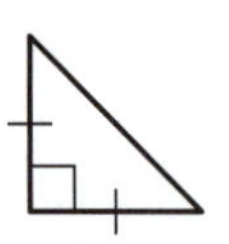

j 

k 

UNDERSTAND THESE TERMS

- Line of symmetry
- Rotational symmetry
- Axis of symmetry
- Centre of rotation
- Plane symmetry
- Cyclic quadrilateral
- Perpendicular bisector
- Subtended angle
- Alternate segment

REFLECTION

How do you know that you have identified all the lines of symmetry and have not counted any twice? What can you do to make sure?

« RECALL AND CONNECT 1 «

Which quadrilaterals always have at least one line of symmetry?

2 State the order of rotational symmetry for each of the shapes in Question 1. If there is no rotational symmetry, write 'none'.

3 **a** Look at the shaded shape in the diagram.

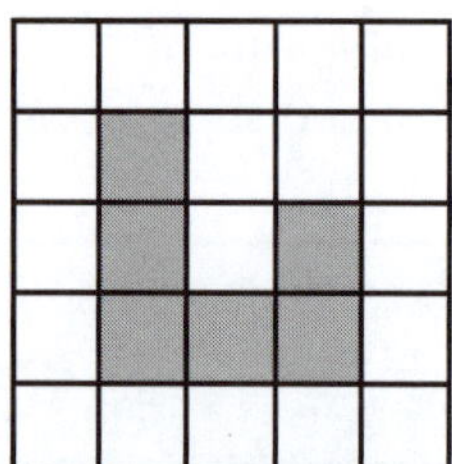

i State the order of rotational symmetry. [1]

ii Copy the diagram and shade one more square, so that the pattern has exactly one line of symmetry. [1]

b Look at the shaded shape in the diagram.

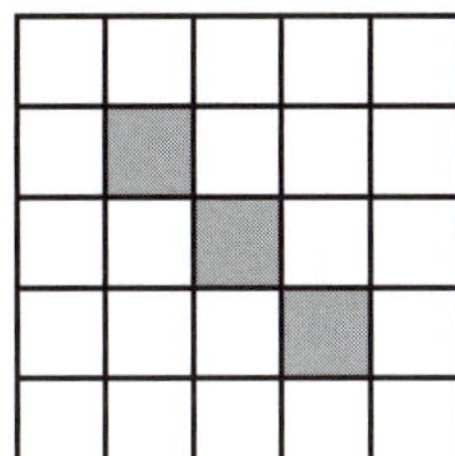

i State the order of rotational symmetry for this pattern. [1]

ii Copy the diagram and shade **two** more squares, so that the order of rotational symmetry remains unchanged. [2]

[Total: 5]

REFLECTION

Mark schemes are provided for the examination skills questions. How well did your solution match the mark schemes? Were there any parts you missed each time? Where there is more than one possible answer, try to work out *all* the possible solutions.

19.2 Symmetry in three dimensions

《 RECALL AND CONNECT 2 《

Draw a diagram to show you understand each of the following terms covered in Chapter 3.

a Complementary angles **b** Supplementary angles

c Angles round a point **d** Vertically opposite angles

e Corresponding angles **f** Alternate angles

g Co-interior angles

1 Write down the number of planes of symmetry for each of the following shapes.

a

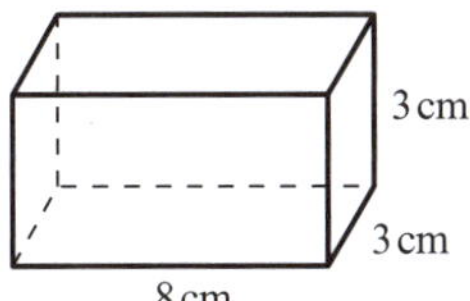

b

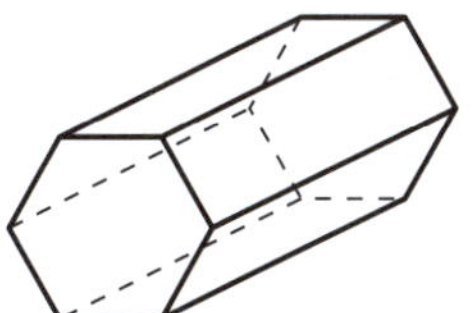

c

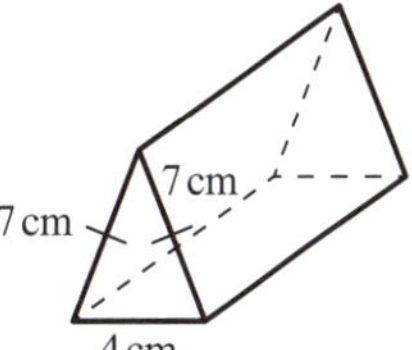

d

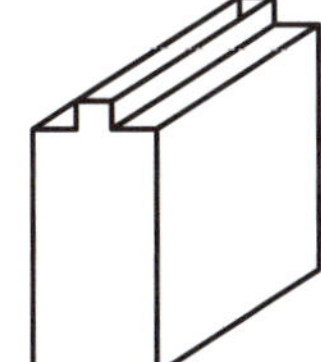

e

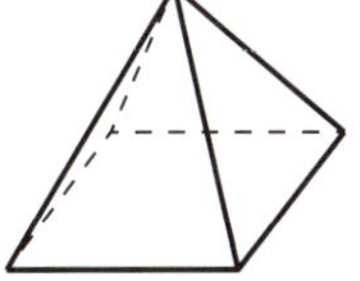

f

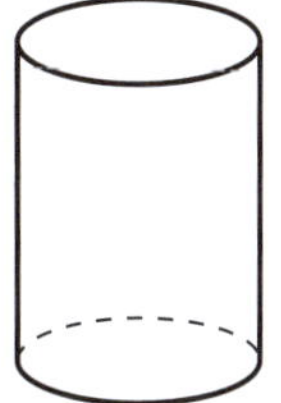

2 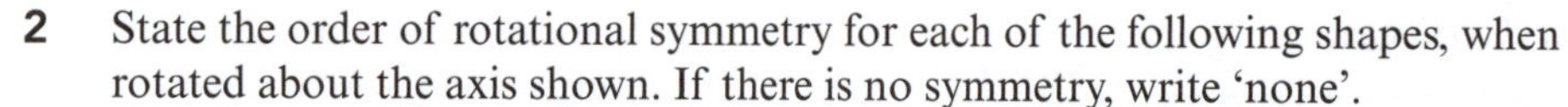
State the order of rotational symmetry for each of the following shapes, when rotated about the axis shown. If there is no symmetry, write 'none'.

a

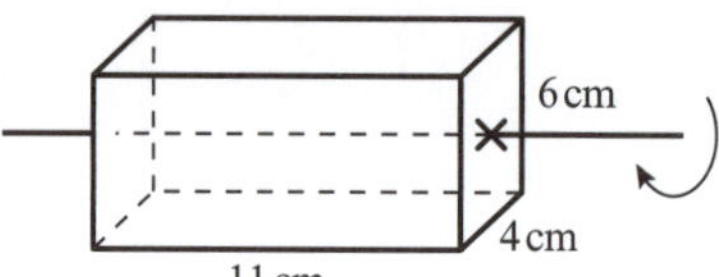

b

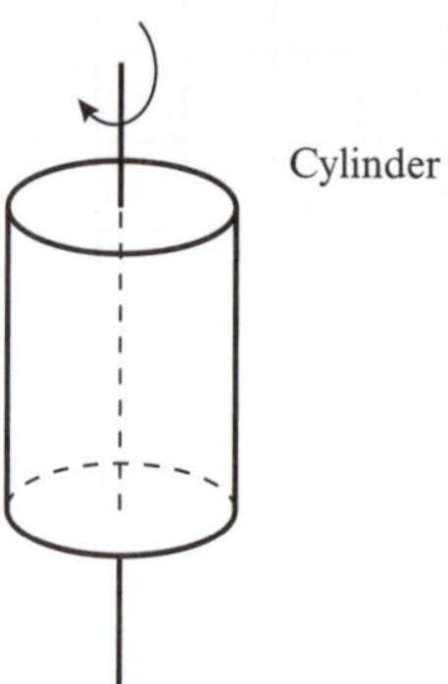

c

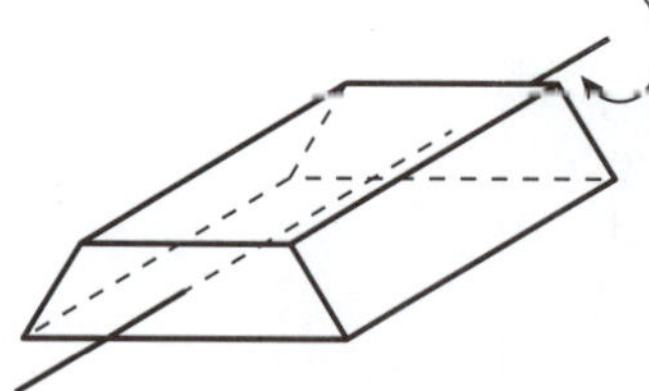

d

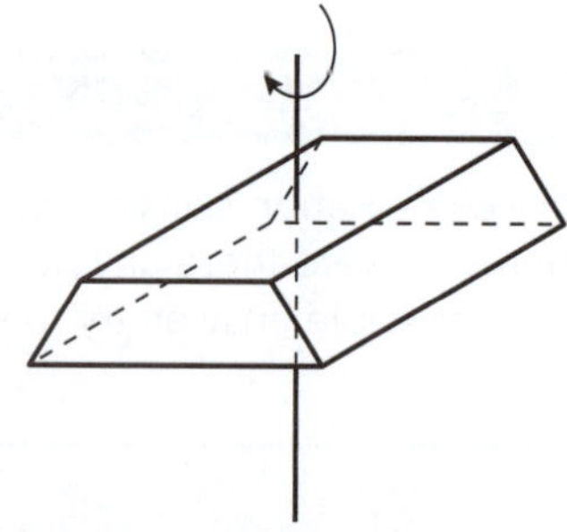

REFLECTION

Have you practised copying diagrams in three dimensions? Sometimes this can be very helpful, so you can add information but still see the original. How well and how quickly can you copy them?

19.3 Symmetry properties of circles

<< RECALL AND CONNECT 3 <<

Use Pythagoras' theorem to calculate the length of the hypotenuse of a right-angled triangle with short sides of length 6.2 cm and 7.9 cm.

1 Calculate d for each diagram.

a

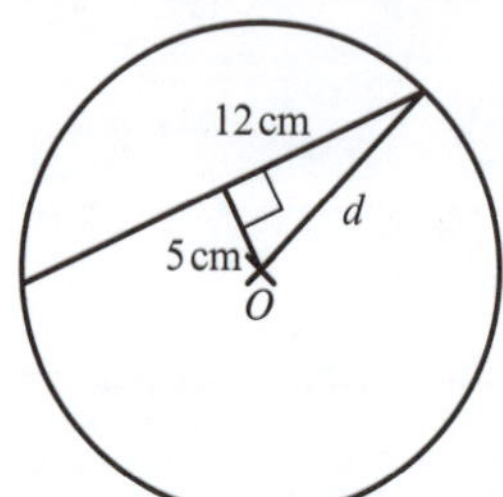

b

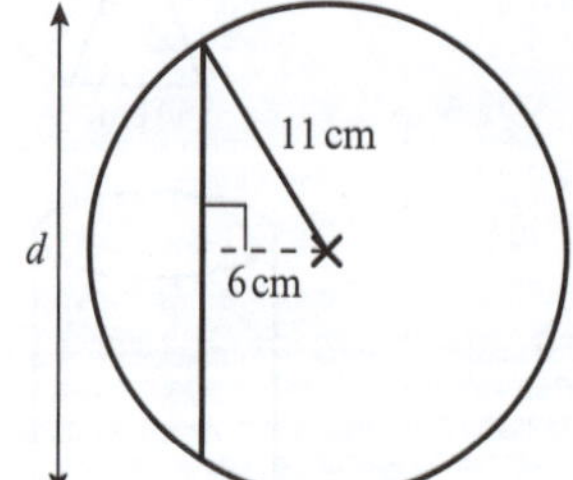

c

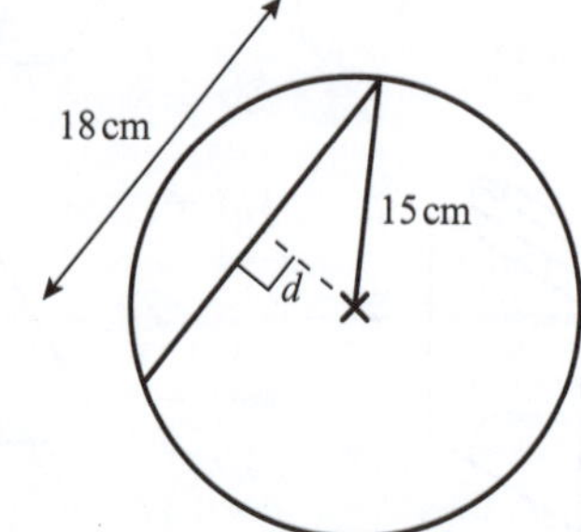

2 Find the length, *d*.

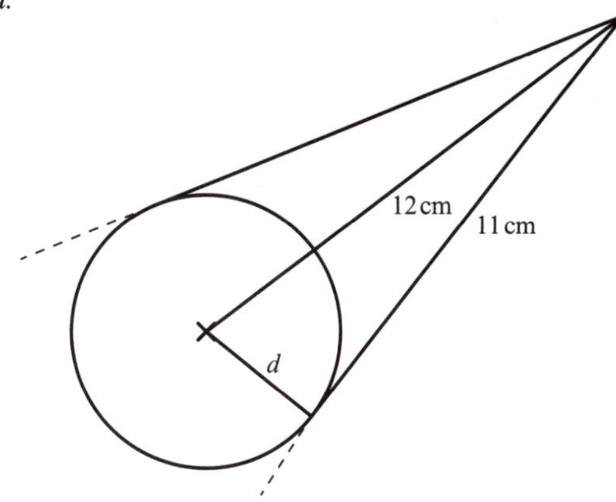

3 Find the length, *d*.

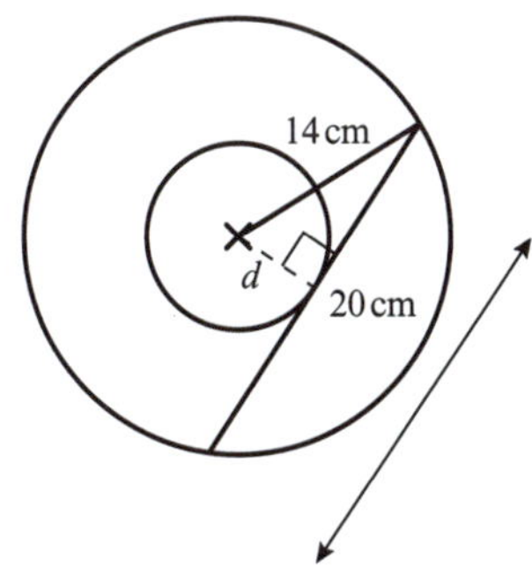

4 Find the length, *d*.

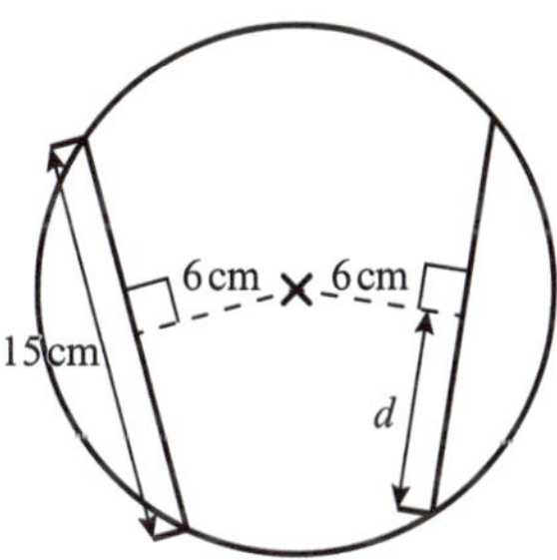

5 In the diagram, the radius of the circle is 7 cm. Points *A* and *B* lie on the circle, and the chord *AB* is 10 cm long.

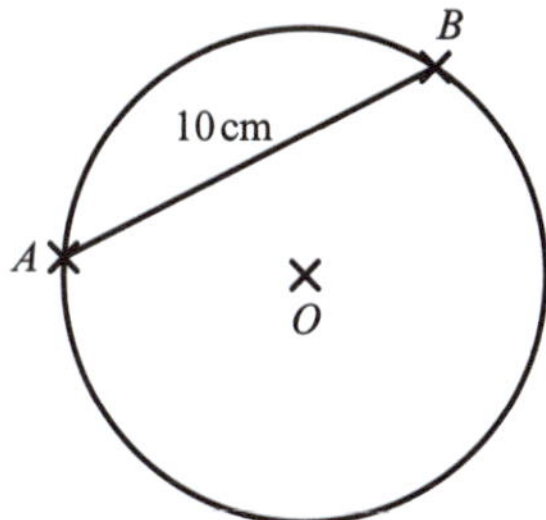

a Show that the perpendicular bisector of *AB* passes through the centre of the circle. [2]

b Calculate the distance from the centre of the circle to the chord *AB*. [2]

[Total: 4]

19.4 Angle relationships in circles

<< RECALL AND CONNECT 4 <<

What is the angle sum in a triangle?

How do you know if a triangle is isosceles?

1 Find the value of x for each of the following diagrams.

a

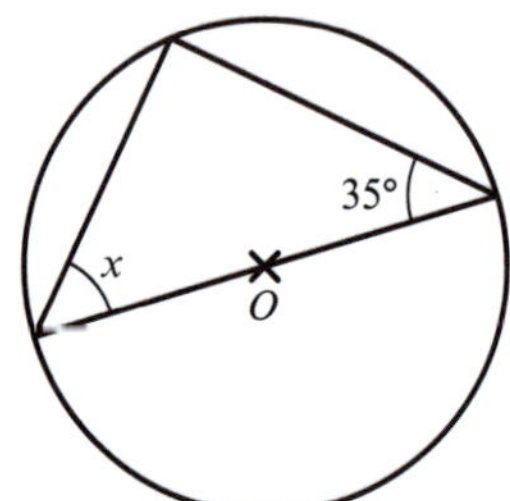

b

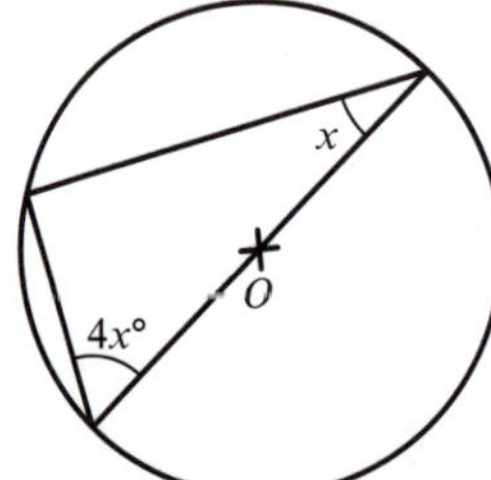

c

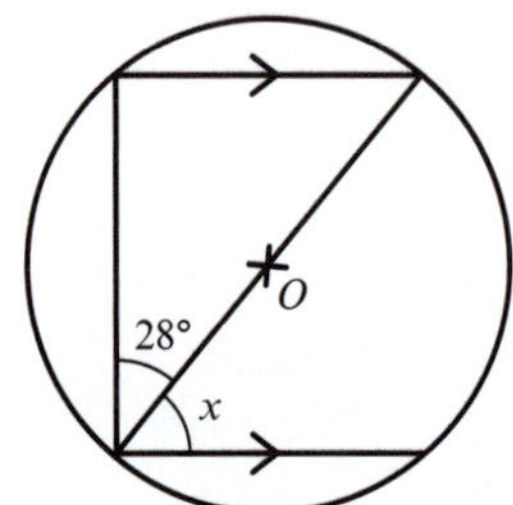

d

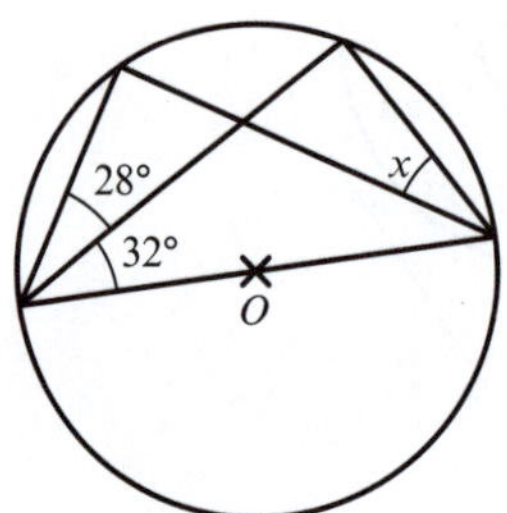

2 Find the value of x for each of the following diagrams.

a

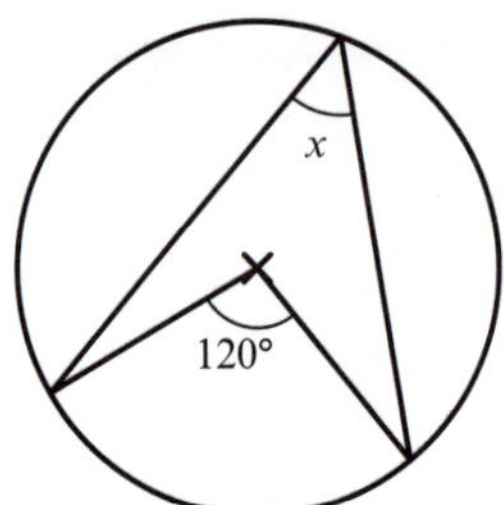

b

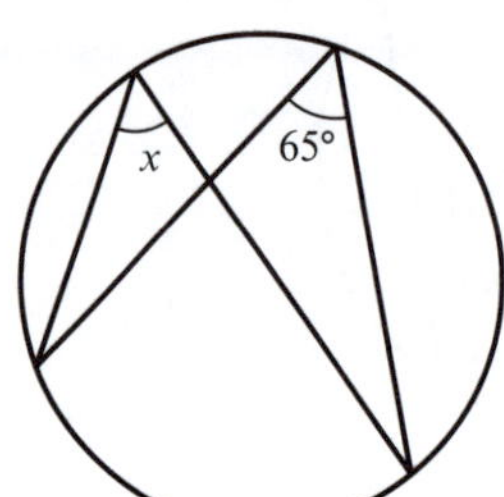

c

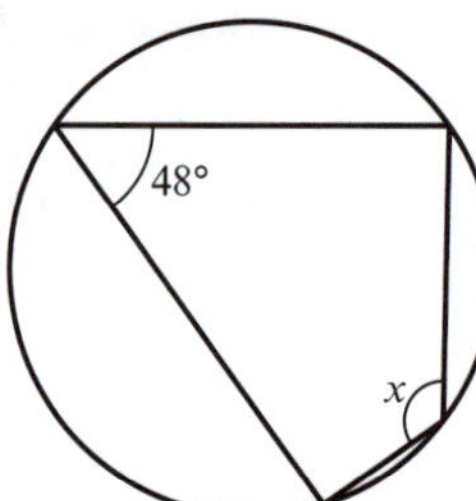

d

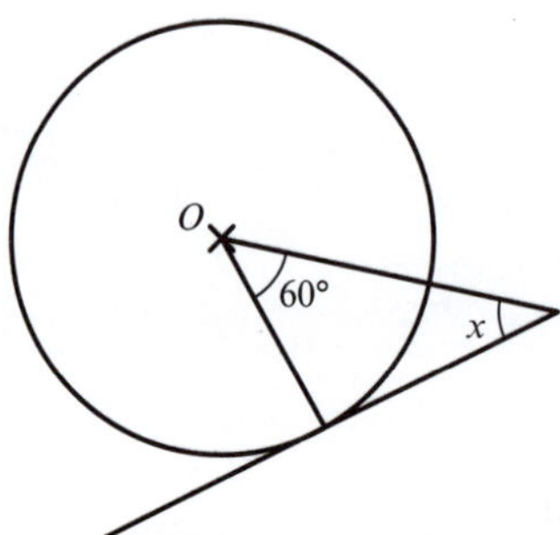

e

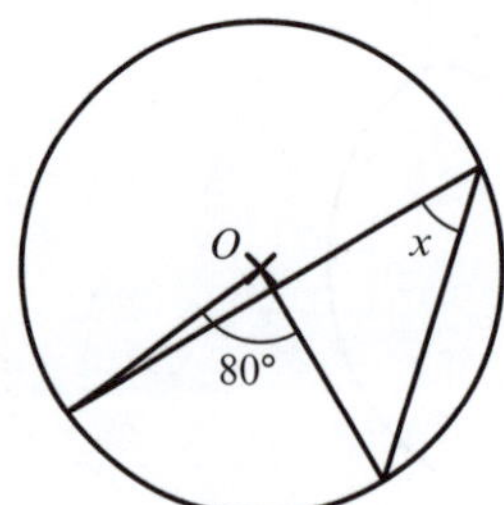

f

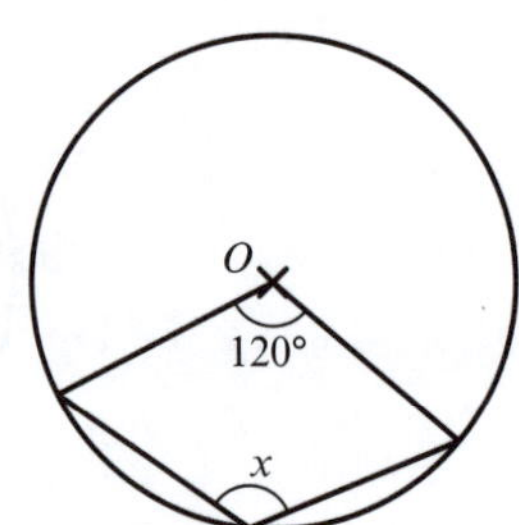

g

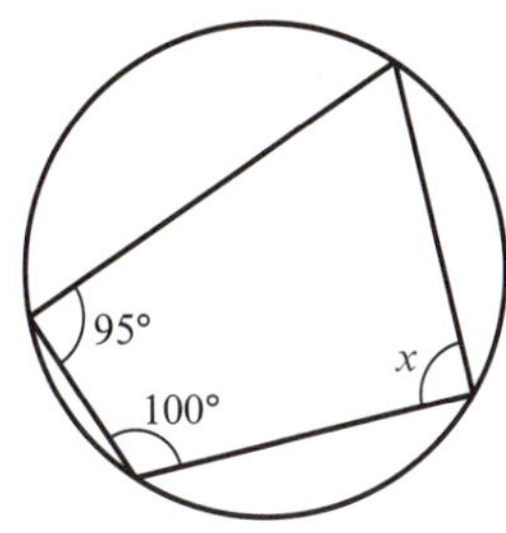

h

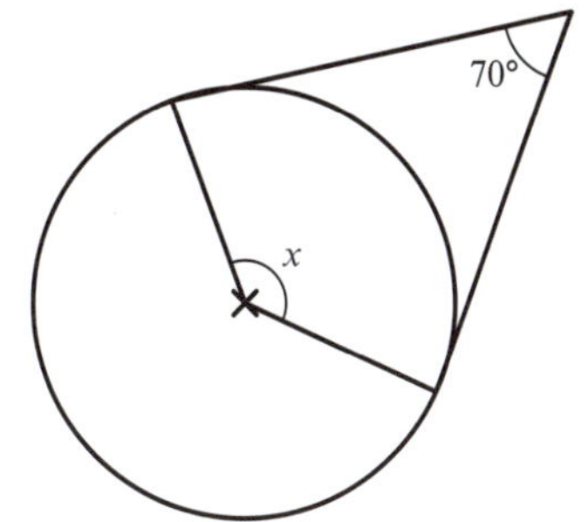

i

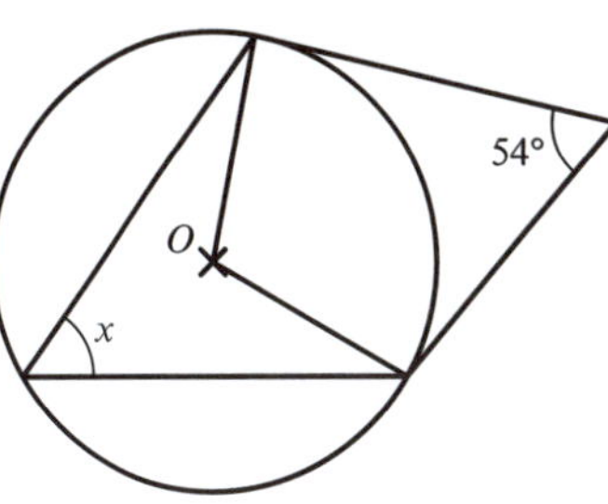

j

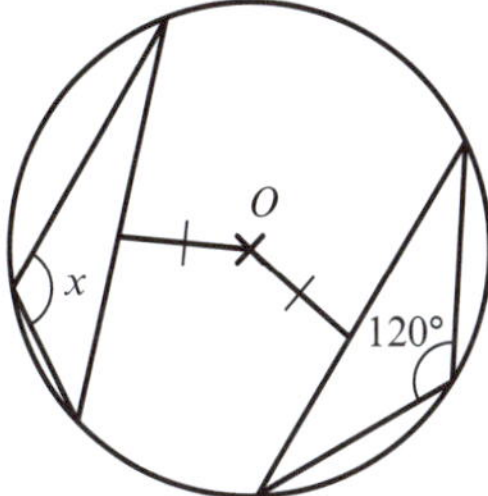

k

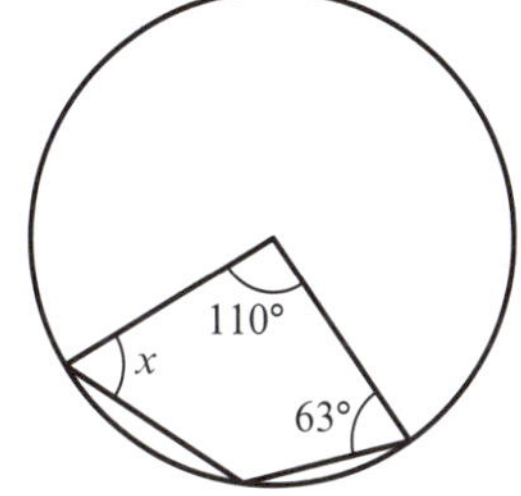

l

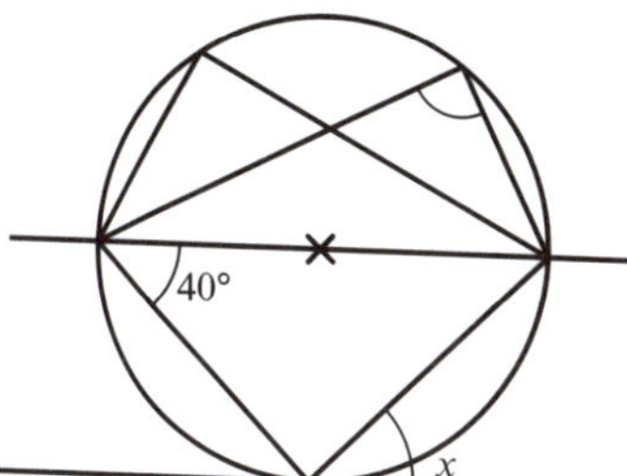

m

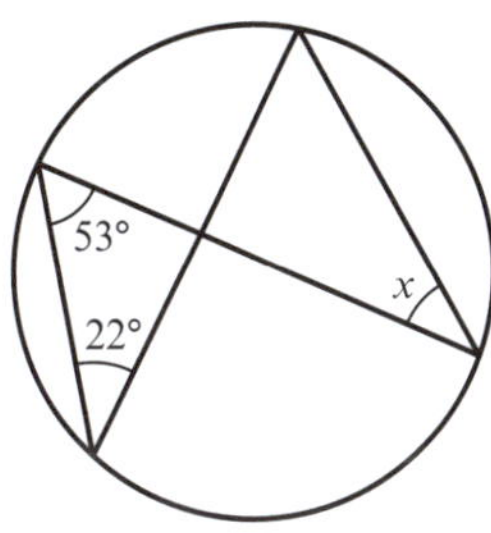

n

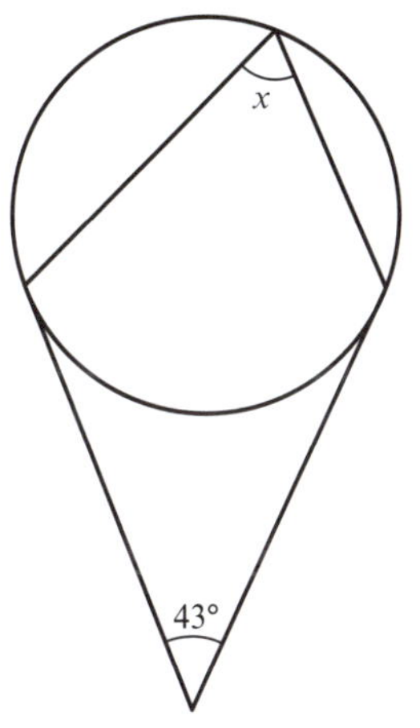

3 Find the value of x for each of the following diagrams.

a

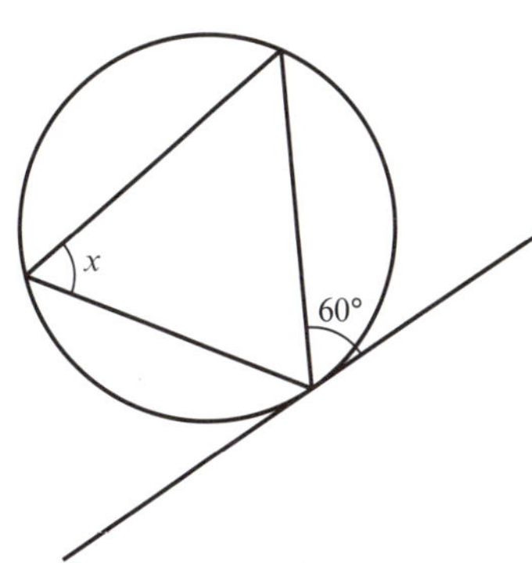

b

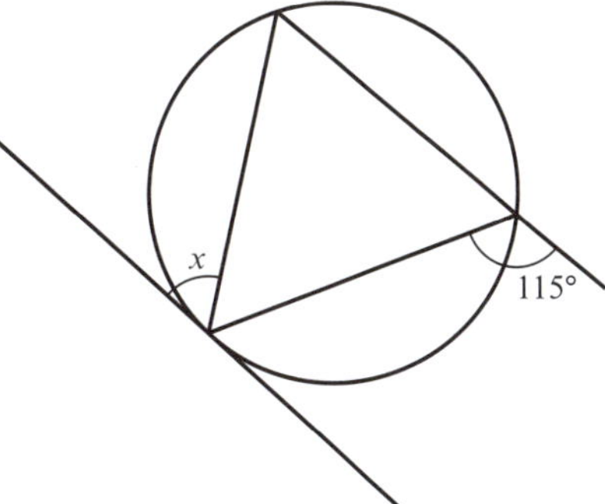

c

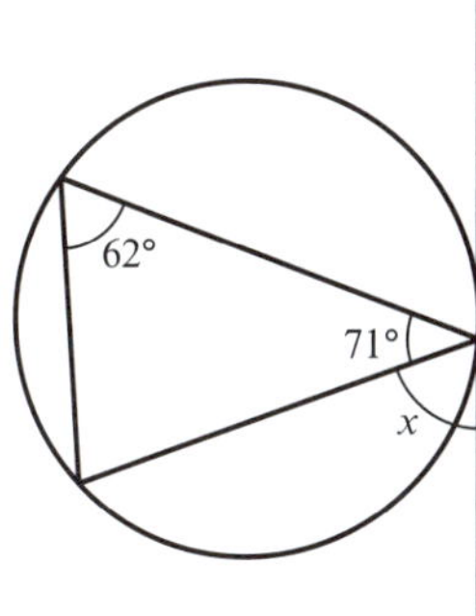

REFLECTION

How do you know for sure if lines are parallel or not? Have you ever assumed they are when they have turned out not to be? How can you remember to check each time?

4 P, Q, S and T are points on the circumference of a circle.

The chords passing through P and Q and through S and T meet at the point R.

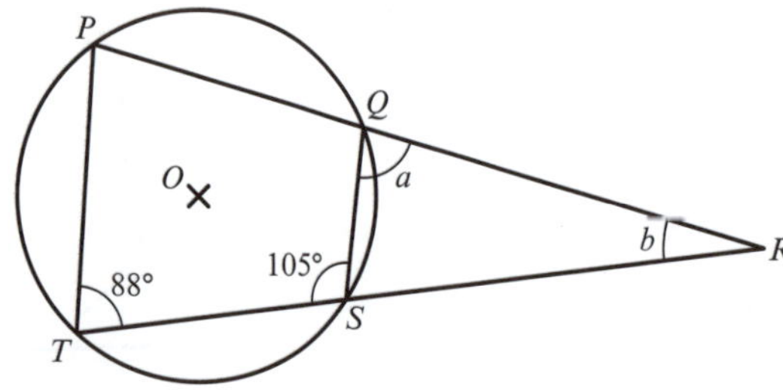

Find the size of a and b. State your reasons clearly and show all working. [4]

[Total: 4]

5

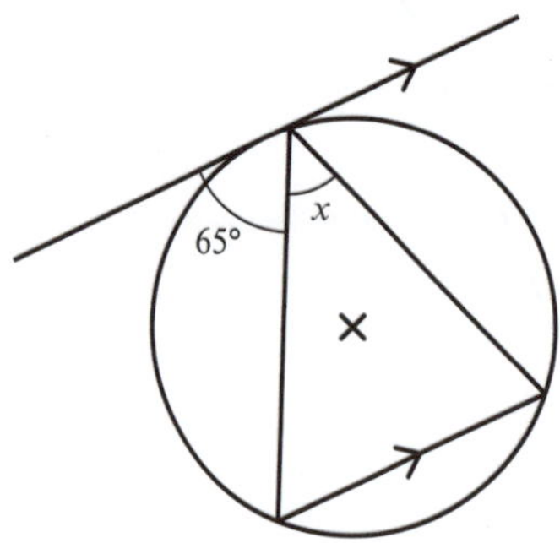

Find the value of x. Explain each step clearly. [3]

[Total: 3]

REFLECTION

How can you tell when a question needs more than just a short answer?

Have you practised writing full explanations using correct mathematical terms, especially when giving reasons for angle facts or symmetry properties?

SELF-ASSESSMENT CHECKLIST

Let's revisit the Knowledge and Exam skills focus for this chapter.
Decide how confident you are with each statement.

	Now I can	Show it	Needs more work	Almost there	Confident to move on
1	identify line symmetry in two-dimensional shapes	Draw lines of symmetry on the diagrams in Section 19.1. Use a mirror to check that the reflections are correct.			
2	find the order of rotational symmetry of two-dimensional shapes	Explain to a classmate how to test for rotational symmetry of any shape. Include what makes a shape have an order of 1.			
3	recognise and use symmetry properties of triangles, quadrilaterals and circles	Choose one diagram from Section 19.4 and write out a full answer, including clear reasons for each step (e.g. 'angle in a semicircle'). Swap answers with a friend and check for missing reasoning.			
4	recognise symmetry properties of prisms and pyramids	Look back at the 3D shapes in Section 19.2. Write a sentence for each, explaining how you know how many planes or orders of symmetry it has.			
5	apply symmetry properties of circles to solve problems	Use one of the circle diagrams in Section 19.3 or 19.4. Write a full 'show that' solution explaining how to find a missing length or angle. Label the diagram and give a clear justification for each step.			
6	identify when a question requires explanation or justification, rather than simple calculation or recall.	Look back at Section 19.4, Questions 4 and 5. Highlight where you gave reasons (e.g. naming the angle rule used) and where you simply calculated. Can you explain why reasoning is required in these questions?			

20 Histograms and cumulative frequency diagrams

KNOWLEDGE FOCUS

In this chapter, you will answer questions on:

- constructing and using histograms with unequal intervals
- drawing cumulative frequency tables
- constructing cumulative frequency diagrams
- estimating and interpreting the median, percentiles, quartiles and interquartile range.

EXAM SKILLS FOCUS

In this chapter you will:

- learn how to work with mark schemes to understand what examiners may be looking for
- recognise what a full answer looks like when interpreting data from diagrams.

In this chapter, you will construct and interpret histograms and cumulative frequency diagrams, and use them to estimate measures such as the median, quartiles and percentiles. These techniques are often assessed in examination questions that include both a graphical task (such as plotting a graph) and interpretation (explaining what the data shows).

It is important not just to get the right answer, but to know how mark schemes award the marks. For example, in Section 20.2, Question 4, you compare two cumulative frequency diagrams. Even if your final answer is not perfect, you may still earn 'method marks' for correctly identifying the median or interquartile range from a graph or making a valid comparison using context.

It may help to construct some mark schemes yourself, to help understand what examiners are looking for.

20.1 Histograms

UNDERSTAND THESE TERMS

- Histogram
- Frequency density

1 When would you use a histogram instead of a bar chart?

Select all the options that apply.

A When the data is continuous.

B When the data is discrete.

C When data is grouped into intervals.

D When comparing categories.

2 Complete the formula for frequency density.

frequency density = ______ ÷ ______

3 Explain why the height of each bar in a histogram does not necessarily give frequencies, as they do in a bar chart.

4 A histogram bar represents a total frequency of 36. Work out the frequency represented by a bar that is:

a the same height, but with twice the class width

b the same class width by three times the height

c twice the class width *and* three times the height

d a quarter of the height, but twice the class width.

5 100 oak saplings are planted in a new woodland. Two years later, Jacob decides to survey the saplings and measures their heights in cm. He records the information in a table.

Height, h (cm)	Frequency	Frequency density
$0 < h \leqslant 20$	12	
$20 < h \leqslant 40$	38	
$40 < h \leqslant 80$	41	
$80 < h \leqslant 120$	9	

a Copy and complete the table by calculating the frequency density for each class.

b Construct a histogram to display the results.

6 The table shows the lifetime of light bulbs before they blow.

Time, t (hours)	Frequency	Frequency density
$0 < t \leqslant 10$	36	
$10 < t \leqslant 20$	28	
$20 < t \leqslant 30$	11	
$30 < t \leqslant 60$	19	
$60 < t \leqslant 100$	3	
$100 < t \leqslant 200$	1	

a Copy and complete the table by calculating frequency densities for each class. [2]

b Plot a histogram for this data. [3]

c Write down the modal class. [1]

[Total: 6]

REFLECTION

How did you decide on the best set of axes to use? How can you work this out quickly, so that you do not waste time during the examination?

≪ RECALL AND CONNECT 1 ≪

Write down the definition of density for a sample of material, in terms of mass and volume. Then write down the definition of frequency density. How are the two definitions related? What does density tell you?

7 Data was collected on the price of cars sold by a showroom.
The histogram shows the results.

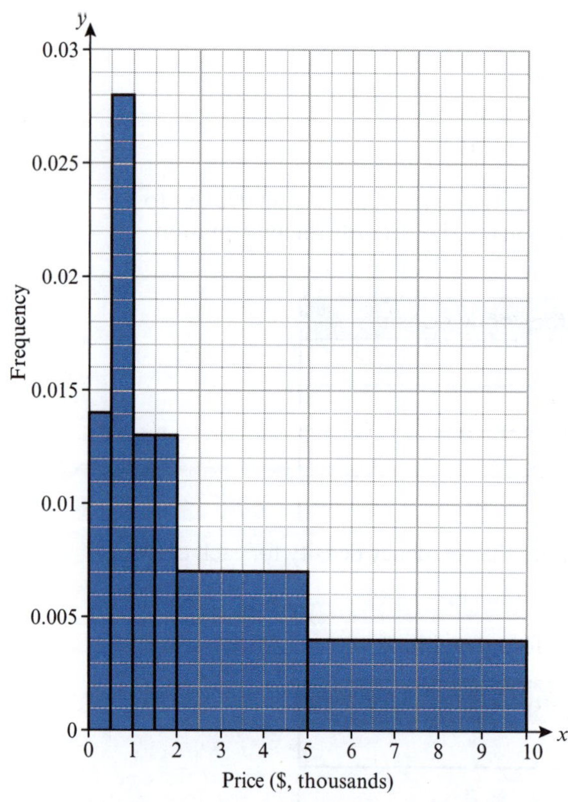

Copy and complete the table. [4]

Price, P ($)	Frequency	Frequency density
$0 < P \leqslant 500$		
$500 < P \leqslant 1000$		
$1000 < P \leqslant 2000$		
$2000 < P \leqslant 5000$		
$5000 < P \leqslant 10\,000$		

[Total: 4]

8 The histogram shows the time taken, t, for a group of 280 children to travel to school.

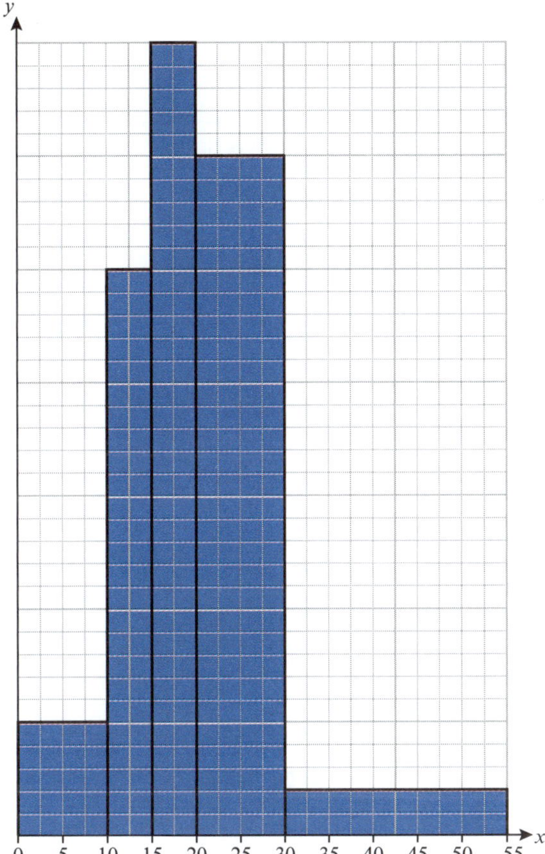

a Work out the frequency density scale. [2]

b Copy and complete the table of frequencies. [3]

Time (t) in minutes	Frequency
$0 < t \leqslant 10$	20
$10 < t \leqslant 15$	50
$15 < t \leqslant 20$	70
$20 < t \leqslant 30$	120
$30 < t \leqslant 55$	20

[Total: 5]

REFLECTION

Look at an official mark scheme for a histogram question.
What common features earn marks? What types of error lead to missed marks?

20.2 Cumulative frequency

UNDERSTAND THESE TERMS

- Cumulative frequency
- Cumulative frequency graph
- Percentiles

1 Match the terms to their definitions.

Term
Cumulative frequency
Median
Cumulative frequency graph
Percentile

Definition
The number halfway through a dataset.
A diagram used to estimate medians and quartiles.
A running total of frequencies up to each class boundary.
A value below which a given percentage of data fall.

2 When are cumulative frequency graphs used?

A To compare data with unequal class widths.

B To estimate averages for grouped data.

C To show how totals build up across intervals.

D To display individual pieces of data.

3 Copy and complete this sentence which describes the method to find the median from a cumulative frequency graph.

To estimate the median, draw a line across at ______ of the total frequency and read the corresponding value on the ______ axis.

4 A large summerhouse showroom has wooden buildings in the following continuous price ranges.

For example, the first group covers prices from \$0 up to but not including \$2000, and the second group covers prices from \$2000 up to but not including \$5000.

Price (\$)	Frequency	Cumulative frequency	Upper class boundary
0–2000	10	10	2000
2000–5000	16		
5000–8000	24		
8000–10 000	40		
10 000–12 000	64		
12 000–15 000	58		
15 000–20 000	28		

a Copy and complete this table.

b Draw a cumulative frequency diagram to represent the data.

c Find an estimate for the median.

d Find an estimate for the interquartile range.

e Bhawna can afford to spend a maximum of \$9000 on a summer house. Approximately how many summer houses can Bhawna choose from?

REFLECTION

How do you make sure you remember to plot cumulative frequencies at the *end-points* of intervals? This can be especially confusing if you have also been asked to estimate a mean, which uses mid-points.

5 A social experiment records the amount of time a person spends using a computer during a 24-hour period. The times are grouped into the following continuous intervals (in hours).

For example, the first group covers 0 hours up to but not including 2 hours, the second covers 2 hours up to but not including 4 hours, and so on.

Hours of sleep	Frequency	Cumulative frequency
0–2	12	
2–4	38	
4–6	68	
6–8	83	
8–10	46	
10–12	33	

a Copy and complete the table. [2]

b Construct a cumulative frequency diagram for the data. [3]

c Estimate the median. [2]

d Estimate the 60th percentile. [2]

[Total: 9]

6 The masses of people about to board a plane are shown in the table.

Mass, m (kg)	Frequency	Cumulative frequency
$50 < m \leqslant 60$	2	
$60 < m \leqslant 70$	8	
$70 < m \leqslant 80$	12	
$80 < m \leqslant 90$	11	
$90 < m \leqslant 100$	8	
$100 < m \leqslant 110$	5	
$110 < m \leqslant 120$	2	

a Complete the cumulative frequency in the table. [2]

b Construct a cumulative frequency diagram for the data. [3]

c Estimate the median mass of people in the survey. [3]

d Estimate the number of people with greater mass than 75 kg, but lower mass than 95 kg. [2]

[Total: 10]

‹‹ RECALL AND CONNECT 2 ‹‹

Write down the definition of median, which you studied in Chapter 12.
Why can you only *estimate* the median in this chapter?

7 Police checked the speeds of cars on two major roads. They checked 100 cars on road P and 60 cars on road Q. The results are shown in the cumulative frequency diagram.

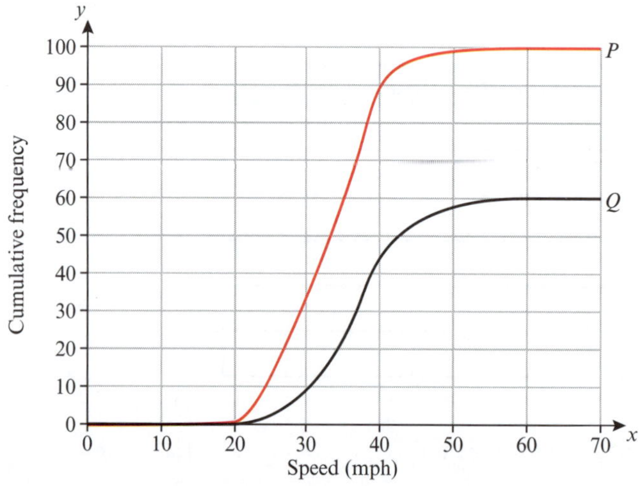

a Find the median speed for road P and for road Q. [2]

b Find the interquartile range for road P and for road Q. [2]

c The speed limit for road Q is 40 mph. Calculate the percentage of cars driving within the speed limit on road Q. [2]

[Total: 6]

REFLECTION

How do you decide the best axes and scale when plotting a histogram or cumulative frequency diagram? What are the risks of choosing poor intervals or scales?

SELF-ASSESSMENT CHECKLIST

Let's revisit the Knowledge and Exam skills focus for this chapter. Decide how confident you are with each statement.

	Now I can	Show it	Needs more work	Almost there	Confident to move on
1	construct and use histograms with unequal intervals	Measure the height of 20 classmates or friends. Group your data into unequal intervals and draw a histogram.			
2	draw cumulative frequency tables	Ask 20 people how many hours of sleep they got last night. Group the results into intervals and complete a cumulative frequency table.			
3	construct cumulative frequency diagrams	Use the sleep data above or research screen time data for teens. Create a cumulative frequency diagram and describe what it shows.			
4	estimate and interpret the median, percentiles, quartiles and interquartile range.	Use your own cumulative frequency diagram to estimate median and quartiles. Write one sentence about what this tells you about the data.			
5	work with mark schemes to increase understanding	Pick any histogram or cumulative frequency question from this chapter or a past paper. Create a mark scheme to explain how each mark is awarded.			
6	recognise what a full answer looks like when interpreting data from diagrams.	Pick one question from this chapter that involves interpreting a diagram. Write a model answer to the question. Then swap with a partner and assess each other's answers.			

Exam practice 5

This section contains past paper questions from previous Cambridge exams, which draw together your knowledge on a range of topics that you have covered up to this point. These questions give you the opportunity to test your knowledge and understanding.

The following question has an example student response and commentary provided. Work through the question first, then compare your answer to the sample response and commentary. Are your answers different to the sample responses?

1 **a** Anil changes \$830 into euros when the exchange rate is 1 euro = \$1.16.
He spends 500 euros.

He then changes the remaining money back into dollars at the same exchange rate.

Work out how much, in dollars, Anil receives. [3]

b In 2021, Anil earns \$37 000.

i He spends \$12 400 on bills in 2021.
Calculate the percentage of his earnings he spends on bills. [2]

ii His earnings of \$37 000 increase by 3.2% in 2022.
Calculate his earnings in 2022. [2]

c Anil invests \$3500 in an account that pays a rate of 2.4% per year compound interest.

i Calculate the total interest earned at the end of 5 years. [3]

ii Find the number of complete years before Anil has at least \$5000 in his account. [3]

Cambridge IGCSE Mathematics (0580) Paper 42 Q2 June 2023 **[Total: 13]**

Example student response	Commentary
a 715.52 euros 215.52 euros left \$250	1 mark for working, but only because it is implied by the correct answer. If the student had got the answer wrong, then no working marks could be awarded. 1 mark for correct final answer. Although it is clear that the student knows what to do, there is no working. Full marks are fortunately awarded because the correct working is implied, but just one error could have meant that no marks were awarded. ***This answer scores 3 out of 3 marks.***

Example student response	Commentary
b i $\frac{12\,400}{37\,000} = 33.5$	1 mark for the correct division and 1 for the correct final answer, though the fraction given does not equal the final answer. An important multiplication is missing and there are no % signs in appropriate places. ***This answer scores 2 out of 2 marks.***
b ii $37\,000 \times 1.032 = 38\,184$	1 mark for the correct multiplier and 1 for the correct final answer. But always include the appropriate units, at least in the final answer. In this question the marks are not awarded for units, but somewhere in the exam paper they will be! ***This answer scores 2 out of 2 marks.***
c i $\$3500 \times 1.024^5 = \$3940.65$	1 mark for multiplying by any power of 1.024. However, the student hasn't then subtracted the principal for 1 mark and so hasn't given the final answer for the third mark. ***This answer scores 1 out of 3 marks.***
c ii $\$3500 \times 1.024^{15} = \$4995.37 < \$5000$ $\$3500 \times 1.024^{16} = \$5115.26 > \$5000$ Anil's account will contain $5000 at some point between 15 and 16 years. So, 15 complete years will have passed.	1 mark for multiplying $3500 by powers of 1.024. 1 mark for showing the $5000 is achieved in between years 15 and 16. However, they have lost a mark because, when 15 years have passed, the total is less than $5000. ***This answer scores 2 out of 3 marks.***

2 Now that you have gone through the commentary, try to write an improved answer for your own solution and edit the sample student response to improve their answer to each part.

3 These are the rates charged by a painter, a plumber and an electrician who do some work for Mr Sharma.

Painter	Plumber	Electrician
$35 per hour	Fixed charge $40 Plus $26.50 per hour	$48 per hour for the first 2 hours Then $32 per hour

a The painter works for 7 hours.

Calculate the amount Mr Sharma pays the painter. [1]

b Mr Sharma pays the plumber $252.

Calculate how many hours the plumber works. [2]

c Mr Sharma pays the electrician \$224.

Calculate how many hours the electrician works. [2]

d Write down the ratio of the amount Mr Sharma pays to the painter, the plumber and the electrician. Give your answer in its lowest terms. [2]

[Total: 7]

Cambridge IGCSE Mathematics (0580) Paper 42 Q1 March 2021

The following question has an example student response and commentary provided. Work through the question first, then compare your answer to the sample response and commentary. Are your answers different to the sample responses?

4 Solve the simultaneous equations.

You must show all your working.

$4y + 3x = 13$

$y = x^2 - 18$ [5]

Cambridge IGCSE Mathematics (0580) Paper 22 Q21 June 2024 **[Total: 5]**

Example student response	Commentary
$4y + 3x = 13$ ① and $y = x^2 - 18$ ② Substitute ② into ①: $4(x^2 - 18) + 3x = 13$ $\Rightarrow 4x^2 + 3x - 72 = 13$ $\Rightarrow 4x^2 + 3x - 85 = 0$ $\Rightarrow (x - 5)(4x + 17) = 0$ $x = 5$ and $y = (5)^2 - 18 = 7$ *or* $x = -\frac{17}{4}$ and $y = \left(-\frac{17}{4}\right)^2 - 18 = \frac{1}{16}$	1 mark for attempting a substitution. 1 mark for obtaining correct quadratic equation. 1 mark for attempting to solve the quadratic, even though the actual solution is incorrect. 0 mark for incorrect x values. 1 mark for corresponding y values (even though they are incorrect, they have been correctly calculated from incorrect x values). ***This answer scores 4 out of 5 marks.***

5 Now that you have gone through the commentary, try to write an improved answer for your own solution and edit the sample student response to improve their answer to each part.

6 Solve the simultaneous equations.

You must show all your working.

$x = 7 - 3y$

$x^2 - y^2 = 39$ [6]

Cambridge IGCSE Mathematics (0580) Paper 22 Q16 March 2020 **[Total: 6]**

The following question has an example student response and commentary provided. Work through the question first, then compare your answer to the sample response and commentary. Are your answers different to the sample responses?

7

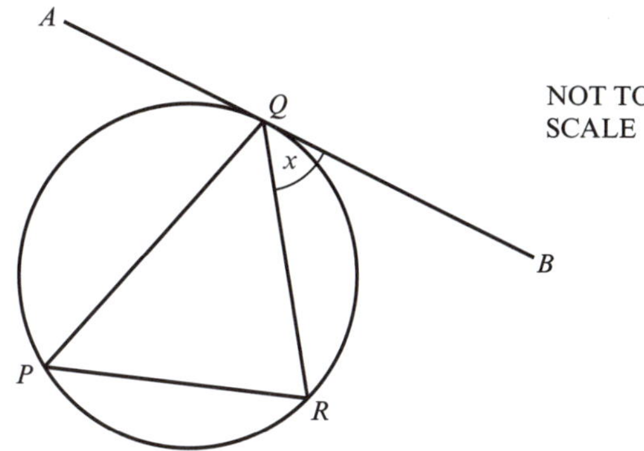

P, R and Q are points on the circle.

AB is a tangent to the circle at Q.

QR bisects angle PQB.

Angle $BQR = x$, with $x < 60$.

Use this information to show that triangle PQR is an isosceles triangle.

Give a geometrical reason for each step of your work. [3]

Cambridge IGCSE Mathematics (0580) Paper 21 Q15 June 2020 **[Total: 3]**

Example student response	Commentary
Angle QPR = angle BQR QR bisects angle PQB, so angle PQR = angle BQR. So, both angles PQR and QPR are equal, giving an isosceles triangle.	0 marks. Although there is a correct use of the alternate segment theorem, the student has not said that this is the theorem used. The mark scheme requires the reasoning in full. 1 mark for recognising that angle PQR = angle BQR. 1 mark for correctly explaining that two equal angles in a triangle show that we have an isosceles triangle. ***This answer scores 2 out of 3 marks.***

8

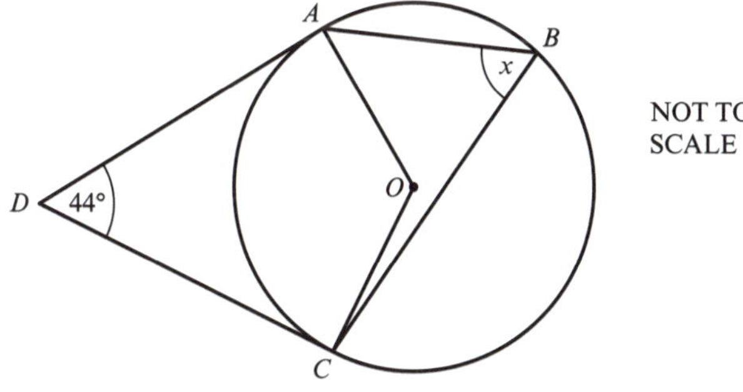

A, B and C are points on a circle, centre O.

DA and DC are tangents.

Angle $ADC = 44°$.

Work out the value of x. [3]

Cambridge IGCSE Mathematics (0580) Paper 22 Q13 June 2021 **[Total: 3]**

The following question has an example student response and commentary provided. Work through the question first, then compare your answer to the sample response and commentary. Are your answers different to the sample responses?

9 The height, h cm, of each of 120 plants is measured. The cumulative frequency diagram shows this information.

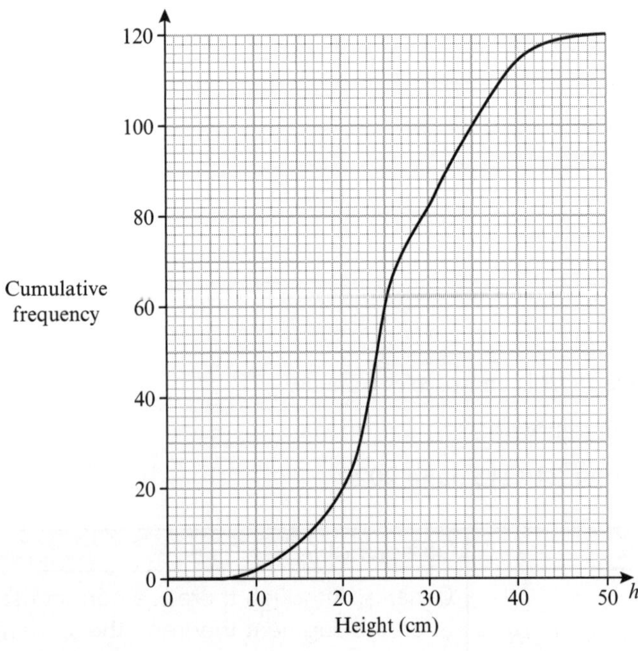

a Use the cumulative frequency diagram to find an estimate of

i the median [1]

ii the interquartile range [2]

iii the 60th percentile [1]

iv the number of plants with a height greater than 40 cm [2]

b The information in the cumulative frequency diagram is shown in this frequency table.

Height, h cm	$0 < h \leqslant 10$	$10 < h \leqslant 20$	$20 < h \leqslant 30$	$30 < h \leqslant 50$
Frequency	2	18	62	38

i Calculate an estimate of the mean height. [4]

ii A histogram is drawn to show the information in the frequency table. The height of the bar representing the interval $10 < h \leqslant 20$ is 7.2 cm.

Calculate the height of the bar representing the interval $30 < h \leqslant 50$. [2]

Cambridge IGCSE Mathematics (0580) Paper 42 Q4 November 2020 **[Total: 12]**

Example student response	Commentary
a i Half the final total = 60, so reading across at 60 we get 26 cm.	1 mark for any answer between 24.5 and 25.5. Unfortunately the student has not been quite careful enough when reading the scale. 0 marks, therefore. ***This answer scores 0 out of 1 mark.***
a ii Read across at 90 and 30 for the upper and lower quartiles. Upper quartile = 32 Lower quartile = 22 Interquartile range = 22 to 32	1 mark for attempting to read off the upper and lower quartiles. 0 marks for final answer. The student has stated an informal range of the data, but the question requires the range to be a single number. ***This answer scores 1 out of 2 marks.***
a iii 60% of 120 = 0.6 × 120 = 72. Read across at 72 to obtain 27.	1 mark for correct answer, though the student has not given units. This is not good practice, even if the mark scheme doesn't require it. ***This answer scores 1 out of 1 mark.***
a iv Reading up at 40 cm to get 114.	1 mark for reading up at 40 cm. This gives the number of plants LESS than 40 cm. 0 marks for final correct answer, which is supposed to be the number MORE than 40 cm. ***This answer scores 1 out of 2 marks.***
b i Mid-points are 5, 15, 25, 40 $\frac{2 \times 5 + 18 \times 15 + 62 \times 25 + 38 \times 40}{4} = \frac{3350}{4}$ $= 837.5\text{ cm}$	1 mark for correct mid-points. 1 mark for attempt at calculating the total. 0 marks for dividing by incorrect total frequency. The student has divided by the number of classes. 0 marks for final answer. ***This answer scores 2 out of 4 marks.***
b ii Frequency density for the interval $10 < h \leqslant 20$ is $18 \div 10 = 1.8$. This is represented by 7.2 cm. 7.2 ÷ 1.8 = 4 cm will represent a frequency density of 1. Frequency density for the new bar is 38 ÷ 20 = 1.9. 1.9 × 4 = 7.6 cm.	1 mark for calculating at least one correct frequency density. 1 mark for scaling and getting the right answer. ***This answer scores 2 out of 2 marks.***

10 a The cumulative frequency diagram shows information about the floor area, $a\,\text{m}^2$, of each of 80 houses.

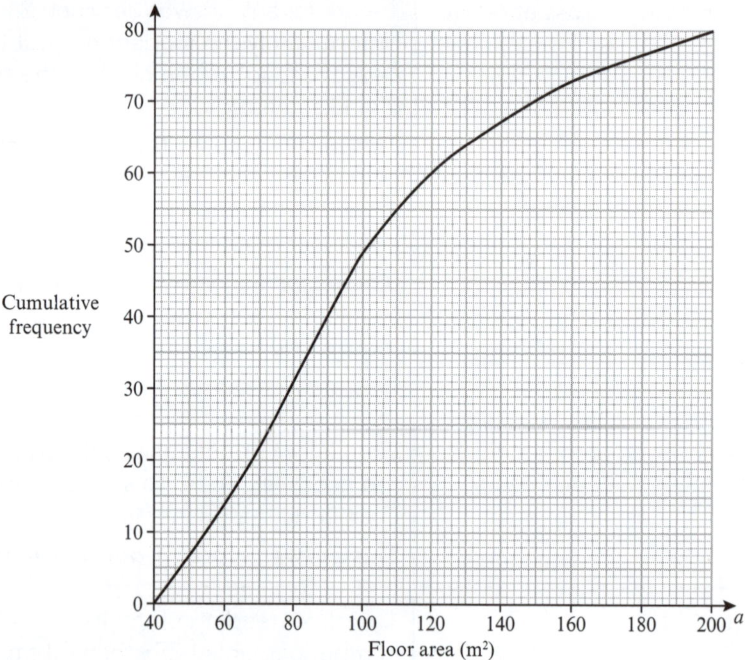

Use the diagram to find an estimate of

i the median [1]

ii the lower quartile [1]

iii the interquartile range [1]

iv the number of houses with a floor area greater than $120\,\text{m}^2$. [2]

b The information about the 80 floor areas is shown in this frequency table.

Floor area (a m^2)	$40 < a \leqslant 60$	$60 < a \leqslant 80$	$80 < a \leqslant 100$	$100 < a \leqslant 130$	$130 < a \leqslant 160$	$160 < a \leqslant 200$
Frequency	14	17	18	15	9	7

i Calculate an estimate of the mean floor area. [4]

ii Complete the histogram to show the information in the frequency table.

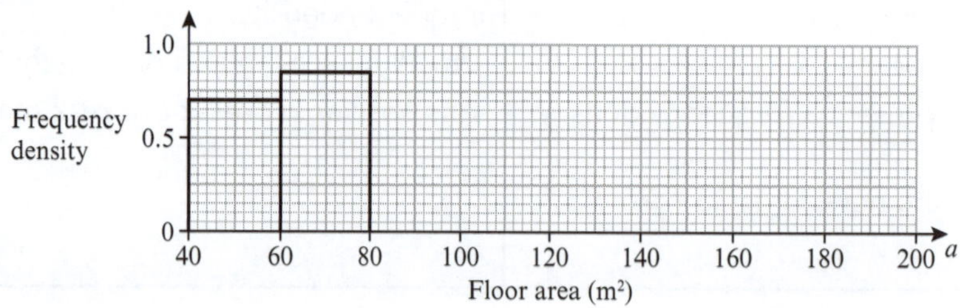

[4]

[Use Figure 4 in the Past Paper Practice Questions Resource Sheet.]

iii Two of the houses are picked at random.

Find the probability that one of the houses has a floor area greater than $130\,\text{m}^2$ and the other has a floor area $60\,\text{m}^2$ or less. [3]

Cambridge IGCSE Mathematics (0580) Paper 42 Q2 November 2021 **[Total: 16]**

21 Ratio, rate and proportion

KNOWLEDGE FOCUS

In this chapter, you will answer questions on:

- recording relationships using ratio notation
- finding one quantity when the other is given
- dividing amounts in a given ratio
- making sense of scales on maps, models and plans
- reading and interpreting rates
- calculating average speed
- using and interpreting distance–time and speed–time graphs
- solving problems using distance–time and speed–time graphs
- understanding what is meant by direct and inverse proportion
- solving problems involving proportionate amounts
- using algebra to express direct and inverse proportion.

EXAM SKILLS FOCUS

In this chapter you will:

- show that you understand what a good answer looks like, and what you can do to maximise your chances of getting good marks in a question
- understand that, in mathematics, 'find' does not mean 'locate'.

Questions that have one mark usually require either only a single step calculation or could be for writing in a different form, for example, 'write the ratio in its simplest form'. Questions with multiple marks available will usually require more calculations or working out. It is helpful to show the stages of your calculations even if you aren't convinced you are right, as there are method marks available even if you make a mathematical mistake. Examiners also can also award 'follow through' marks, if your initial answer has a mistake but is then used in the correct way later in the question. You won't get any marks for a blank response!

Mathematics exams use specific 'command words' to ask the questions. It is important to understand the responses that the examiner is looking for, as this will be directly related to the mark scheme. You will have learnt about the command words in previous chapters, but it is important to recognise them and their meanings.

Work out	calculate from given facts, figures or information with or without the use of a calculator.

One of the terms that can cause confusion is 'find'. In a mathematics examination it does not mean 'locate', it means 'work out' or 'find out'. 'Work out' has a very specific meaning.

21.1 Working with ratio

1 Express each of these ratios in their simplest form.

a 24 : 16 b 36 : 21 c 5 cm to 15 mm

d 20 cents to $3 e 1.2 m to 80 cm f 2.4 kg to 1800 g

2 Find the unknown values, x, in the following equivalent ratios.

a $3:4=6:x$ b $x:7=9:21$ c $6:x=42:35$

d $5:8=x:32$ e $7:x=28:40$ f $x:12=15:20$

3 a Copy and reorder the steps involved in the unitary method.

- Multiply the values in the ratio by the quantity per part to find the value of each part.
- Divide the quantity by the total number of parts to find the quantity per part (the value of one part).
- Add the values in the ratio to find the total number of parts involved.

b Copy and reorder the steps involved in the ratio method.

- Express each part of the ratio as a fraction of the total parts.
- Multiply the quantity by the fraction to find the value of each part.
- Add the values in the ratio to find the total number of parts involved.

4 Albert, Baz and Chen are sharing some sweets in the ratio A : B : C = 2 : 3 : 4.

There are 72 sweets in total.

Work out how many sweets each person gets. [2]

[Total: 2]

5 Sandhya and Munira share an apartment and pay rent in the ratio Sandhya : Munira = 7 : 5.

Sandhya pays $70 more than Munira per month.

Work out how much each of them pays. [3]

[Total: 3]

⟪ RECALL AND CONNECT 1 ⟪

a What are the similarities and differences between fractions and ratios?

b What can you do with a ratio that you can also do with a fraction?

REFLECTION

What do you recall about the unitary method and the ratio method?
How did you decide whether to use the unitary method or the ratio method in Question 5? What made one method more suitable than the other?

21.2 Ratio and scale

1 Write each of the scales in the following two forms.

i $1:n$

ii $n:1$

a	2 cm to 3 m	**b**	5 cm to 1 km	**c**	1.5 cm to 2 m
d	25 mm to 3 km	**e**	4 cm to 5.6 m	**f**	6 mm to 1.2 km

2 A map has a scale 1 : 25 000.

Find the real distance in km of the following lengths on the map.

a	3 cm	**b**	35 mm	**c**	12.5 cm
d	7 mm	**e**	9.6 cm	**f**	42 mm

3 A map is drawn to a scale of 1 : 125 000.

How long will each of these real lengths be on the map?

a 25 km [1]

b 15 km [1]

c State whether it is likely that you could see a distance of 275 km on a paper copy of the map.

Explain your answer. [2]

[Total: 4]

4 The scale of a map is 1 : 40 000.

The distance between two towns on the map is 29 cm.

Calculate the actual distance between the two towns.

Give your answer in kilometres. [2]

[Total: 2]

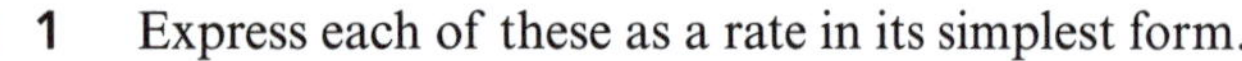

REFLECTION

How did you approach the map and scale drawing question you just completed? Did you use a method like the unitary method to connect map measurements to real-life distances? Why did that method work well (or not) for you?

21.3 Rates

1 Express each of these as a rate in its simplest form.

- a 35 kg for $45
- b 275 km for 75 kW
- c 1200 litres in 90 seconds
- d 100 m in 12.5 seconds
- e 660 g in 5.5 min
- f $84 for 210 items

2 How long would it take to complete a journey of 350 km at each of these speeds?

- a 70 km/h
- b 50 km/h
- c 75 km/h
- d 350 m/min
- e 87.5 km/h
- f 2.5 km/min

3 A plane flies 1065 km in 3 hours. If it continues to fly at the same average speed, how far will it fly in 4 hours and 30 minutes?

4 A factory has a machine that fills bottles at a rate of 24 bottles per minute.

Calculate the number of bottles it will fill

- a in one day [2]
- b in one week. [2]

[Total: 4]

5 A train travels at a speed of 108 km/h.

Work out this speed in m/s. [2]

[Total: 2]

« RECALL AND CONNECT 2 «

- a What does a rate mean?
- b How do you give the units of a rate?

REFLECTION

What method did you use to calculate the answer to Question 3? Did you use the unitary method to find out how far the plane travelled in 1 hour? Was this an effective method? Is there another way of calculating the distance travelled in 4 hours and 30 minutes?

21.4 Kinematic graphs

UNDERSTAND THESE TERMS

- Kinematics
- Distance–time graph
- Speed–time graph
- Travel graph

1 Josh goes for a run.

He leaves his house at 9.30 a.m. and runs for 5 km at an average speed of 15 km/h.

He then runs a time trial, where he covers a further 10 km in 35 minutes.

He then has a 20 minute rest.

One of his friends drives him the 15 km back to his house, which takes another 20 minutes.

a Draw a distance–time graph to show Josh's journey.

b What time does Josh get home?

c What is Josh's speed in m/s when he is running his time trial? Give your answer to 3 significant figures.

d What is the average speed in km/h of his journey home?

2 The speed–time graph below shows a racing car on a test track.

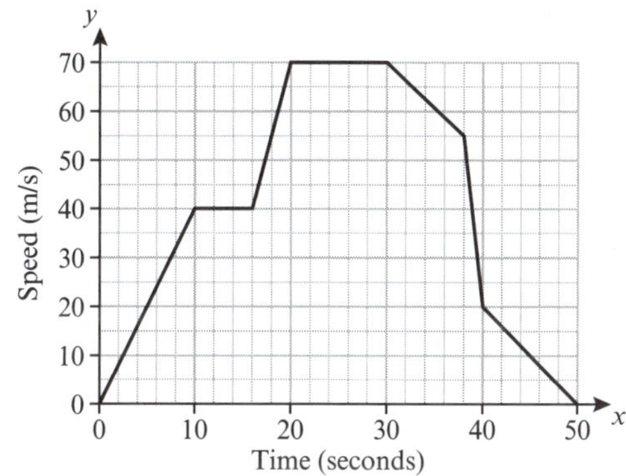

a What is the average rate of acceleration in the first 10 seconds?

b What is the speed of the car at 11 seconds?

c What happens after 30 seconds?

d When is the car decelerating the most?

3 Lucia is going on holiday.

She leaves her home and drives to her holiday destination.

The distance–time graph shows her journey.

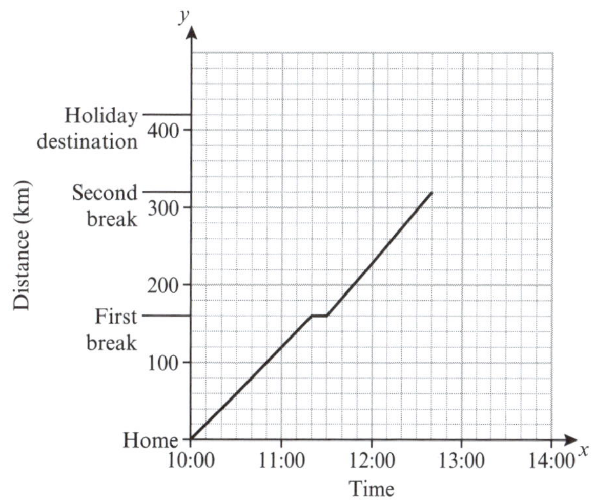

a Calculate her average speed in km/h from home to her first break. Give your answer to the nearest km/h. [1]

b Identify the length of time she spends on her first break. [1]

c Work out the difference between her average speed from home to her first break and her average speed from her first to second break. [2]

Lucia takes a 20-minute break before continuing to her destination.

She completes her journey at an average speed of 120 km/h.

d **i** Work out how long she takes to get from her second break to her destination. [2]

ii Complete the distance–time graph to show this final part of the journey. [1]

[Total: 7]

4 The diagram shows a speed–time graph of part of a train journey.

a Find the acceleration of the train between 0 and 7 seconds (to 3 significant figures). [1]

b Calculate the total distance travelled from 0 to 20 seconds. [3]

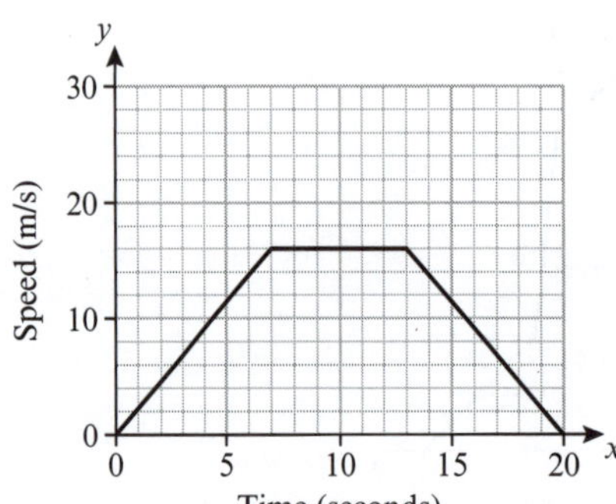

[Total: 4]

≪ RECALL AND CONNECT 3 ≪

Which shapes do you often need to use to calculate the total area under a speed–time graph?

21.5 Proportion

UNDERSTAND THESE TERMS

- Direct proportion
- Inverse proportion

1 The recipe for a simple sponge cake is given in the table.

Sugar	200 g
Butter	180 g
Eggs	4
Flour	210 g
Baking powder	10 g
Milk	30 ml

This recipe serves 12 people.

a Write out the recipe for 18 people.

b A chef only has seven eggs but plenty of the other ingredients.

How many people could he make a cake for?

2 Four workers are digging holes in the road to lay a new cable.

It takes them six hours to dig eight equal-sized holes.

How long would it take two workers to dig the same number of holes?

3 The extension of a spring is measured with different masses attached to the end of it.

The results are shown in the table.

Extension (cm)	8	14	20	36
Mass (kg)	18	31.5	45	81

a State and explain whether the relationship is proportional or inversely proportional. [2]

b Estimate the extension of the spring when a mass of 126 kg is applied. [2]

[Total: 4]

4 The time, t (in seconds), to heat water is inversely proportional to the heater's power, P (in watts).

A 3000 W heater takes 175 seconds to heat water from 20 °C to 100 °C.

Calculate the time required for a 600 W heater to do the same. [2]

[Total: 2]

REFLECTION

Look at your answer to Question 3. What would a graph of this relationship look like?

What would a graph of the relationship in Question 4 look like?

Were you confident in identifying whether the relationship was direct or inverse proportion?

How could checking the shape of the graph help you avoid common errors in an examination?

21.6 Direct and inverse proportion in algebraic terms

UNDERSTAND THIS TERM

- The symbol for proportionality is ∝

1 y is proportional to x^2. If $y = 234$ when $x = 6$, find the following.

a The constant of proportionality (k).

b The value of y when:

i $x = 7$ ii $x = 4$ iii $x = 9$

c The value of x when:

i $y = 936$ ii $y = 1664$ iii $y = 79.625$

2 y is inversely proportional to x^3. If $y = 15$ when $x = 3$, find the following.

a The constant of proportionality.

b The value of y when:

i $x = 6$ ii $x = 5$ iii $x = 1$

c The value of x when:

i $y = 10\,935$ ii $y = \frac{5}{9}$ iii $y = 3240$

3 y is directly proportional to the square of $(x + 2)$.

When $x = 3$, $y = 125$.

Find y when $x = 7$. [3]

[Total: 3]

4 a is inversely proportional to the square of $(b - 3)$.

$a = 12$ when $b = 9$.

Find a when $b = 11$. [3]

[Total: 3]

REFLECTION

What are the similarities between finding k (the constant of proportionality) and solving an equation?

SELF-ASSESSMENT CHECKLIST

Let's revisit the Knowledge and Exam skills focus for this chapter.
Decide how confident you are with each statement.

	Now I can	Show it	Needs more work	Almost there	Confident to move on
1	record relationships using ratio notation	Write the relationship between two quantities as a ratio, such as 2 : 3.			
2	find one quantity when the other is given	Calculate a missing quantity using its ratio to another quantity.			
3	divide amounts in a given ratio	Create and solve your own ratio-sharing question, then explain it to a partner.			

CONTINUED

	Now I can	Show it	Needs more work	Almost there	Confident to move on
4	make sense of scales on maps, models and plans	Use a ruler and scale to estimate a real distance on a map.			
5	read and interpret rates	Answer a rate question, for example, how much is \$5 worth if the exchange rate is \$1 = €1.50?			
6	calculate average speed	Draw your own distance–time graph for a journey and label average speed.			
7	use and interpret distance–time and speed–time graphs	Complete and understand distance–time graphs.			
8	solve problems using distance–time and speed–time graphs	Write a multi-step exam-style question based on a speed–time graph and create a mark scheme.			
9	understand what is meant by direct and inverse proportion	Understand the difference between quantities that are proportional and quantities that are inversely proportional.			
10	solve problems involving proportionate amounts	Solve a proportions question, for example, if a recipe uses three eggs to make six cakes, how many will be needed to make twelve cakes?			
11	use algebra to express direct and inverse proportion	Express proportions using the correct symbol and equation, for example, if $y \propto x^2$ then $y = kx^2$.			
12	show that I understand what a good answer looks like, and how you can make sure you get maximum marks in a question	Annotate one of your answers from the chapter to show where you earned method marks and could improve.			
13	understand that, in mathematics, 'find' means 'work out' and does not mean 'locate'.	Collect examples of 'find' questions and explain what each one requires.			

22 More equations, formulae and functions

KNOWLEDGE FOCUS

In this chapter, you will answer questions on:

- making your own equations and using them to solve worded problems
- constructing and transforming more complex formulae
- using function notation to describe simple functions and their inverses
- forming composite functions.

EXAM SKILLS FOCUS

In this chapter you will:

- think about ensuring that you keep time well during examinations
- recognise the different ways equations are used in exam questions and how to respond to each.

Taking examinations can be stressful and it can feel that there is not enough time to get everything done. This can lead to students feeling overloaded, so that they rush and make simple errors.

The best advice is to keep calm and to work steadily through the questions, keeping your focus on the question you are doing at the time.

Your mathematics exams have either 80 marks or 100 marks available. The 80-mark paper lasts 90 minutes, so there is more than a minute to gain each mark. The 100-mark paper lasts 120 minutes, so again there is more than a minute to gain each mark.

A simple one- or two-mark question should not take you longer than 1 or 2 minutes, but you can allow yourself longer on the questions that have greater numbers of marks available. Usually, you have plenty of time to complete calculations, so spend a little time ensuring that you read the question carefully and understand what it is you are being asked to do.

As you prepare for your examination, monitor how long it takes you to answer questions and check whether you are working towards gaining approximately one mark every minute. This is particularly important when you are trying the past paper questions, and you can see how many marks each section has available.

Equations do not always behave the same way – and neither do questions about them! Sometimes you are asked to form an equation, or solve an equation, or rearrange a formula to make a different variable the subject. Recognising what kind of equation question you are facing helps you choose the right approach from the start, saving you time and helping you avoid mistakes.

22.1 Setting up equations to solve problems

UNDERSTAND THIS TERM

- Equation

1 There are 81 stones in 3 piles.

The second pile has 26 more stones than the first pile.

The third pile has three times as many stones as the first pile.

How many stones are there in each pile?

2 A rectangle with an area of 48 cm^2 has one side 8 cm longer than the other.

a Form an equation that represents the area of the rectangle.

b Solve the equation and find the values of the two sides.

3 A right-angled triangle has side lengths $(x + 2)$ cm, $4x$ cm and a hypotenuse of $(5x - 2)$ cm.

Find the value of x and state the length of the three sides.

4 The product of two consecutive even integers is 168.

a Write an equation to show this. [1]

b Solve the equation and hence find the values of the integers. [3]

[Total: 4]

REFLECTION

Look back at your answer to Question 3 in Section 22.1. What steps did you take to form the equation, and how did you know it was correct? What clues helped you realise it involved Pythagoras' theorem?

How did you recognise what kind of equation you were working with in other questions – for example, rearranging in Question 2?

How do you check that your solution is correct? Could you use substitution, estimation or graphing to confirm your answer?

22.2 Using and rearranging formulae

1 Make x the subject of each equation.

a $c = a(x - b)$

b $b = \frac{\sqrt{x}}{c}$

c $b = \sqrt{\frac{x}{c}}$

d $b = \frac{c}{\sqrt{x}}$

e $a = \frac{c\sqrt{x}}{b}$

f $y = \frac{a}{bx^2}$

2 Make c the subject of each equation.

a $b + c = bc + d$

b $d = \frac{2c}{c - 7}$

c $ac^2 = bc^2 - 4$

d $x = \frac{c + 2}{1 - c}$

e $\frac{x}{5} = \frac{c}{4} - 1$

f $x = y + \frac{4c}{3}$

3 The formula for the surface area of a sphere is $A = 4\pi r^2$.

Rearrange the equation to make r the subject. [2]

[Total: 2]

4 The speed of a wave on a string is given by $v = \sqrt{\frac{T}{\mu}}$.

Rearrange the equation to make μ the subject. [3]

[Total: 3]

RECALL AND CONNECT 1

What are the inverse operations for $+$, $-$, $\times$, $\div$, $\sqrt{\ }$, $\sqrt[3]{\ }$, squared and cubed?

22.3 Functions and function notation

UNDERSTAND THESE TERMS

- Function
- Domain
- Range

1 $f(x) = 5x-1$

Find each of the following.

a $f(2)$ b $f(-2)$ c $f(0)$

d $f\left(\frac{1}{2}\right)$ e $f(5)$ f $f(-1.5)$

2 $f(x) = (x + 1)^2$

Find each of the following.

a $f(1)$ b $f(-2)$ c $f(5)$

d $f(-5)$ e $f\left(\frac{1}{2}\right)$ f $f\left(-\frac{1}{2}\right)$

3 $g(x) = \sqrt{3x + 1}$

Find x when $g(x) = 8$.

4 Given that $f(x) = (x^2 - 1)$ and $g(x) = 2x - 1$, find the following.

a $fg(x)$ b $gf(x)$ c $ff(x)$ d $gg(x)$

5 $f(x) = 2x + 3$

The domain of $f(x)$ is $\{-3, 3, 11\}$.

Find the range. [2]

[Total: 2]

6 $f(x) = 3x + 4$, $g(x) = 4 - 3x$

a Find

i $f(-5)$ [1]

ii $gf(-5)$ [2]

b Find $g^{-1}(x)$. [2]

c Find x when $ff(x) = 79$. [3]

d Find x when $f^{-1}(x) = 3$. [2]

[Total: 10]

≪ RECALL AND CONNECT 2 ≪

What are the other ways that you can represent functions?

REFLECTION

Reflect on how you managed your time while answering the exam-style questions. What strategies did you use to keep track of time? How did you decide how much time to spend on each question? How did you approach Question 6? Did you notice anything that helped or hindered you in terms of timing while working through that question?

SELF-ASSESSMENT CHECKLIST

Let's revisit the Knowledge and Exam skills focus for this chapter.
Decide how confident you are with each statement.

	Now I can	Show it	Needs more work	Almost there	Confident to move on
1	make your own equations and use them to solve worded problems	For example, Iqbal is 3 years older than his sister. If their total ages add up to 27, how old is his sister?			
2	construct and transform more complex formulae	Change the subject of a formula involving powers and roots.			
3	use function notation to describe simple functions and their inverses	Draw a diagram of $f(x)$, $f^{-1}(x)$ and $gf(x)$. Explain it to a friend.			
4	form composite functions	Combine two or more functions in the form $gf(x)$.			

CONTINUED

	Now I can	Show it	Needs more work	Almost there	Confident to move on
5	think about how to keep time well during examinations	Set a timer to attempt Section 22.1, Question 6 in under 10 minutes.			
6	recognise the different ways equations are used in exam questions and how to respond to each.	Make a set of flashcards about the different equation 'actions' (e.g. form, solve, rearrange, substitute into). On the back, write what the action means, what method you use and an example question.			

23 Transformations and vectors

KNOWLEDGE FOCUS

In this chapter, you will answer questions on:

- reflecting, rotating, translating and enlarging plane shapes
- recognising and describing transformations
- using vectors to describe translations
- recognising and using combined transformations
- precisely describing transformations using coordinates
- adding and subtracting vectors and multiplying them by scalars
- calculating the magnitude of a vector
- representing vectors in conventional ways
- using the sum and difference of vectors to express them in terms of coplanar vectors
- using position vectors.

EXAM SKILLS FOCUS

In this chapter you will:

- show that you know how to answer questions that ask you to 'draw' or 'describe'
- show that you know what a good answer looks like in transformation and vector questions.

When working with geometry, examination questions sometimes ask you to draw and sometimes ask you to describe.

Describe	state the points of a topic / give characteristics and main features.

If you are asked to 'draw' the result of a transformation, you will have a grid or a pair of axes on which to draw it.

If you are asked to 'describe' a transformation, you must give all of the information required for the transformation to be correctly enacted rather than drawing it yourself. The question will often ask you to 'describe fully'.

Understanding how marks are awarded in transformation and vector questions is essential. In this chapter, you will practise describing transformations fully and use vector notation. Describing fully means giving all the mathematical information required, such as the centre, angle and direction in a rotation. Using exact vector form will help you write precise answers.

23.1 Simple plane transformations and 23.2 Further transformations

≪ RECALL AND CONNECT 1 ≪

Which letters does convention say that we use for reflection, rotation, translation and enlargement?

UNDERSTAND THESE TERMS

- Reflection
- Rotation
- Translation
- Enlargement
- Vector
- Position vector
- Column vector
- Magnitude

1 Describe fully the single transformation that has transformed shape A to shape B.

a

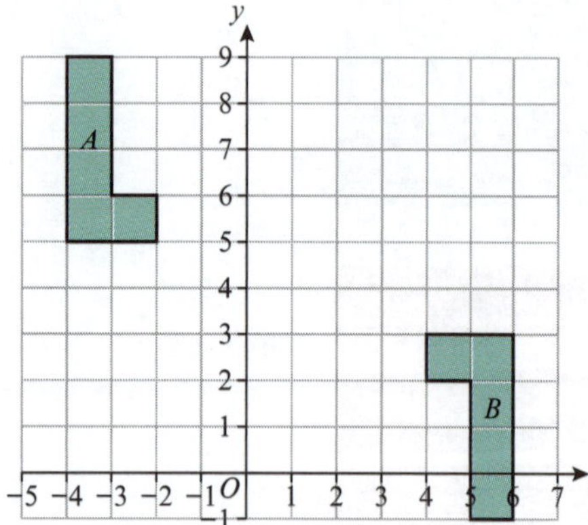

b

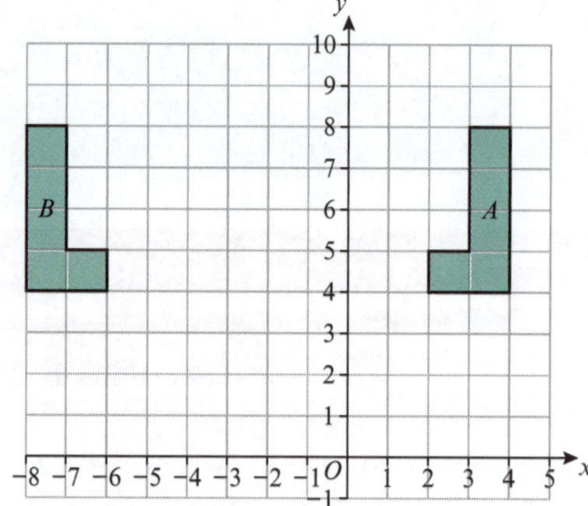

c

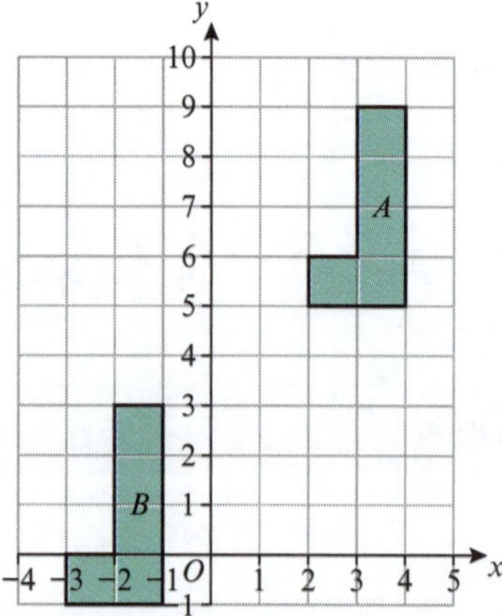

d

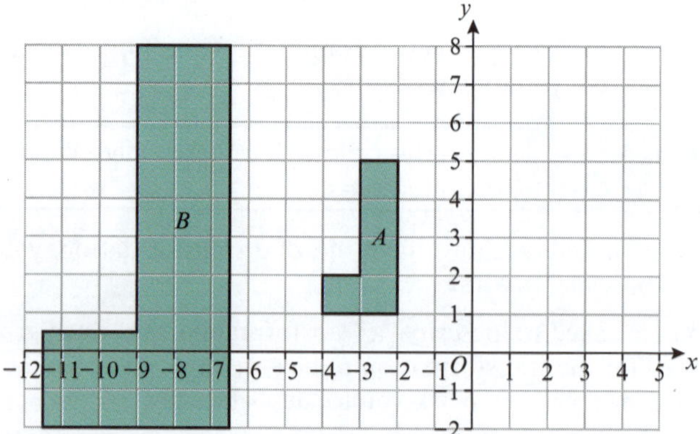

2 Copy the diagram onto squared paper.

Some transformations are defined as follows.

- **T**: A translation by the vector $\begin{pmatrix} -4 \\ -5 \end{pmatrix}$.
- **R**: A rotation 90° anticlockwise about the point (1, 1).
- **M**: A reflection about the line $x = -1$.
- **E**: An enlargement with scale factor 2 and centre (−1, 3).

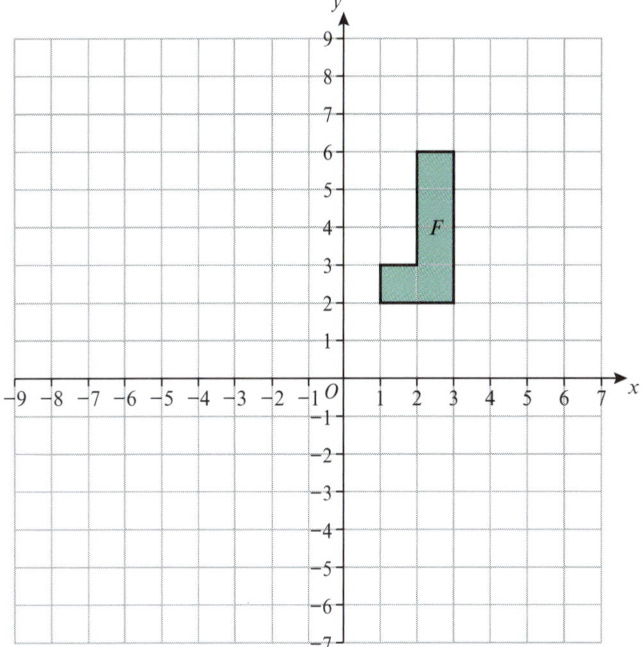

a Draw the image of F after transformation **T**, followed by transformation **M**.

b Draw the image of F after transformation **E**, followed by transformation **R**.

c Draw the image of F after transformation **M**, followed by transformation **E**.

3 Write down the equation of the mirror line that has been used to reflect the object P to create the image Q.

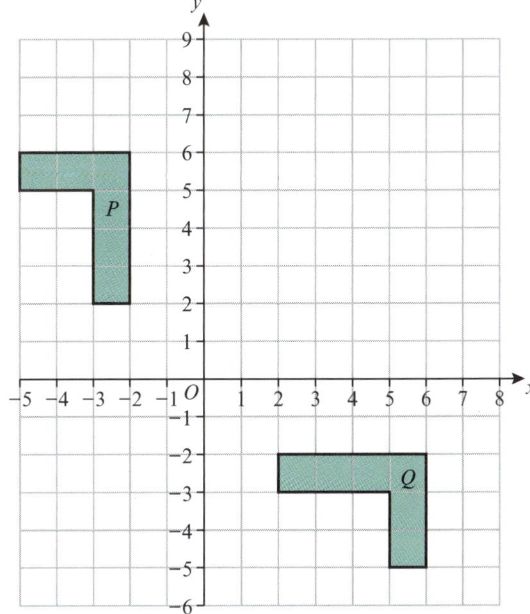

4 The shape S has been enlarged to create the image S'.

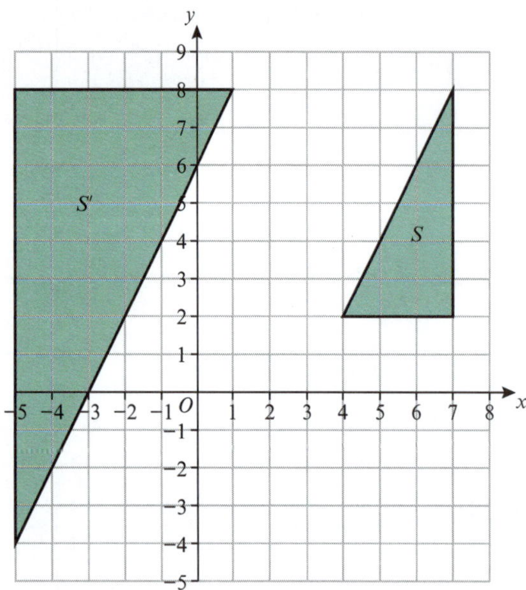

Write down the scale factor and centre of enlargement.

5 Which of the following statements are true of reflection?

A The object and image are congruent.

B Reflection can only be done with horizontal or vertical lines.

C The mirror cannot pass through the shape.

D The orientation of the object is reversed in the image .

6 Which transformations preserve congruence?

7 **a** Describe fully the single transformation that maps shape P onto shape Q. [3]

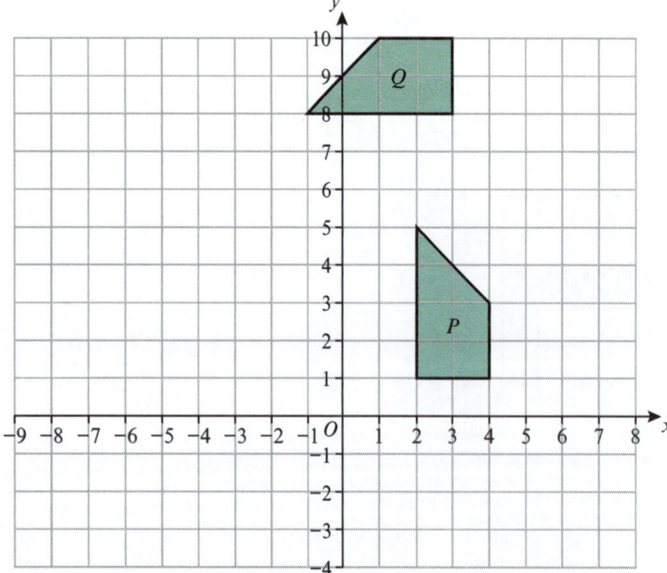

b Copy the grid.

i Draw P', the image of shape P after an enlargement of scale factor $-\frac{1}{2}$ with centre $(-2, 5)$. [2]

ii Draw P'', the image of shape P after a translation by the vector $\begin{pmatrix} -5 \\ -2 \end{pmatrix}$. [2]

[Total: 7]

8

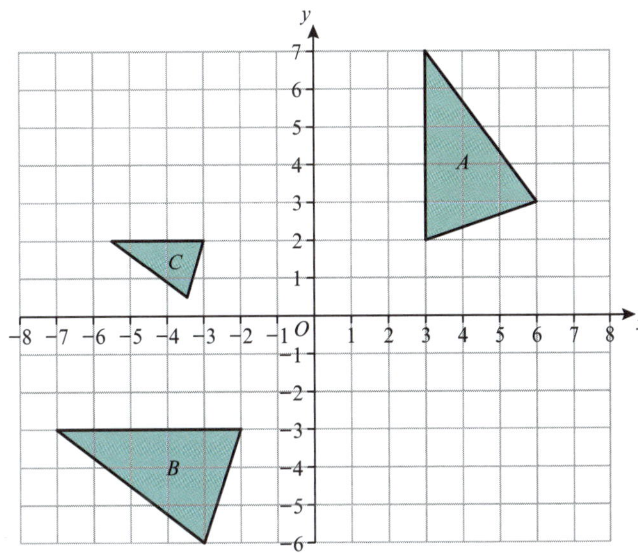

a Describe fully the single transformation that maps

i triangle A to triangle B [2]

ii triangle B onto triangle C. [3]

b Draw triangle A', the image of triangle A after a rotation of 90° clockwise about the point $(-1, 1)$. [2]

c Describe fully a single transformation that would map triangle B to triangle A'. [2]

[Total: 9]

REFLECTION

Reflect on how you carried out the transformations in the questions above.

Are you clear on the information needed to complete each transformation?

Are you able to describe each transformation fully?

What can you say about the orientation and the size of a shape after each transformation?

23.3 Vectors

1 Which of the following are examples of vector quantities?

mass, velocity, time, speed, force, acceleration

2 $\mathbf{a} = \begin{pmatrix} 3 \\ -2 \end{pmatrix}$ $\mathbf{b} = \begin{pmatrix} -4 \\ -5 \end{pmatrix}$ $\mathbf{c} = \begin{pmatrix} -7 \\ 4 \end{pmatrix}$

Express the following in column vector form.

a $3\mathbf{a}$ b $\mathbf{a} + \mathbf{c}$ c $2\mathbf{b} - \mathbf{c}$

d $3\mathbf{a} + 2\mathbf{b}$ e $2(\mathbf{a} - \mathbf{c})$

3 $\mathbf{p} = \begin{pmatrix} 4 \\ -3 \end{pmatrix}$ $q = \begin{pmatrix} -5 \\ 6 \end{pmatrix}$ $r = \begin{pmatrix} -2 \\ -3 \end{pmatrix}$

Find the following to 2 decimal places.

a $|p|$ b $|p + q|$ c $|3r|$ d $|2q + r|$

4 $OBCA$ is a parallelogram in which $\overrightarrow{OA} = \mathbf{a}$ and $\overrightarrow{OB} = \mathbf{b}$.

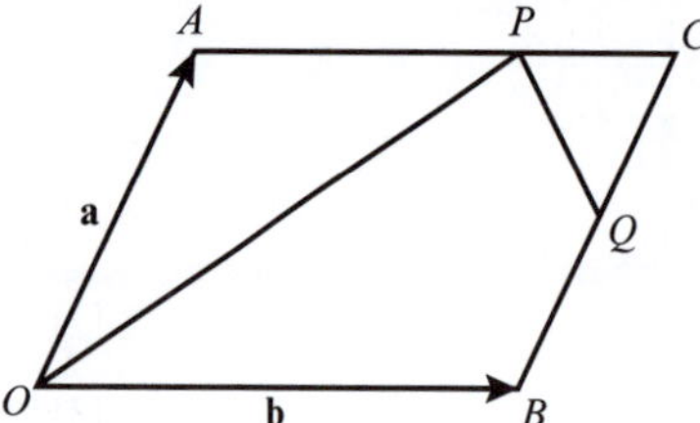

Q is the midpoint of BC.

P is a point on AC such that $AP : PC = 2 : 1$

Find the following in terms of **a** and **b**.

a $\overrightarrow{OC}$ b $\overrightarrow{OQ}$ c $\overrightarrow{OP}$

d $\overrightarrow{PQ}$ e $\overrightarrow{QP}$

5 $\mathbf{p} = \begin{pmatrix} -3 \\ 5 \end{pmatrix}$ and $\mathbf{q} = \begin{pmatrix} 10 \\ -2 \end{pmatrix}$

Find

a $2\mathbf{p} - \mathbf{q}$ [2]

b $|\mathbf{q}|$ [2]

[Total: 4]

6 O is the origin and $OACB$ is a parallelogram.

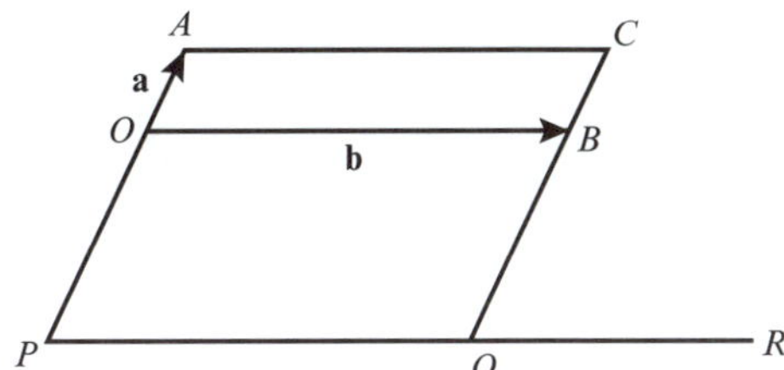

P is a point such that $PO:OA = 3:1$.

Q is a point such that $QB:BC = 3:1$.

PQR is a straight line and $PQ:QR = 4:3$.

a Find, in terms of **a** and **b**, in its simplest form

i the position vector of Q [2]

ii $\overrightarrow{BR}$. [1]

b Show that AQ is parallel to BR. [2]

[Total: 5]

REFLECTION

Think about how you answered the transformation and vector-based questions. Did you include all the required detail in your descriptions? Were your answers clearly set out and accurate? Could someone unfamiliar with the question follow your method and reach the same conclusion? What would you improve next time to make sure your answers earn all the available marks?

‹‹ RECALL AND CONNECT 2 ‹‹

a Write down all the vector notation that you know.

b What can you say about the coordinates of the point A if the position vector $\mathbf{a} = \begin{pmatrix} 3 \\ -2 \end{pmatrix}$?

SELF-ASSESSMENT CHECKLIST

Let's revisit the Knowledge and Exam skills focus for this chapter.
Decide how confident you are with each statement.

	Now I can	Show it	Needs more work	Almost there	Confident to move on
1	reflect, rotate, translate and enlarge plane shapes	Transform a shape in a plane, given the correct information.			

CONTINUED

	Now I can	Show it	Needs more work	Almost there	Confident to move on
2	recognise and describe transformations	Draw your own shape, apply two transformations and describe what you did.			
3	use vectors to describe translations	Describe the translation that moves an object to its image by using a vector in the form $\begin{pmatrix} a \\ b \end{pmatrix}$.			
4	recognise and use combined transformations	Determine which combinations of transformations have taken place on a shape in a plane.			
5	precisely describe transformations using coordinates	Give the coordinates of an image after a transformation.			
6	add and subtract vectors and multiply them by scalars	Create and solve a vector path problem using a diagram.			
7	calculate the magnitude of a vector	Use Pythagoras' theorem to calculate the length of a vector.			
8	represent vectors in conventional ways	Represent vectors as $\overrightarrow{AB}$, $\underset{\sim}{a}$, $\mathbf{a}$, $\begin{pmatrix} a \\ b \end{pmatrix}$.			
9	use the sum and difference of vectors to express them in terms of coplanar vectors	For example, if $p = \begin{pmatrix} 2 \\ -3 \end{pmatrix}$ and $q = \begin{pmatrix} 1 \\ 3 \end{pmatrix}$, express $2p + q$ in column vector form.			
10	use position vectors	Understand that position vectors start from the origin.			
11	use the command words 'draw' and 'describe'	Answer a question with one or both of these command words, for example, Section 23.2, Question 8.			
12	describe what a good answer looks like in transformation and vector questions.	Annotate one of your answers to highlight where marks would be awarded. Then write a tip for a friend about how to get full marks on a similar question.			

24 Probability using tree diagrams and Venn diagrams

KNOWLEDGE FOCUS

In this chapter, you will answer questions on:

- using tree diagrams and Venn diagrams to show all possible outcomes of combined events
- calculating the probability of simple combined events using tree diagrams and Venn diagrams
- using tree diagrams, Venn diagrams and two-way tables to calculate conditional probability.

EXAM SKILLS FOCUS

In this chapter you will:

- think about techniques to help deal with test anxiety
- show that you understand how different representations of probability relate to each other.

It is normal to be anxious about examinations, but the most effective way to deal with test anxiety is to make sure that you arrive at the examination well prepared. This should involve practising questions from past papers, revising your knowledge thoroughly and well in advance.

In the examination, try to stay as relaxed as you can, take deep breaths and try to focus only on the question you are doing.

It also helps to make sure that you are eating healthily, exercising properly and getting enough sleep in the period leading up to the examinations.

Probability questions often use different formats: tree diagrams, Venn diagrams, sample spaces or two-way tables. These may look different, but they all represent the same kinds of information. If you can make links between them and choose the best one for a question, you will save time and increase your accuracy.

24.1 Using tree diagrams to show outcomes and 24.2 Calculating probability from tree diagrams

UNDERSTAND THESE TERMS

- Conditional probability
- Tree diagram

1 Micha has a bag with three different colours of tokens within it.

Four are red, six are blue and three are yellow.

a Draw a tree diagram to show the possible outcomes when one token is drawn out at random and replaced, and then another token is drawn.

b How many different possible outcomes are there?

c How many outcomes include at least one yellow token?

d How many outcomes do not include blue tokens?

2 A bag contains different coloured counters. There are six green, seven blue and four yellow.

Two counters are drawn out at random. The first counter is replaced before the second one is drawn.

a Draw a tree diagram to show all possible outcomes.

b What is the probability of drawing the following?

i Two yellow counters.

ii One green counter and one yellow counter.

c What is the most likely outcome?

3 Two differently biased coins, coin A and coin B, are flipped.

The probability of coin A landing on heads is 0.6

The probability of coin B landing on heads is 0.3

a Copy and complete the tree diagram. [2]

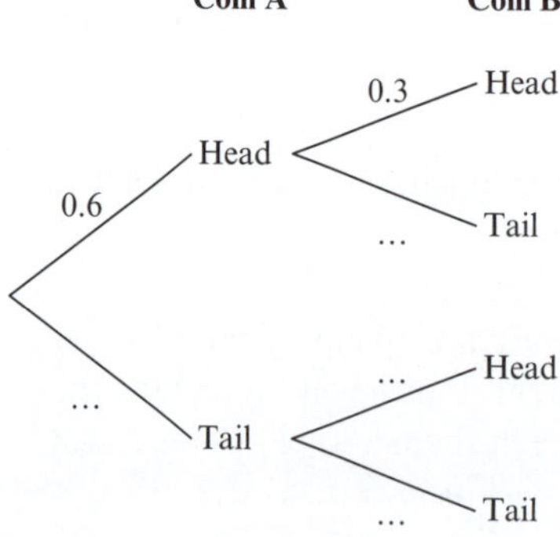

b A student tosses both coins. Find the probability that:

i both coins land on tails [2]

ii there is one head and one tail. [2]

[Total: 6]

24.3 Calculating probability from Venn diagrams

UNDERSTAND THIS TERM

- Venn diagram

1 In a class of 30 students, 14 take history, 17 take geography and 7 take neither history nor geography.

a Draw a Venn diagram to show this information.

b Use the Venn diagram to calculate the probability that a student chosen at random from this class:

i takes geography but not history

ii takes geography or history

iii takes geography and history.

2 Students can access their homework on a tablet (T), laptop (L) or phone (P).

A survey was conducted with 50 students to determine which devices they used to complete their homework over the course of a week. The results of the survey were then represented in a Venn diagram.

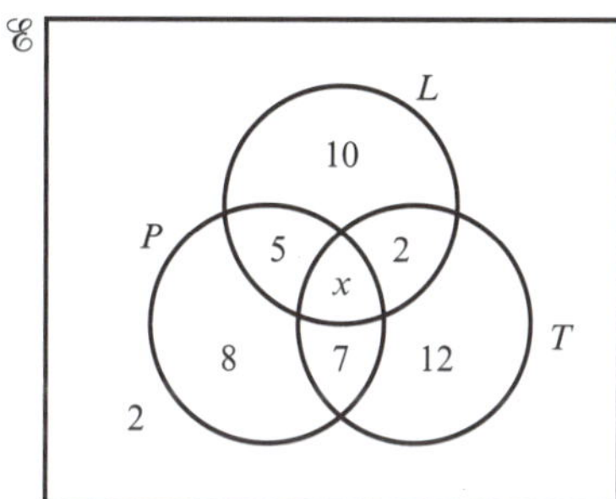

a Determine the value of x.

b Calculate the following.

i $n(P \cup L)$ ii $n(T \cap P)$ iii $n(T' \cap L')$

c Find the probability that a student chosen at random:

i did not do their homework using a phone, tablet or laptop

ii only used a phone

iii used a phone, a tablet and a laptop

iv never used a phone.

3 There are 40 students in a class.

- 6 do not play cricket or football
- 15 play football
- 24 play cricket

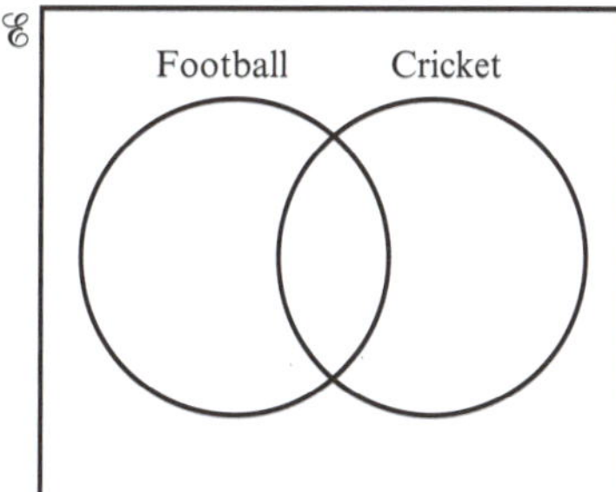

a Complete the Venn diagram to show this information. [2]

b A student is chosen at random.

Find the probability that the student plays cricket but not football. [1]

c A student who plays football is chosen at random.

Find the probability that this student also plays cricket. [1]

[Total: 4]

4 The Venn diagram shows the numbers of students in a group of 35 who have sisters (S), cousins (C) or brothers (B).

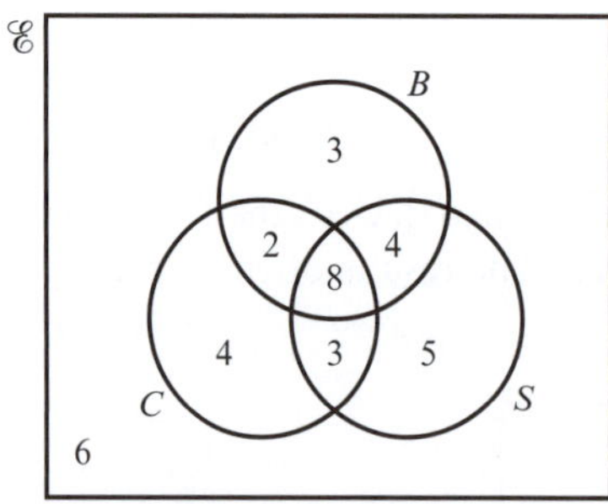

a One student is picked at random from the group.

i Write down the probability that this student has brothers. [1]

ii Write down the probability that this student has sisters but no brother. [1]

b Two students are picked at random from the students that have cousins.

Calculate the probability that both have sisters. [3]

[Total: 5]

≪ RECALL AND CONNECT 1 ≪

If events A and B are independent, how would you calculate:

- $P(A \cap B)$?
- $P(A \cup B)$?

Which region(s) on a Venn diagram would be shaded for each?

REFLECTION

What strategies have you got in place to minimise examination anxiety? Are you making sure you get enough sleep? Are you eating healthily? Are you practising answering past paper questions and building your confidence? How did working through conditional probability problems help you feel more confident for the exam?

24.4 Conditional probability

UNDERSTAND THESE TERMS

- Conditional probability
- Mutually exclusive
- Independent events
- Venn diagram

1 There are some coloured disks in a bag.

Seven are blue, five are red and eight are green.

A disk is selected at random and not replaced.

A second disk is selected at random.

Find the probability that:

a two blue disks are selected

b no red disks are selected

c the first disk is red and the second is green.

2 A card is selected at random from a pack of 52 playing cards and the card is not replaced.

Then a second card is randomly selected.

Find the probability that:

a both cards are hearts

b both cards are Kings

c both cards are red

d both cards are picture cards (King, Queen or Jack)

e the first card is a spade and the second card is a heart.

3 A box contains a set of snooker balls.

It has 15 reds and one each of yellow, green, brown, blue, pink and black (known as the colours) and a white cue ball.

A ball is selected at random, and is either a red, a colour or the white cue ball.

The ball is not replaced, and a second ball is selected.

a Copy and complete the tree diagram to show the probability of each event. Show each probability as a fraction its simplest form.

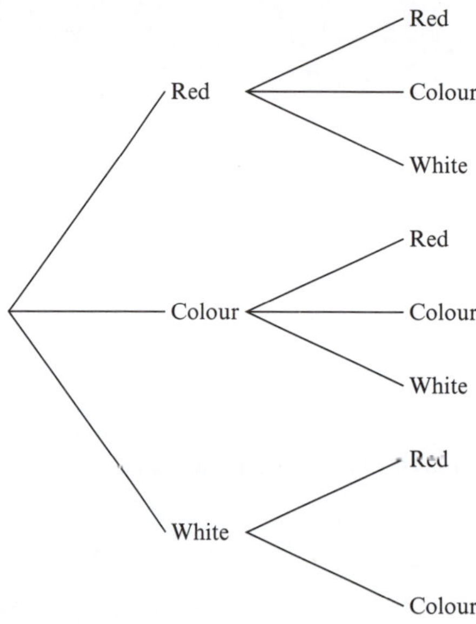

b Find the probability that:

i both balls are red

ii both balls are colours

iii the white ball is one of the two balls selected

iv the first ball is a colour and the second ball is white

v at least one of the balls is red.

4 A sock drawer contains five red socks and three blue socks.

a Arshad pulls a sock out of the drawer without looking and replaces it.

Find the probability that the sock was blue. [1]

b Marina picks a sock at random from the same drawer and replaces it.

She does this 160 times.

Calculate how often she would expect the sock to be blue. [1]

c Nigel picks a sock at random from the drawer, replaces it and picks a second sock at random.

Find the probability that both socks are:

i the same colour [3]

ii a different colour. [1]

d Ranvir picks two socks at random without replacing the first one.

Find the probability she picks a pair of socks the same colour. [3]

[Total: 9]

5 On any day, the probability that Mica wakes up before 07:00 is 0.4.

When he wakes before 07:00, the probability that he will go for a run is 0.6.

When he does not wake before 07:00, the probability that he will go for a run is 0.2.

a Work out how often Mica expects to wake before 07:00 during a 90-day period. [1]

b Copy and complete the tree diagram. [2]

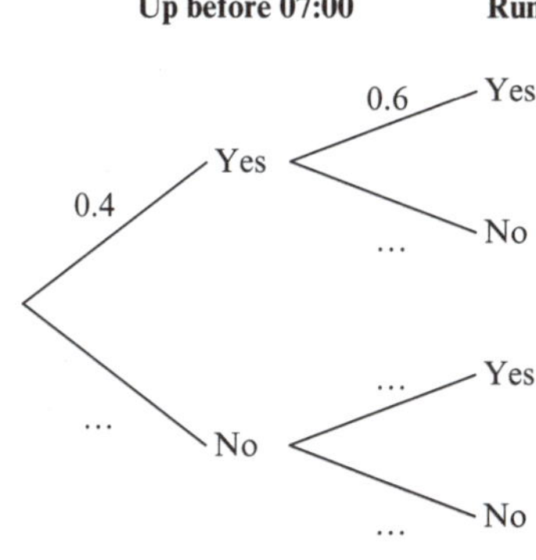

c Find the probability that, on any day, Mica does not run. [3]

[Total: 6]

REFLECTION

When working with Venn diagrams and tree diagrams, did you notice any similarities in how probabilities were calculated? Do you find either of them easier or harder to work with? How confident are you that you will be able to answer questions using these representations in the examination?

SELF-ASSESSMENT CHECKLIST

Let's revisit the Knowledge and Exam skills focus for this chapter. Decide how confident you are with each statement.

	Now I can	Show it	Needs more work	Almost there	Confident to move on
1	use tree diagrams and Venn diagrams to show all possible outcomes of combined events	Create your own tree diagram for a situation with three colours of marbles and explain it to a partner.			
2	calculate the probability of simple combined events using tree diagrams and Venn diagrams	Use a tree diagram to show the probability of selecting two different coloured counters if the counter is replaced.			

CONTINUED

	Now I can	Show it	Needs more work	Almost there	Confident to move on
3	use tree diagrams, Venn diagrams and two-way tables to calculate conditional probability.	Use a tree diagram to show the probability of selecting two different coloured counters if the counter is not replaced.			
4	think about techniques to help deal with test anxiety	Practise a full past-paper question under timed conditions, then reflect on how you managed your anxiety level.			
5	show that you understand how different representations of probability relate to each other.	Take a tree diagram question and rewrite it as a Venn diagram or table. Then explain to a classmate how both diagrams show the same probability structure.			

Exam practice 6

This section contains past paper questions from previous Cambridge exams, which draw together your knowledge on a range of topics that you have covered up to this point. These questions give you the opportunity to test your knowledge and understanding.

The following question has an example student response and commentary provided. Work through the question first, then compare your answer to the sample response and commentary. Are your answers different to the sample responses?

1 **a** y is directly proportional to $(x - 1)^2$.

When $x = 4$, $y = 3$.

Find y when $x = 7$. [3]

b m is inversely proportional to the square root of p.

Explain what happens to the value of m when the value of p is multiplied by 9. [1]

Cambridge IGCSE Mathematics (0580) Paper 22 Q19 June 2024 **[Total: 4]**

Example student response	Commentary
a $y = k(x - 1)^2$ $3 = k(4 - 1)^2$ $\frac{3}{(4 - 1)^2} = k$ $k = \frac{1}{3}$	1 mark for $y = k(x - 1)^2$ Student has successfully found the value of k but hasn't then used it to find y when $x = 7$. ***This answer scores 1 out of 3 marks.***
b $m = \frac{k}{\sqrt{p}}$ $\sqrt{9} = 3$ Multiplied by 3	Student has written a correct equation for the inverse proportion relationship, and found the square root of 9 but confused multiplying by three (trying to solve the equation). ***This answer scores 0 out of 1 mark.***

2 m is inversely proportional to the square of $(t + 2)$.

$m = 0.64$ when $t = 3$.

Find m when $t = 8$. [3]

Cambridge IGCSE Mathematics (0580) Paper 22 Q19 June 2023 **[Total: 3]**

The following question has an example student response and commentary provided. Work through the question first, then compare your answer to the sample response and commentary. Are your answers different to the sample responses?

3 The distance from town A to town B on a map is 3.5 cm.

The scale on the map is 1 : 250 000.

Find the actual distance, in kilometres, from town A to town B. [2]

Cambridge IGCSE Mathematics (0580) Paper 22 Q4 June 2023 **[Total: 2]**

Example student response	Commentary
1 : 250 000 means that 1 cm on a map is 250 000 cm in real life $\frac{3.5 \times 250\,000}{100 \times 100}$ 87.5 km	1 method mark for $\frac{3.5 \times 250\,000}{100 \times 100}$ Student has correctly identified the scale but has not converted from cm to km accurately. ***This answer scores 1 out of 2 marks.***

4 Now that you have gone through the commentary, try to write an improved answer for your own solution and edit the sample student response to improve their answer to each part.

The following question has an example student response and commentary provided. Work through the question first, then compare your answer to the sample response and commentary. Are your answers different to the sample responses?

5 **a** Solve.

$10 - 3p = 3 + 11p$ [2]

b Make m the subject of the formula.

$mc^2 - 2k = mg$ [3]

c Solve.

$\frac{1}{x-3} + \frac{4}{2x+3} = 1$ [5]

Cambridge IGCSE Mathematics (0580) Paper 42 Q8a–c June 2022 **[Total: 10]**

Example student response	Commentary
a $10 - 3p = 3 + 11p$ $10 = 3 + 14p$ $7 = 14p$ $p = 2$	1 method mark for $7 = 14p$. The student has made an error at the final stage, calculating 14 ÷ 2. ***This answer scores 1 out of 2 marks.***
b $mc^2 - 2k = mg$ $mc^2 = mg + 2k$ $mc^2 - mg = 2k$ $m(c^2 - g) = 2k$	1 method mark for isolating m terms, and another mark for correct factorising of $mc^2 - mg = 2k$ The student has rearranged and factorised but hasn't completed the rearrangement. ***This answer scores 2 out of 3 marks.***

c $\frac{2x + 3 + 4x - 12}{2x^2 + 3x - 6x - 9} = 1$ $6x - 9 = 2x^2 - 3x - 9$ $2x^2 - 9x = 0$	4 marks for $2x^2 - 9x = 0$. Student has found common denominator and correct numerator, then rearranged equation correctly. Equation not solved as it has not been factorised. ***This answer scores 4 out of 5 marks.***

6 Now that you have gone through the commentary, try to write an improved answer for your own solution and edit the sample student response to improve their answer to each part.

The following question has an example student response and commentary provided. Work through the question first, then compare your answer to the sample response and commentary. Are your answers different to the sample responses?

7

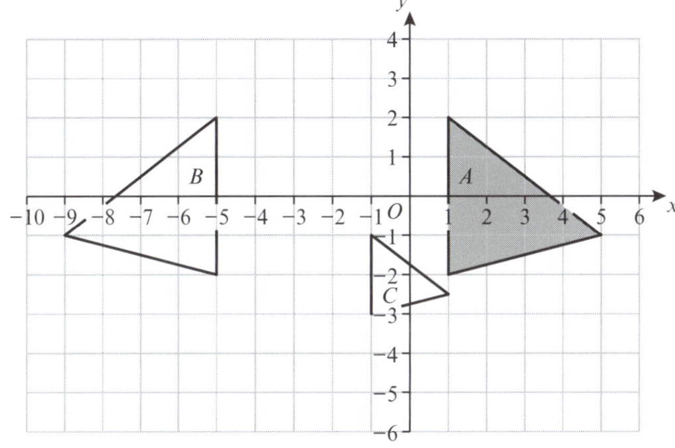

a Describe fully the **single** transformation that maps

  i triangle A onto triangle B [2]

  ii triangle A onto triangle C. [3]

b Draw the image of triangle A after a rotation, 90° clockwise, about (1, 3). [3]

[Use Figure 5 on the Past Paper Practice Questions Resource Sheet.]

Cambridge IGCSE Mathematics (0580) Paper 22 Q15 March 2024 **[Total: 8]**

Example student response	Commentary
a **i** Reflection in the line $y = -3$	Student has identified the correct transformation (reflection) for 1 mark but given incorrect line of reflection. ***This answer scores 1 out of 2 marks.***
a **ii** Enlargement scale factor 2 centre of enlargement (−3, −4)	Student receives 1 mark for 'enlargement' and 1 mark for (−3, −4). But the question asks for A to C and they have described the transformation from C to A. ***This answer scores 2 out of 3 marks.***

Example student response	Commentary
b 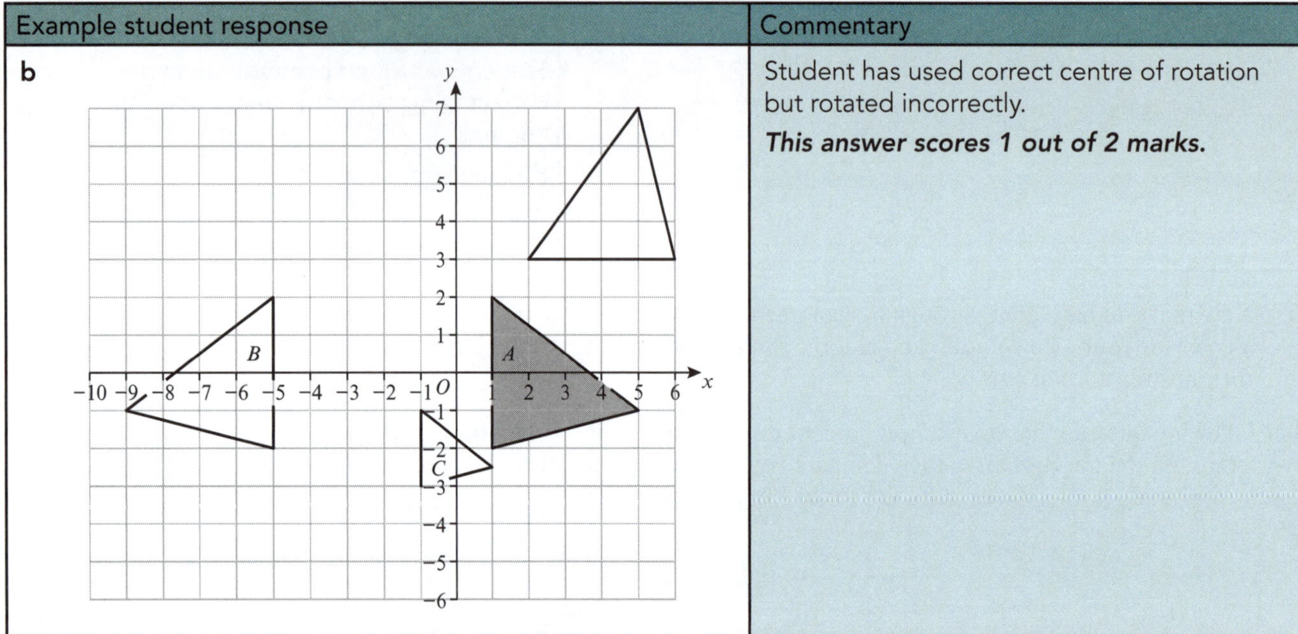	Student has used correct centre of rotation but rotated incorrectly. ***This answer scores 1 out of 2 marks.***

8 **a** Draw the lines of symmetry of the rectangle.

[2]

[Use Figure 6 on the Past Paper Practice Questions Resource Sheet.]

b

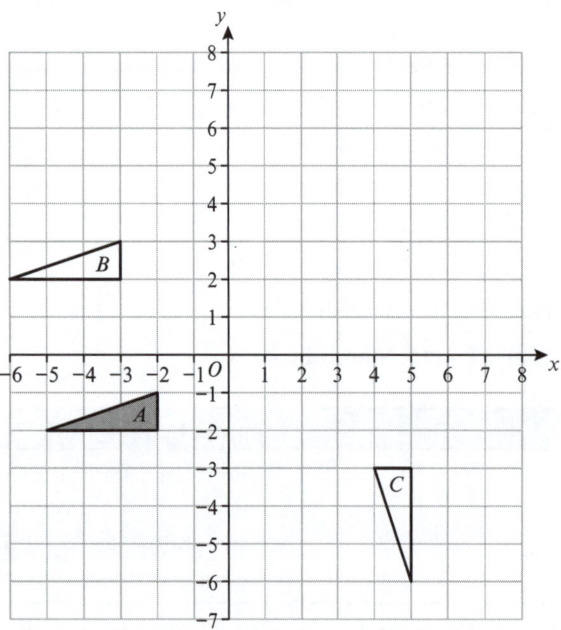

Describe fully the **single** transformation that maps

i triangle A onto triangle B [2]

ii triangle A onto triangle C. [3]

c Draw the image of triangle A after reflection in $y = 2$. [2]

[Use Figure 7 on the Past Paper Practice Questions Resource Sheet.]

d Draw the image of triangle A after enlargement by scale factor -2, centre $(-1, 1)$. [2]

Cambridge IGCSE Mathematics (0580) Paper 42 Q5 June 2022 **[Total: 11]**

The following question has an example student response and commentary provided. Work through the question first, then compare your answer to the sample response and commentary. Are your answers different to the sample responses?

9 **a** $\mathbf{p} = \begin{pmatrix} 4 \\ 5 \end{pmatrix}$ $\mathbf{q} = \begin{pmatrix} -2 \\ 7 \end{pmatrix}$

i Find $2\mathbf{p} + \mathbf{q}$. [2]

ii Find $|\mathbf{p}|$. [2]

b A is the point $(4, 1)$ and $\overrightarrow{AB} = \begin{pmatrix} -3 \\ 1 \end{pmatrix}$.

Find the coordinates of B. [1]

c The line $y = 3x - 2$ crosses the y-axis at G.

Write down the coordinates of G. [1]

d

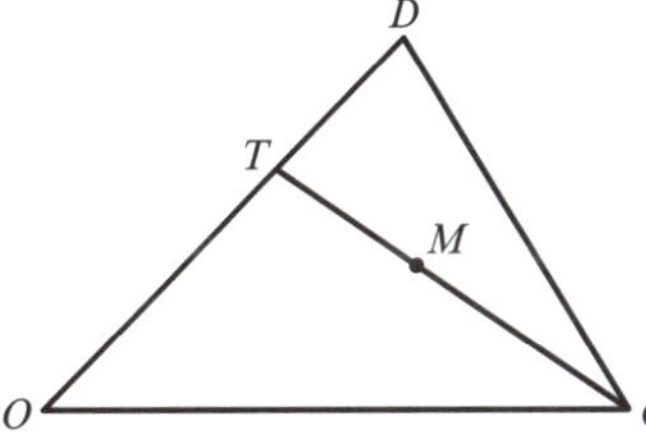

NOT TO SCALE

In the diagram, O is the origin, $OT = 2TD$ and M is the midpoint of TC.

$\overrightarrow{OC} = \mathbf{c}$ and $\overrightarrow{OD} = \mathbf{d}$

Find the position vector of M.

Give your answer in terms of $\mathbf{c}$ and $\mathbf{d}$ in its simplest form. [3]

Cambridge IGCSE Mathematics (0580) Paper 42 Q2 June 2020 **[Total: 9]**

Example student response	Commentary
a **i** $2\begin{pmatrix} 4 \\ 5 \end{pmatrix} + \begin{pmatrix} -2 \\ 7 \end{pmatrix}$ $= \begin{pmatrix} 8 \\ 10 \end{pmatrix} + \begin{pmatrix} -2 \\ 7 \end{pmatrix}$ $= \begin{pmatrix} 6 \\ 17 \end{pmatrix}$	The student answered correctly. ***This answer scores 2 out of 2 marks.***

Example student response	Commentary
a **ii** $\|\mathbf{p}\| = 4^2 + 5^2$ $\|\mathbf{p}\| = 41$	1 mark for $4^2 + 5^2$. The student has recognised the need to use Pythagoras' theorem to find the magnitude but has not completed the calculation. ***This answer scores 1 out of 2 marks.***
b $\begin{pmatrix} -3 \\ 1 \end{pmatrix}$ applied to (4, 1) = (1, 2)	The student answered correctly. ***This answer scores 1 out of 1 mark.***
c (0, −2)	Student answered correctly. ***This answer scores 1 out of 1 mark.***
d $\overrightarrow{TC} = \mathbf{c} - \frac{2}{3}\mathbf{d}$	1 mark for $\overrightarrow{TC} = \mathbf{c} - \frac{2}{3}\mathbf{d}$ Student has found a vector for TC but not the point M. ***This answer scores 1 out of 3 marks.***

10 **a** F is the point (5, −2) and $\overrightarrow{FG} = \begin{pmatrix} -2 \\ 3 \end{pmatrix}$.

Find

i the coordinates of point G [1]

ii $5\overrightarrow{FG}$ [1]

iii $|\overrightarrow{FG}|$ [2]

b

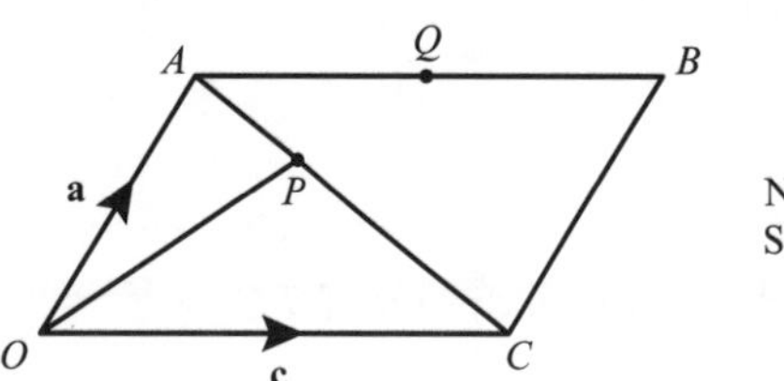

NOT TO SCALE

$OABC$ is a parallelogram.

P is a point on AC and Q is the midpoint of AB.

$\overrightarrow{OA} = \mathbf{a}$ and $\overrightarrow{OC} = \mathbf{c}$.

i Find, in terms of **a** and/or **c**.

a $\overrightarrow{AQ}$ [1]

b $\overrightarrow{OQ}$ [1]

ii $\overrightarrow{OP} = \frac{2}{3}\mathbf{a} + \frac{1}{3}\mathbf{c}$

a Show that O, P and Q lie on a straight line. [2]

b Write down the ratio $OP : OQ$.
Give your answer in the form $1 : n$. [1]

Cambridge IGCSE Mathematics (0580) Paper 42 Q9 November 2021 **[Total: 9]**

The following question has an example student response and commentary provided. Work through the question first, then compare your answer to the sample response and commentary. Are your answers different to the sample responses?

11 Tanya plants some seeds.

The probability that a seed will produce flowers is 0.8.

When a seed produces flowers, the probability that the flowers are red is 0.6 and the probability that the flowers are yellow is 0.3.

a Tanya has a seed that produces flowers.

Find the probability that the flowers are not red and not yellow. [1]

b **i** Complete the tree diagram.

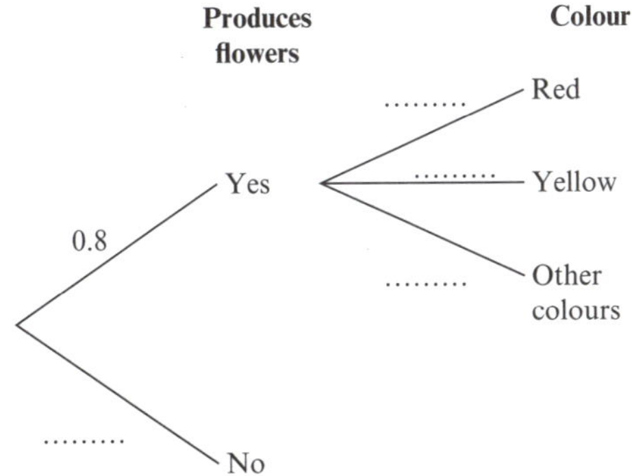

[2]

[Use Figure 8 on the Past Paper Practice Questions Resource Sheet.]

ii Find the probability that a seed chosen at random produces red flowers. [2]

iii Tanya chooses a seed at random.

Find the probability that this seed does not produce red flowers and does not produce yellow flowers. [3]

c Two of the seeds are chosen at random.

Find the probability that one produces flowers and one does not produce flowers. [3]

Cambridge IGCSE Mathematics (0580) Paper 42 Q7 June 2020 **[Total: 11]**

Example student response	Commentary
a 0.1	The student answered correctly. ***This answer scores 1 out of 1 mark.***
b **i** Tree diagram: 0.8 → Yes; 0.2 → No; Yes: 0.6 → Red, 0.3 → Yellow, 0.1 → Other colours	The student answered correctly. ***This answer scores 2 out of 2 marks.***

Example student response	Commentary
b ii 0.8	The student has not considered the conditional aspect of the probability. ***This answer scores 0 out of 2 marks.***
b iii Not red = 0.4 Not yellow 0.7	The student has not considered the conditional aspect of the probability. ***This answer scores 0 out of 3 marks.***
c 0.8 and 0.2	Misunderstanding of the conditional nature of the probability. ***This answer scores 0 out of 3 marks.***

12 a The probability that Shalini is late for school on any day is $\frac{1}{6}$.

i Complete the tree diagram for Monday and Tuesday.

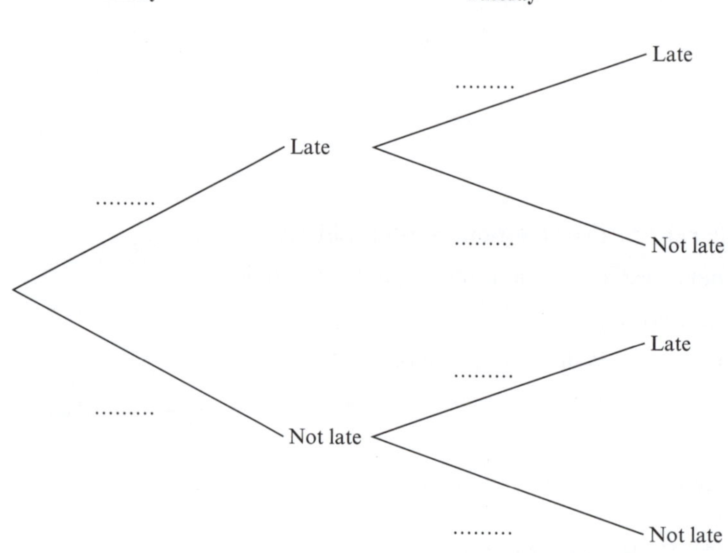

[2]

[Use Figure 9 on the Past Paper Practice Questions Resource Sheet.]

ii Calculate the probability that Shalini is late on Monday but is not late on Tuesday. [2]

b The Venn diagram shows the number of students in a group of 50 students who wear glasses (G), who wear trainers (T) and who have a mobile phone (M).

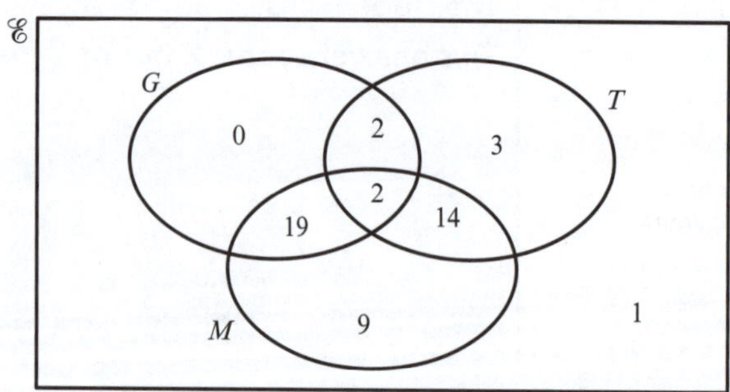

i Use set notation to describe the region that contains only one student. [1]

ii Find $n(T' \cap (G \cup M))$). [1]

iii One student is picked at random from the 50 students.

Find the probability that this student wears trainers but does not wear glasses. [1]

iv Two students are picked at random from those wearing trainers.

Find the probability that both students have mobile phones. [3]

Cambridge IGCSE Mathematics (0580) Paper 42 Q11, March 2022 **[Total: 10]**

The following question has an example student response and commentary provided. Work through the question first, then compare your answer to the sample response and commentary. Are your answers different to the sample responses?

13

4	6	3	4	2	3
Red	Yellow	Blue	Blue	Yellow	Blue

The diagram shows six discs.

Each disc has a colour and a number.

a One disc is picked at random.

Write down the probability that

i the disc has the number 4, [1]

ii the disc is red and has the number 3, [1]

iii the disc is blue and has the number 4. [1]

b Two of the six discs are picked at random **without** replacement.

Find the probability that

i both discs have the number 3, [2]

ii both discs have the same colour. [3]

c Two of the six discs are picked at random **with** replacement.

Find the probability that both discs have the same colour. [3]

Cambridge IGCSE Mathematics (0580) Paper 42 Q6 November 2020 **[Total: 11]**

Example student response	Commentary
a i $\frac{2}{6}$	Correct but not simplified. ***This answer scores 1 out of 1 mark.***
a ii 0 as no reds have a 3	Correct answer. ***This answer scores 1 out of 1 mark.***
a iii $\frac{1}{6}$	Correct answer. ***This answer scores 1 out of 1 mark.***

<table>
<tr><th>Example student response</th><th>Commentary</th></tr>
<tr><td>b i $\frac{2}{6} \times \frac{1}{6} = \frac{1}{18}$</td><td>Student has multiplied probabilities correctly but has the incorrect denominator for the second fraction.
This answer scores 0 out of 2 marks.</td></tr>
<tr><td>b ii $\frac{2}{6} \times \frac{1}{6} + \frac{3}{6} \times \frac{2}{6} = \frac{2}{9}$</td><td>Student has accounted for one less on the numerator but not one less on the denominator for the second selection.
This answer scores 0 out of 3 marks.</td></tr>
<tr><td>c
<table>
<tr><th></th><th></th><th colspan="3">Second pick</th></tr>
<tr><td></td><td></td><td>Blue</td><td>Red</td><td>Yellow</td></tr>
<tr><td rowspan="3">First pick</td><td>Blue</td><td>BB</td><td>BR</td><td>BY</td></tr>
<tr><td>Red</td><td>RB</td><td>RR</td><td>RY</td></tr>
<tr><td>Yellow</td><td>YB</td><td>YR</td><td>YY</td></tr>
</table>
$\frac{3}{9} = \frac{1}{3}$</td><td>Student has drawn a sample space but has not accounted for the numbers of blue and yellow counters, so the correct number of possibilities has not been identified.
This answer scores 0 out of 3 marks.</td></tr>
</table>

14 a A bag contains 24 coloured beads.

Some are red, some are blue and 10 are yellow.

One bead is picked at random from the bag.

Find the probability that

i the bead is yellow [1]

ii the bead is not yellow. [1]

b Another bag contains 5 green marbles, 6 white marbles and 4 black marbles.

Meera picks 2 marbles at random from the bag, without replacement.

Find the probability that

i the first marble is black and the second marble is white [2]

ii both marbles have different colours. [4]

Cambridge IGCSE Mathematics (0580) Paper 42 Q8 November 2024 **[Total: 8]**

The following question has an example student response and commentary provided. Work through the question first, then compare your answer to the sample response and commentary. Are your answers different to the sample responses?

15 80 students are asked whether they play a musical instrument, M, and whether they play for a sports team, S.

The Venn diagram shows the results.

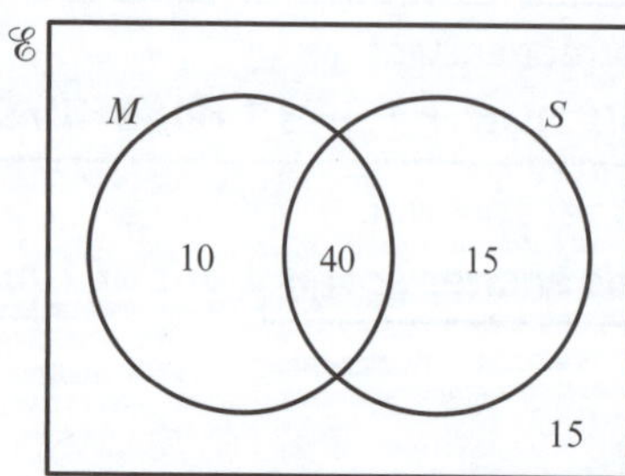

A student is chosen at random from those who play a musical instrument.

Find the probability that this student also plays for a sports team. [1]

[Total: 1]

Example student response	Commentary
$\frac{40}{80} = \frac{4}{8}$	The student has made an error with the denominator, considering all 80 students instead of just those who play a musical instrument. ***This answer scores 0 out of 1 mark.***

16 The Venn diagram shows the number of students in a class of 40 who study physics (P), mathematics (M) and geography (G).

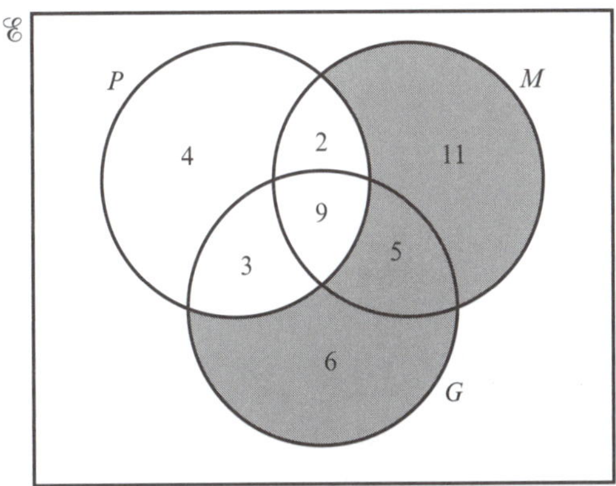

a Use set notation to describe the shaded region. [1]

b Find $n((P \cap G) \cup M')$. [1]

c A student is chosen at random from those studying geography.

Find the probability that this student also studies physics or mathematics but not both. [2]

Cambridge IGCSE Mathematics (0580) Paper 22 Q16 June 2022 **[Total: 4]**

The following question has an example student response and commentary provided. Work through the question first, then compare your answer to the sample response and commentary. Are your answers different to the sample responses?

17 $f(x) = 7x - 8$ $\qquad g(x) = \frac{4}{x} + 5$ $\qquad h(x) = 2^x + 1$

a Find $f^{-1}(x)$. [2]

b Find the value of x when $h(x) = g\left(\frac{1}{3}\right)$. [2]

Cambridge IGCSE Mathematics (0580) Paper 22 Q19 June 2022 **[Total: 4]**

Example student response	Commentary
a $\frac{x - 8}{7}$	The student has made an error with a sign. No working out is shown, so no method marks can be awarded. ***This answer scores 0 out of 2 marks.***

Example student response	Commentary
b $2^x + 1 = 4 \div \frac{1}{3} + 5$ $2^x + 1 = 17$ $2^x = 16$ $x = 8$	1 mark for $4 \div \frac{1}{3} + 5$ The student has correctly substituted $\frac{1}{3}$ into g(x) and formed the correct equation. The student has failed to solve $2^x = 16$ correctly. ***This answer scores 1 out of 2 marks.***

18 **a** Solve $3x - 8 = 6 - 4x$. [2]

b Factorise fully $10a^2 + 5a$. [2]

c Factorise fully $(2x - 3)^2 - 9$. [2]

d $f(x) = \frac{1}{4x - 1}, x \neq \frac{1}{4}$ $\qquad$ $g(x) = 3^x$

i Find f(4). [1]

ii Find gg(2). [2]

iii Find k when $g(k) = f(7)$. [2]

Cambridge IGCSE Mathematics (0580) Paper 42 Q7 June 2024 **[Total: 11]**

The following question has an example student response and commentary provided. Work through the question first, then compare your answer to the sample response and commentary. Are your answers different to the sample responses?

19

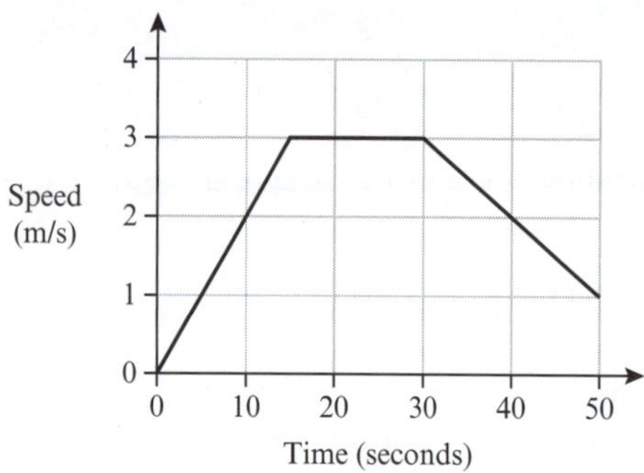

Adhrit goes for a ride on his scooter.

The diagram shows the speed–time graph for his journey.

a Find his acceleration between 0 and 15 seconds, in m/s^2. [1]

b Find the total distance that Adhrit travelled, in metres. [3]

[Total: 4]

Example student response	Commentary
a Speed at 0 seconds is 0 m/s Speed at 15 seconds is 3 m/s Acceleration is $3 \div 15 = 0.2$ m/s^2	Correct answer. ***This answer scores 1 out of 1 mark.***

Example student response	Commentary
b $\frac{1}{2} \times 15 \times 3 + 3 \times 15 + \frac{1}{2}(3-1) \times 20 = 87.5\,\text{m}$	1 mark for $4 \div \frac{1}{3} + 5$ The student gains 1 mark for the method (they have used 'distance = area under the speed–time graph' and split the graph into sections). They gain another mark for calculating each section but lose a mark because they have incorrectly calculated the third section, so the final answer is incorrect. ***This answer scores 2 out of 3 marks.***

20 a A car starts its journey by accelerating from rest at a constant rate of $0.7\,\text{m/s}^2$ for 20 seconds, before reaching a constant speed of 14 m/s.

It then travels at 14 m/s for a distance of 210 m.

The car then decelerates at a constant rate of $1.4\,\text{m/s}^2$ before coming to a stop.

On the grid, complete the speed–time graph for the car's journey.

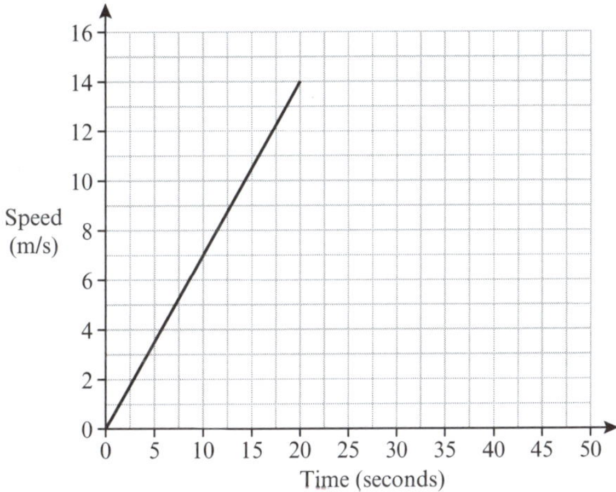

[3]

[Use Figure 10 on the Past Paper Practice Questions Resource Sheet.]

Cambridge IGCSE Mathematics (0580) Paper 22 Q11 November 2021 **[Total: 3]**